Cloud Computing in Medical Imaging

Today's healthcare organizations must focus on a lot more than just the health of their clients. The infrastructure it takes to support clinical-care delivery continues to expand, with information technology being one of the most significant contributors to that growth. As companies have become more dependent on technology for their clinical, administrative, and financial functions, their IT departments and expenditures have had to scale quickly to keep up. However, as technology demands have increased, so have the options for reliable infrastructure for IT applications and data storage. The one that has taken center stage over the past few years is cloud computing. Healthcare researchers are moving their efforts to the cloud because they need adequate resources to process, store, exchange, and use large quantities of medical data.

Cloud Computing in Medical Imaging covers the state-of-the-art techniques for cloud computing in medical imaging, healthcare technologies, and services. The book focuses on

- Machine-learning algorithms for health data security
- Fog computing in IoT-based health care
- Medical imaging and healthcare applications using fog IoT networks
- Diagnostic imaging and associated services
- Image steganography for medical informatics

This book aims to help advance scientific research within the broad field of cloud computing in medical imaging, healthcare technologies, and services. It focuses on major trends and challenges in this area and presents work aimed to identify new techniques and their use in biomedical analysis.

Cloud Computing in Medical Imaging

Edited by
Ayman El-Baz
Jasjit S. Suri

CRC Press
Taylor & Francis Group
Boca Raton London New York

CRC Press is an imprint of the
Taylor & Francis Group, an **informa** business
AN AUERBACH BOOK

First Edition published 2023
by CRC Press
6000 Broken Sound Parkway NW, Suite 300, Boca Raton, FL 33487-2742

and by CRC Press
4 Park Square, Milton Park, Abingdon, Oxon, OX14 4RN

CRC Press is an imprint of Taylor & Francis Group, LLC

© 2023 Taylor & Francis Group, LLC

ISBN: 978-0-367-70239-7 (hbk)
ISBN: 978-1-032-43894-8 (pbk)
ISBN: 978-1-003-14518-9 (ebk)

DOI: 10.1201/9781003145189

Typeset in Garamond
by MPS Limited, Dehradun

With love and affection to my mother and father, whose loving spirit sustains me still

Ayman El-Baz

To my late loving parents, immediate family, and children

Jasjit S. Suri

Contents

Acknowledgements ix
Preface xi
Editors xiii
Contributors xv

1 Cloud Computing in Healthcare and Medical Imaging: A Brief
   Overview 1
   SARAH M. AYYAD, MOHAMED SHEHATA, ALI H. MAHMOUD,
   MOHAMMED GHAZAL, JASJIT S. SURI, AND AYMAN EL-BAZ

2 ISM and DEMATEL Analysis of H4.0 Enablers in the Indian
   Healthcare Industry 23
   PADMAKALI BANERJEE, VINEET JAIN, AND PUNEETA AJMERA

3 Machine Learning Algorithms for Health Data Security:
   A Systematic Review 53
   NAIF AL MUDAWI, ABDULWAHAB ALAZEB,
   MOHAMMED S. ALSHEHRI, AND SULTAN ALMAKDI

4 Fog Computing in IoT-Based Healthcare Systems 79
   AZADEH ZAMANIFAR AND ALI YAMINI

5 Medical Imaging and Healthcare Applications Using 5G 91
   ENJIE LIU, YOUBING ZHAO, AND ABIMBOLA EFUNOGBON

6 The Application of Cloud-Computing Technology to Improve
   Patients' Medical History Access to Clinicians for Quality of
   Care in the Fourth Industrial Revolution 111
   NGOAKO SOLOMON MARUTHA

7 Diagnostic Imaging and Associated Services: Toward
   Interoperability and Cloud Computing 125
   CEZAR MIRANDA PAULA DE SOUZA
   AND ITAMIR DE MORAIS BARROCA FILHO

8 Health Monitoring Based on the Integrated Offer of Cloud-IoT Sensing Services 147
GABRIEL NEAGU

9 Sleep-Stage Identification Using Recurrent Neural Network for ECG Wearable-Sensor Systems.................................. 163
NICO SURANTHA AND VINCENT VALENTINE JANSEN

10 Classification of Methods to Reduce Clinical Alarm Signals for Remote Patient Monitoring: A Critical Review 173
TEENA ARORA, VENKI BALASUBRAMANIAN, ANDREW STRANIERI,
MAI SHENHAN, RAJKUMAR BUYYA, AND SARDAR M.N. ISLAM

11 Cloud Computing in Medical Imaging, Healthcare Technologies, and Services 195
ARUSHI ANANTHAKRISHNAN, ARYA AGRAWAL, ASMI DHULL,
MANAN GUPTA, DHANUSH SRIKANTH, SHREEMANTO LAHIRI,
DIVYANSH SRIVASTAVA, AND UTKARSH CHADHA

12 An Insight into Image Steganography for Medical Informatics 217
ASHA DURAFE AND VINOD PATIDAR

Index 243

Acknowledgements

The completion of this book could not have been possible without the participation and assistance of so many people whose names may not all be enumerated. Their contributions are sincerely appreciated and gratefully acknowledged. However, the editors would like to express their deep appreciation and indebtedness particularly to Dr. Ali H. Mahmoud and Dr. Heba Kandil for their endless support.

Ayman El-Baz
Jasjit S. Suri

Preface

The book covers the state-of-the-art techniques for cloud computing in medical imaging, healthcare technologies, and services. Currently, healthcare organizations should focus a lot more on the infrastructure, in addition to the health of their clients. The infrastructure it takes to support clinical-care delivery continues to grow rapidly, and a lot of research is being performed in this area. This book will focus on cloud computing in medical imaging, healthcare technologies, and services. Among the topics discussed in the book are ISM and DEMETAL analysis of H4.0 enablers in the Indian healthcare industry; machine-learning algorithms for health data security; fog computing in IoT-based health care; medical image and healthcare applications using 5G; the application of cloud-computing technology to improve patients' medical history access to clinicians for quality of care in the fourth industrial revolution; healthcare infrastructure; diagnostic imaging and associated services; health monitoring based on the integrated offer of cloud IoT-sensing services; sleep stage identification using recurrent neural network for ECG wearable-sensor system; classification of methods to reduce clinical alarm signals for remote patient monitoring; and image steganography for medical informatics.

In summary, the main aim of this book is to help advance scientific research within the broad field of cloud computing in medical imaging, healthcare technologies and services. The book focuses on major trends and challenges in this area, and it presents work aimed to identify new techniques and their use in biomedical analysis.

Ayman El-Baz
Jasjit S. Suri

Editors

Ayman El-Baz is a distinguished professor at University of Louisville, Kentucky, United States, and University of Louisville at AlAlamein International University (UofL-AIU), New Alamein City, Egypt. Dr. El-Baz earned his BSc and MSc degrees in electrical engineering in 1997 and 2001, respectively. He earned his PhD in electrical engineering from the University of Louisville in 2006. Dr. El-Baz was named a Fellow for Coulter, AIMBE, and NAI for his contributions to the field of biomedical translational research. Dr. El-Baz has almost two decades of hands-on experience in the fields of bio-imaging modeling and non-invasive computer-assisted diagnosis systems. He has authored or coauthored more than 700 technical articles (209 journals, 53 books, 104 book chapters, 262 refereed-conference papers, 216 abstracts, and 38 US patents and disclosures).

Jasjit S. Suri is an innovator, scientist, visionary, industrialist, and an internationally known world leader in biomedical engineering. Dr. Jasjit S. Suri has spent over 25 years in the field of biomedical engineering/devices and its management. He received his PhD from the University of Washington, Seattle, and his business management sciences degree from Weatherhead, Case Western Reserve University, Cleveland, Ohio. Dr. Jasjit S. Suri was crowned with the President's Gold medal in 1980 and made Fellow of the American Institute of Medical and Biological Engineering for his outstanding contributions. In 2018, he was awarded the Marquis Lifetime Achievement Award for his outstanding contributions and dedication to medical imaging and its management.

Contributors

 I am **Arya Agrawal**, currently pursuing computer science engineering. I have always been interested in engineering, basically building machines, along with having an affinity for economics. Both my associations somewhere indulge me to work in various interdisciplinary engineering and social sciences. I recently started working on robotics projects, focusing mainly on machine learning and ROS as a result of my curiosity about integrating automation in robotics. I've been part of the Women's Indian Chamber of Commerce and Industry cyber-security team, along with being a part of Ex-Curia International, working on dispute resolution and ADR, mainly associated with Law. I am an avid sportsperson, having represented Haryana Team in girls U-17 basketball at the state level. I carry a vast experience in Model UN because I aim to become an Indian diplomat someday.

 **Dr. Puneeta Ajmera** is working as an associate professor in the Department of Public Health, School of Allied Health Sciences, Delhi Pharmaceutical Sciences and Research University, New Delhi. She has done her PhD in healthcare management. She has total experience of 16 years that includes around 13 years of teaching and 3 years of industry experience. She has published more than 50 research papers in peer-reviewed international journals and presented papers in national and international conferences. She has filed two patents and authored three books on healthcare system and health policy. Her areas of interest include maternal and child health, globalization of healthcare, industry 4.0 and lean management in healthcare, decision making in healthcare with expertise in MADM (AHP, TOPSIS, VIKOR) approaches and structural modelling techniques like ISM, TISM etc. She can be contacted at puneeta_22@yahoo.com.

Abdulwahab Alazeb received his BS degree in computer science from King Khaled University, Abha, Saudi Arabia in 2007, MS degree in computer science from the Department of Computer Science, University of Colorado, USA in 2014, and PhD degree at the University of Arkansas, USA in 2021. His research interests include cybersecurity, cloud- and edge-computing security, and Internet of Things.

Sultan Almakdi received the BS degree in computer science from King Khalid University, Abha, Saudi Arabia, in 2010, the MS degree in computer science from the University of Colorado Denver, Denver, USA, in 2014, and the PhD degree in computer science from the University of Arkansas, Fayettiville, USA, in 2020. He is currently working as an assistant professor with the Department of Computer Science and Information Systems, Najran University, Saudi Arabia. His research interests include cloud security, fog security, edge-computing security, IoT security, and computer security. He received a graduate certificate in cybersecurity from the University of Arkansas in 2020.

Mohammed S. Alshehri received a BS degree in computer science from King Khalid University, Abha, KSA, in 2010. Mohammed received an MS degree in computer science from the University of Colorado, Denver, USA, in 2014, and a PhD degree in computer science from the University of Arkansas, Fayettiville, USA, in 2021. Mohammed recieved a graduate certificate in cybersecurity from the University of Arkansas, Fayetteville, USA, in 2021. Mohammed joined moderator volunteer, IEEE CS DVP-SYP Virtual Conference. Mohammed has gained multiple professional certificates during his graduate life, such as: Security+, Network+, and CISM.

I'm **Arushi Ananthakrishnan**, pursuing a B.Tech degree in electronics and communication. I am a curious and driven individual who is always looking for opportunities to learn a new skill or to enhance my current skill set. I additionally am a quick learner and enjoy working with people. I also do not give up on problems easily and would work on them until I get them right. While reading a biography of Elon Musk, I found my interest in autonomous vehicles and have since started working on building my knowledge for the same. Autonomous vehicles require various fields to come together and work to function the way it is. It requires a deep understanding of not just the field you are in but others as well It requires a deep understanding of concepts such as Python and ML, which are precisely what I have applied for as well. Non-technically, I'm a good listener and able to naturally engage people in a conversation. Furthermore, I also tend to grasp concepts and software quickly. I have an integrated understanding, and my skills are involved not only in my branch but also in other branches such as mechanical and computer science. Being a part of a team like AutoZ, specializing in the research and development of autonomous vehicles, we built a prototype of an actual electric vehicle that was both cost-effective and efficient. Since understanding my passion for the subject, I have used most of my time harnessing the skills required for the same and have also joined groups with similar interests. Non-technically, I'm also proficient with vocal music and classical dance. I was also a part of my badminton school team. I have also got into a team at my university where I am able to build my skills firsthand and work on physical projects. I am additionally a quick learner and am hoping to make it an opportunity for me to learn and grow as a person.

Teena Arora is doing her PhD degree in wireless body area network using the sensors for remote healthcare-monitoring applications using the cloud computing. Her area of interest is healthcare, cloud computing, remote patient monitoring.

Sarah M. Ayyad is a graduate research assisstant at computer engineering and control system department, Faculty of Engineering, Mansoura University. She received her BSc in 2014 from Mansoura University and received her master's in 2019. She is currently pursuing her PhD at Mansoura University, and she had been working and collaborating widely with the bioImaging lab, bioengineering department at the University of Louisville for more than two years. Her main research interests include medical-image analysis using the state-of-the-art machine and deep-learning techniques for different medical conditions, e.g., prostate cancer. She had published more than seven technical publications, including journal articles, book chapters, and abstracts.

Venki Balasubramanian received the PhD degree in body area wireless sensor network (BAWSN) for remote healthcare-monitoring applications. He is currently with the School of Science, Engineering and Information Technology, Federation University, Mount Helen, VIC, Australia. He is also the pioneer in building (pilot) remote healthcare-monitoring application (rHMA) for pregnant women with the New South Wales Healthcare Department. He also founded Anidra Tech Ventures Pty Ltd., a smart remote patient monitoring system. His research establishes a dependability measure to evaluate rHMA that uses BAWSN. His research opens up a new research area in measuring time-critical applications. He contributed immensely to eResearch software research and development that uses cloud-based infrastructure. He is also a core member for the project sponsored by the Nectar Australian Research Cloud Provider. He contributed heavily in the field of healthcare informatics, sensor networks, and cloud computing.

Dr. Padmakali Banerjee is a thought leader and life coach, Vice Chancellor, Sir Padampat Singhania University, Udaipur, India. Padmakali Banerjee has over 30 years of experience in research, teaching and training, and academic administration. She has extensive experience as an executive, life coach, and psychologist. Her areas of interest are psychology, health management, and research methodology. She has authored of The Power of Positivity Optimism and the 7th Sense, SAGE publication.

Dr. Rajkumar Buyya is a fellow of IEEE, professor of computer science and software engineering and director of the Cloud Computing and Distributed Systems (CLOUDS) Laboratory at the University of Melbourne, Australia. He is also serving as the founding CEO of Manjrasoft, a spin-off company of the university, commercializing its innovations in cloud computing. He has authored over 525 publications and seven text books, including *Mastering Cloud Computing* published by McGraw Hill, China Machine Press, and Morgan Kaufmann for Indian, Chinese, and international markets, respectively. He is one of the highly cited authors in computer science and software engineering worldwide (h-index = 109, g-index = 230, 58,300+ citations). Microsoft Academic Search Index ranked Dr. Buyya as #1 author in the world (2005–2016) for both field rating and citations evaluations in the area of distributed and parallel computing. *A Scientometric Analysis of Cloud Computing Literature* by German scientists ranked Dr. Buyya as the world's top-cited (#1) author and the world's most productive (#1) author in cloud computing. Recently, Dr. Buyya is recognized as 2016 Web of Science Highly Cited Researcher by Thomson Reuters. Software technologies for grid and cloud computing developed under Dr. Buyya's leadership have gained rapid acceptance and are in use at several academic institutions and commercial enterprises in 40 countries around the world. Manjrasoft's Aneka cloud technology developed under his leadership has received the "2010 Frost & Sullivan New Product Innovation Award." Recently, Dr. Buyya received the "Mahatma Gandhi Award" along with Gold Medal for his outstanding and extraordinary achievements in the information technology field and services rendered to promote greater friendship and India-International cooperation. He served as the founding editor-in-chief of the IEEE Transactions on Cloud Computing. He is currently serving as co-editor-in-chief of *Journal of Software: Practice and Experience,* which was established over 45 years ago. For further information on Dr. Buyya, please visit his cyberhome: www.buyya.com.

Utkarsh Chadha is an undergraduate student of mechanical engineering from VIT University, Vellore, India, with varied research domains, within healthcare applications. From artificial intelligence implementation to IoT in wearable sensors for hospital applications to ease a patient's recovery.

Other than healthcare, his core domain of research is materials science, composites, artificial intelligence and machine learning in mechanical applications and process precision, human error reduction, and wastage reduction.

I'm **Asmi Dhull** currently pursuing Btech in electrical and electronics engineering at VIT, Vellore. I have always had an inclination toward science in general. Engineering is a branch of science that basically refers to building new things, and that is exactly what fascinates me about it. I have always loved building up things or coming up with ideas to solve the most random problems that one may face in their day-to-day life. Nikola Tesla has been a great inspiration for me since childhood. Something I learned from reading about him was his ability to prognosticate future technology and sustainability. My core is electrical and electronics engineering, and what interests me most about it is that everything that exists in today's world from nano-sized things to massive devices that gives us comfort or saves our time fundamentally depends and works on electricity. Electric vehicles and automation are something I'm highly intrigued by. I'd taken part in IBM's one million one billion competition in which I had developed a prototype of an AI-enabled drone that used UV rays and thermal temperature techniques to detect microplastics in the environment. From my school days till today, research has always intrigued my curiosity; however, coming into college has given me the opportunity to pursue it. During my schooling, I've participated in various projects and competitions which required research. In college, I'm a part of Team AutoZ, which is also VIT's first autonomous vehicle team. I have worked on various projects with the team, which required the integration of software skills, and mechanical and electrical skills combined. Although I work in the EEE/ECE domain of the team, I also explore other content creation and management areas like web development and team social media management. The design of battery systems and PCBs is my area of expertise. I'm proficient in using EagleCAD, Fusion360, proteus, and MATLAB. I feel I'm a person who is willing to learn new skills and work consistently. I'm well aware of the fact that success comes through working hard. There is a quote by Vincent Van Gogh that stuck with me "Normality is a paved road. It's comfortable to walk but no flowers grow."

Asha Durafe is a PhD research scholar in the electronics and communication department at Sir Padampat Singhania University, Rajasthan, India. She is also working as assistant professor in Shah and Anchor Kutchhi Engineering College, India for the last 16 years. She has earned the Best Research Project by CSI Technext in Sept. 2019. Her areas of interests are computer security, digital image processing, IoT security, computer networks, IPR and patenting, power electronics and digital communication.

Abimbola Efunogbon is an experienced software engineer with over 15 years of commercial experience across mobile, web, desktop, and distributed applications. She has a BSc degree in chemical and polymer engineering and a MSc degree in computing and entrepreneurship from the University of Bedfordshire. During her undergraduate studies, she was awarded best female engineering student by Association of Professional Women Engineers of Nigeria (APWEN). She is currently undergoing her PhD research at the University of Bedforshire and leads the team of application engineers at Coleparmer Scientific.

Itamir de Morais Barroca Filho was born in Natal, Brazil. He is a professor at Universidade Federal do Rio Grande do Norte (UFRN). His PhD is in computer science, his master's degree in systems and computing in software engineering, and he is a specialist in computer networks. He developed information systems and mobile applications, playing the role of systems analyst, development manager, and software architect. He is currently chief of information officer (CIO) at UFRN's Instituto Metrópole Digital (IMD).

Mohammed Ghazal (Senior Member, IEEE) received the BSc degree in computer engineering from the American University of Sharjah (AUS) in 2004 and the MASc and PhD degrees in electrical and computer engineering (ECE) from Concordia University, Montreal, QC, Canada, in 2010 and 2006, respectively. He is currently an associate professor and the chair of ECE with Abu Dhabi University and an adjunct associate professor of bioengineering with the University of Louisville. He has authored or coauthored over 40 publications in recognized international journals and conferences, including the *IEEE Transactions in Image Processing, IEEE Transactions in Circuits and Systems for Video Technology, IEEE Transactions in Consumer Electronics, Elsevier's Renewable Energy Reviews,* and *Springer's Multimedia Tools and Applications.* His research interests include bioengineering, image and video processing, and smart systems. He is also a member of ACM and BMES. He was a recipient of multiple awards, including the Distinguished Faculty Award of Abu Dhabi University in 2017 and 2014, a Special Innovation Award of AED 1 000 000 by the Office of Prime Minister of the UAE, the NSERC's Alexander Graham Bill's Scholarship, AUS's Presidents Cup, and the Ministry of Education Shield for Creative Thinking.

I am **Manan Gupta**, currently pursuing BTech in computer science engineering from VIT Vellore and BSc in programming and data science from IIT-M. I am a passionate individual with a constant desire to learn and work on challenging projects. I started working on electronics in my childhood and built my foundation upon it. In school, I have worked in numerous competitions over the years and have gathered experience to work on larger and more demanding projects. I have participated in the World Robot Olympiad up to the nationals in 2014, 2015, and 2016, First Tech Challenge up to nationals in 2014 and 2015. I have also won inter-school competitions called Robotronics in 2015 (1st) and 2016 (2nd). I self-learned Arduino and related microcontrollers in 2016 and participated in Odyssey of the mind in which, as a part of a team, we made a semi-humanoid robot to mimic human tasks using Arduino. This helped us win the first prize in the national round. We went to Michigan State University in 2017 for the international round and represented our nation. The experience gained from these competitions showed me how much there is to be learned in these fields, and this strengthened my decision of pursuing sciences for my +2. I have experience with Lego Mindstorms, Arduino, Raspberry pi, Esp-32, and other related boards. I am self-taught in all these technologies and continue to learn new things every day.

I have worked on many small side projects, which are a measure of DIY-ing a lot of devices that I can buy. This gives me experience and works as a way for me to apply my mind to something productive. I also configure and build servers and computers as a hobby. I recycle a lot of old electronics and repurpose them into useful devices that everyone can use. I also fix a lot of my own electronics because of the experience I have gained. As I am pursuing my undergraduate degrees, I am working on autonomous vehicles and their development.

 **Professor Sardar M.N. Islam** currently is a Professor at Victoria University's Institute for Sustainable Industries and Liveable Cities. He was a Professor of Business, Economics and Finance from 2007 to 2017, and has had many years of academic work experience in teaching, supervision, and multidisciplinary research. He has published articles in leading international journals including:

- *Review of Quantitative Finance and Accounting,*
- *Journal of Optimisation Theory and Applications*
- *Journal of Management and Industrial Optimisation*
- *Annals of Operations Research, Applied Mathematical Modelling, Economic Modelling*
- *Journal of Modelling in Management.*

He has published a large number of research books in artificial intelligence and digitalisation, game theory, operations research, supply chain management, accounting, finance, business, economics and law. The following are the areas of his interest and expertise for supervision and mentoring of, and collaboration with, students and colleagues/professors:

- Artificial intelligence, machine learning and data analytics
- Game theory, agency theory and mechanism design
- Finance
- Advanced econometrics
- Economics/health economics
- Accounting and corporate governance
- Management science/applied quantitative methods (applied operations research methods, applied econometrics, structural equation modeling, etc.)
- Supply chain management/applied industrial engineering/operations management, engineering analytics and management
- Business and Marketing Analytics
- Law.

Dr. Vineet Jain is working as a professor & HOD in the Department of Mechanical Engineering, Mewat Engineering College, Haryana Waqf Board, Government of Haryana, Palla, District Nuh, Haryana-122107, India. He received the PhD degree in mechanical engineering at the Department of Mechanical Engineering, YMCA University of Science and Technology, Faridabad, India. He completed his BE mechanical with honours from NIT Kurukshetra, India and M. Tech (manufacturing and automation) with honours from the YMCA Institute of Engineering, Faridabad, India. His areas of interest are manufacturing technology, operation research, and decision making with expertise in ISM, GTMA, EFA, CFA, SPSS, AMOS, ANFIS, GA, TLBO and MADM, like AHP, TOPSIS, VIKOR, PROMETHEE, MOORA,PSI, CMBA, ELECTRE, WEDBA etc. He possesses more than 21 years' experience in teaching and industry. He has written three books in mechanical engineering published with Dhanpat Rai Publication New Delhi, India. He has published 31 papers in international journal like Elsevier, Springer, Emerald, Inderscience, Taylor & Francis, Growing Science, etc. and presented paper in international and national conferences. Editorial Board Member of International Journal of Data and Network Science, Scopus (Elsevier) indexed: ISSN 2561-8156 (Online) - ISSN 2561-8148 (Print). Reviewer of 26 international journals (indexed SCI/Scopus/Web of Science), technical program committee member of 25 international conferences, which were held abroad. Dr Vineet Jain can be contacted at: vjdj2004@gmail.com. (Orchid id: 0000-0002-4662-3081 and Scopus id: 57198886405).

Vincent Valentine Jansen is a graduate student on Bina Nusantara University, BINUS Graduate Program, Master of Computer Science. Currently, he is working as a full-time software engineer.

I am **Shreemanto Lahiri,** currently pursuing BTech in information technology from VIT Vellore. I have always had an interest in science and engineering. I am a person who loves to code and work on challenging projects. I believe that most problems in the world can be solved just with some hardware and a few lines of code, and I aspire to solve the same. I'm particularly interested in machine learning and robotics. I am also a part of VIT's first autonomous vehicle team, AutoZ, where I have contributed in the domain of ROS and machine learning.

Working on autonomous vehicles and learning about them has been a very enriching experience. During my schooling, I was the captain of the boys U-17 volleyball team and have taken part in many state-level tournaments. I am also an A-certificate holder in NCC and NSS. I've always been interested in CSE because of the numerous chances and fields it offers, and I'm currently exploring the app development side of it. I have also worked on blockchain technology and Dapps and am an avid Web3 enthusiast.

Dr. Enjie Liu received her first degree in computer science from Southwestern University in China in 1987. She then worked as assistant lecturer for two years, and then worked for joint-venture of Nortel networks from 1989 to 1998. She moved to UK, and in 2002, she received her PhD from Queen Mary, University of London in telecommunication networks. From 2003, she started to work for the University of Bedfordshire and now is a reader in network applications. Since 2003, she has been working on several EU funded projects in healthcare applications. Her interests include 5G vertical applications, 5G slice and slice management, and 5G non-public networks.

Ali H. Mahmoud received his BS and MS degrees in electrical engineering from Alexandria University, Egypt, in 2005 and 2009, respectively. Also, he received his PhD degree in electrical engineering from the University of Louisville, Louisville, USA in 2014. He is currently working as a postdoctoral research associate at the bioengineering department at the University of Louisville. His research interests include computer vision and image processing, object detection and tracking, medical imaging, and facial biometrics.

Prof. Ngoako Solomon Marutha is working as a Full Professor in the Department of Information Science at the University of South Africa (UNISA). He also serves as a representative of the Unisa Department of Information Science on the International Council on Archives (ICA) and he is an ICA Regular Member of Section on University and Research Institution Archives (ICA/SUV), where he also serve as an executive member for bureau. He is also a regular member for ICA section for Archival education (ICA-SAE) and section for the National Assembly. He is also a member of the South African Society of Archivists and serves on the National Executive Committee as editor-in-chief of the *Journal of the South African Society of Archivists.* He is also a review editor for the journal Frontiers in *Research Metrics and Analytics.* He has published several books, chapters and articles in different national and international publications and presented conference papers. His research interest includes knowledge, archives, and records management, especially on patients and hospital records, electronic records, cloud computing, Blockchain technology, enterprise content management, big data management and police case records security. The other field of his interest includes library management and marketing as well as Open Distance electronic learning (ODeL). His professional industry background includes working as an information and records manager as well as librarian in several public and private institutions over 13 years. He has been in the academic industry over five years so far. He holds Bachelor of Information studies and Bachelor of Information Studies honour from University of the North (UNIN)-now known as University of Limpopo (UL), Master of Information Science and Doctor of literature and philosophy from University of South Africa (UNISA). He serves as external examiner for masters and doctoral research studies for over seven universities.

Dr. Naif Al Mudawi, assistant professor, Department of Computer Science and Information system, Najran University. He holds a PhD from the Collage of Engineering and Informatics at University of Sussex in Brighton, UK with distinction with honours in a delicate specialization in adopting of cloud computing in online system for public organisation in 2018. He graduated from the Australian La Trobe University with a master's degree in computer science in (2011) during his academic journey to obtain a master's degree, he was a member of the Australian Computer Science committee. Dr. Naif has also attended many specialized courses in management and courses in team building, time management, and project management. He has many published and peer-reviewed research and scientific papers in many prestigious journals in various disciplines of computer science.

Gabriel Neagu, PhD, National Institute for Research and Development in Informatics – I.C.I. Bucharest, received his PhD in Applied Informatics at the University Politehnica of Bucharest. In 1993, he was a visiting researcher on advanced decision support in manufacturing at the Centre for Manufacturing Systems - Institute of Technology, New Jersey, the Robotics Institute – Carnegie Mellon University, and the Laboratory for Industrial Process Control – Purdue University, with an IREX (USA) grant support. Since 1995, G. Neagu is scientific researcher first degree. During this period, he has been director of 10 competition-based national partnership research projects and beneficiary of two research grants awarded by the Romanian Academy and the Romanian Ministry of Research, respectively. In the same period, he has been national representative in 13 research projects funded by various European research programs. His list of memberships includes IFAC 5.1 Technical Committee (since 1996), Research Data Alliance (since 2017), European e-Infrastructure Reflection Group (2008–2011),

International Society for Productivity Enhancement (1992-2000). He is author/co-author of more than 100 published articles and conference papers. He has been scientific evaluator for national and EU research programs, IPC member for more than 70 International conferences, invited session organizer and chair at nine international conferences, reviewer for 14 ISI journals. His current research interests include advanced data architectures, data-analytics techniques, e-infrastructures, agile approaches for hierarchical and distributed system development, eHealth services, decision support based on discrete event modeling and simulation, and open research data management.

Prof. Dr. Vinod Patidar is presently professor of Physics and Dean, Research at Sir Padampat Singhania University (SPSU), Udaipur, India. He is also the head of Physics Department at SPSU since July 2011. Prior to his present position, he has served as associate dean research (October 2018–January 2019), associate professor & head (2011–2015), and assistant professor (2008–2011) at SPSU and as a senior lecturer (2007–2008) and lecturer (2005–2007) in the Department of Physics, Banasthali University, Banasthali, India. He has about 20 years of research and teaching experience. He has been the principal investigator in a Young Scientist research project on the "Application of chaotic dynamical systems in developing secure cryptosystems and their cryptanalysis" funded by the Department of Science and Technology, Government of India (2009–2012). Presently, he is principal investigator in the MATRICS project "Development of new designs of secure image encryption schemes utilizing robust chaos and fractional integral transforms" funded by the SERB, government of India (2019–2022).

Mohamed Shehata (Member, IEEE) received his BSc degree in computer engineering and control systems from Mansoura University, Egypt, 2009. In 2014, he joined the BioImaging Lab at the University of Louisville. In 2016, Mohamed has been awarded his MSc degree from the Electrical and Computer Engineering Department at the University of Louisville, and directly enrolled in his PhD program in computer engineering and computer science department. He has actively been working on medical-imaging analysis, specifically, design of computer-aided diagnostic (CAD) systems for detection/classification of acute renal transplant rejection from diffusion-weighted and BOLD-MRIs. In addition, he is working on developing new techniques for the early diagnosis, detection, and prediction of different types of cancers such as renal cancer, liver cancer, spine cancer, breast cancer, prostate cancer, Wilms tumors, etc. Mohamed has been authored in more than 50 technical peer-reviewed publications (e.g., *IEEE Transaction on Biomedical Engineering, Scientific Reports: Nature, Medical*

Physics, PLOS One, Insights into Imaging, Sensors, The British Journal of Radiology, MICCAI, IEEE ISBI, IEEE ICIP, IEEE ICPR, etc.). He has also received many international and local prestigious awards.

Mai Shenhan is doing his master's in research degree in wireless body area network using the sensors for remote healthcare-monitoring applications. His area of interest is healthcare, cloud computing, remote patient monitoring.

Cezar Miranda Paula de Souza was born in Natal, Brazil. He has a degree in computer engineering from Universidade Federal do Rio Grande do Norte (UFRN) and a master's in business administration (MBA) in strategic and economic project management from Fundação Getúlio Vargas (FGV) (Summa Cum Laude). He was involved in software engineering in several capacities on a number of companies and institutions, developing systems with varying requirements, architectural styles and on several platforms, acting in positions such as full-stack developer, technical leader, software designer, coordinator, project manager, and finally, chief technology officer (CTO), a position held until recently on a tech startup that provides healthcare cloud solutions under the QuarkClinic moniker. Currently, he's a visiting researcher at UFRN's Instituto Metrópole Digital (IMD) - a local IT business incubator covering initiatives from the public, private, and academic sectors - acting as an advisor and technical leader in software innovation projects developed in partnership with large multinational companies in the hardware and telecommunications segments. He's also a master's student at UFRN's Programa de Pós Graduação em Tecnologia da Informação (PPGTI) masters program.

Dhanush Srikanth, I am currently an undergraduate pursuing Mechanical Engineering with Specialization in Automotive Engineering from Vellore Institute of Technology. My primary interests are Computational Fluid Dynamics (CFD), Mechatronics and Autonomous Vehicles. I am quite passionate about electric vehicles and furthering their implementation in modern day society. I am open to all forms of science and technology as I am very inquisitive by nature as such I believe that Science can push horizons we may never have imagined and continue to change our understanding of the universe.

I am **Divyansh Srivastava**, For as long as I can recall, I had this passion to invent new things and implement unique solutions to real-life problems; in the process, I stumbled across tech stacks such as Robotic and Automation. The sheer scope of such technologies filled me with immense joy that I could not comprehend. That experience planted the seed of curiosity in my mind to understand how robots function and what goes into the implementation of such technology. My drive for knowledge led me to excel in academics and ultimately graduate with a bachelor's degree in mechanical engineering. I like to innovate new things and solve challenges faced in various industries by implementing automation-oriented solutions. I have hands-on experience with 3D printing, sheet metal fabrication, and metal fabrication like lathe and milling. Apart from these, I'm certified in SIX SIGMA GREEN BELT and fluent in MS Excel, MATLAB, Simulink, and the majority of the CAD software like CATIA, SolidWorks, and Fusion 360. I regularly find new projects and teams to work with, in my pursuit to gain and pass on as much knowledge as I can. As a result, I was awarded the "GD NAIDU YOUNG SCIENTIST AWARD" for my work in the Fast-Track Research Initiative, where I presented a prototype for an autonomous coconut-harvesting machine known as the "Cocobot." Apart from this, I was part of the Autonomous Research Center (ARC), with net funding of 7 crore rupees working on developing autonomous vehicles. I recently worked on a Defense Research & Development Organization (DRDO) funded project, which was a collaboration between Vellore and IIIT-DM to make an autonomous anti-tank mine-detecting rover. I'm also collaborating with scientists from Vikram Sarabhai Space Center (VSSC), Indian Space Research Organization (ISRO), and Trivandrum, to work on two research papers. Additionally, I have various publications published or under review in reputed journals, two of which are published in reputed journals like the *Journal of the Electrochemical Society* (IF:4.316) and *Advances in Materials Science and Engineering* (IF:1.726). I have received "The Raman Research award" for the same; along with that, I have a filled patent on "Adjustable positioning system design for Bistatic Ground Penetrating Radar Antenna in buried object detection applications" (design patent) IN 335429-001 Filled on Dec 10, 2020.

Andrew Stranieri is an AI researcher at the Federation University Australia. Dr Stranieri's expertise in health informatics spans data analytics in health, complementary and alternative medicine informatics, remote patient monitoring, telemedicine, and intelligent decision support systems. Andrew is the author of over 200 peer-reviewed journal and conference articles and has published three books. In 2016, he co-founded Anidra Tech Ventures Pty Ltd, a company that performs remote vital signs monitoring in Indian hospitals. The technology processes data from sensors worn by patients to detect a deterioration and alert remotely-located doctors and nurses to view vital signs in real time. Andrew is associate professor in information technology at the Federation University and currently leads the Health Informatics Laboratory. Prior to commencing at the University of Ballarat (now Federation University), he completed his PhD at La Trobe University and was awarded an Australian Research Council Australian Post-doctoral Award (Industry).

Nico Surantha received his B Eng (2007) and M Eng (2009) from Institut Teknologi Bandung, Indonesia. He received his PhD degree from Kyushu Institute of Technology, Japan, in 2013. Currently, he serves as a full-time faculty member at the Department of Electrical, Electronic and Communication Engineering, Tokyo City University, Japan. He is is also a part-time lecturer at the computer science department, Binus Graduate Program, Bina Nusantara University, Indonesia. His research interest includes ubiquitous intelligent system, Internet of Things, health monitoring, and system on chip design. He is an IEEE member.

Ali Yamini is a BS studying software engineering at Science and Research Branch, Islamic Azad University, Iran. His research interests are machine learning, computer vision, natural language processing, cloud computing, and distributed systems.

Azadeh Zamanifar is currently assistant professor of software engineering in the science and research branch of Azad University, Tehran, Iran. She received her PhD in software engineering from Shahid Beheshti University of Tehran in 2016. She received her MSc in computer engineering (software) in 2008 from Iran University of Science and Technology (IUST), Tehran, Iran. She received her BSc in computer engineering (hardware) in 2002 from Tehran University. Her main interest is Internet of Things and healthcare systems.

Dr. Youbing Zhao received his PhD degree from State Key Lab of CAD&CG, Zhejiang University, China. After working as an innovator in Siemens Research Shanghai for three years, he joined Center for Computer Graphics and Visualisation in University of Bedfordshire UK as a research fellow. He participated in more than 10 EU and EPSRC projects on healthcare and visualisation. At present, he is also helping Communication University of Zhejiang on projects of mobile app-assisted reminiscence and breast cancer data analysis. His research interests include medical and healthcare data mining, visualisation, and VR/AR.

Chapter 1

Cloud Computing in Healthcare and Medical Imaging: A Brief Overview

Sarah M. Ayyad[1], Mohamed Shehata[2],
Ali H. Mahmoud[2], Mohammed Ghazal[3],
Jasjit S. Suri[4], and Ayman El-Baz[2]

[1]Computers and Systems Department, Faculty of Engineering, Mansoura University, Mansoura, Egypt
[2]BioImaging Laboratory, Bioengineering Department, University of Louisville, Louisville, KY, USA
[3]Department of Electrical and Computer Engineering, College of Engineering, Abu Dhabi University, Abu Dhabi, UAE
[4]ATHEROPOINT, Roseville, CA, USA

Contents

1.1 Introduction 1
1.2 Adopting Cloud for Healthcare 4
1.3 Related Work 4
1.4 Conclusion 6
References 6

1.1 Introduction

Research in the life sciences, as well as clinical practice in biomedicine, is increasingly dependent on the large data sets generated by the high-throughput platforms used to

DOI: 10.1201/9781003145189-1

examine the human body, e.g., computed tomography (CT) [1–4], magnetic resonance imaging (MRI) [5–8], and optical coherence tomography (OCT) [9–12]. This considerable rise in medical imaging produces a great challenge for healthcare providers as they have to process, share, and manage this data with cost savings [13]. Additionally, chronic diseases have become more complicated, and new developments in bioengineering and research have aided the growth of new and efficient diagnostic and treatment techniques [14]. As a result, the logistics behind managing such operations have turned more complex and consume high costs. Moreover, competitions in the healthcare industry have increased. There is a significant rise in demand for healthcare solutions, but the deficiencies in professional healthcare specialists, such as nurses, pharmacists, and doctors, constitute one of the biggest issues that healthcare providers tackled [14].

The use of cloud computing in healthcare is attracting great interest from the public sector, the scientific community, and healthcare providers [15]. The term "cloud computing" means accessing hosted services using the Internet for data storage, analytics, aggregation, networking, and recovery, along with the ability to work on the data using computerized techniques and software packages [16]. Adopting a cloud-computing solution in healthcare providers such as hospitals and doctor's clinics with inadequate information technology (IT) resources or hardware infrastructure delivers opportunities to access required IT services using a pay-as-you-go pricing policy [15].

Cloud services come in three varieties: internal (private), outsourced (public), or hybrid [14,17]. The variety depends on the user requirements and the required infrastructure. For a typical healthcare provider, a dedicated private cloud infrastructure is the most ideal mode for ensuring quality, reliability, and privacy of services, but this mode carries a high cost [17]. Figure 1.1 reveals a typical

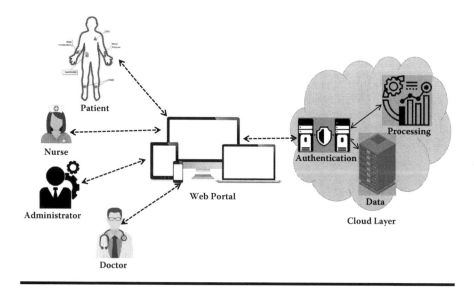

Figure 1.1 Cloud-Computing Architecture for Healthcare.

architecture of a healthcare cloud-computing platform. The cloud-computing model is composed of six main features: (i) resource pooling; (ii) on-demand service; (iii) large network access; (iv) rapid elasticity; (v) security; and (vi) measured services. Nowadays, there exist many cloud services providers like Amazon web service, Google cloud platform, Microsoft Azure, Rackspace, Salesforce, Apache Hadoop [13,18].

Generally, cloud-computing platforms consist of three service types, namely, Software as a Service (SaaS), Platform as a Service (PaaS), and Infrastructure as a Service (IaaS) (as shown in Figure 1.2) [13,14,19]. SaaS offers cloud-based software solutions, e.g., clinical systems and customer relationship management where consumers such as healthcare providers, finance brokers, and insurance brokers can dynamically access the services on the cloud [14,16]. On the other hand, PaaS extends the core infrastructure with high-level integrated environment to design, build, update, deploy, and test online healthcare services [14]. PaaS enhances scalability by providing an online working environment when users demand [19]. In this case, users do not have to worry about keeping their operating system (OS) and programs updated or virus-free [16]. In contrast, IaaS or "cloud infrastructure services" works by a virtualization mechanism that allows several virtual machines to work on top of a single physical hardware infrastructure in an isolated way [16,20]. Users do not handle the cloud infrastructure but may have control over applications, OS, and storage.

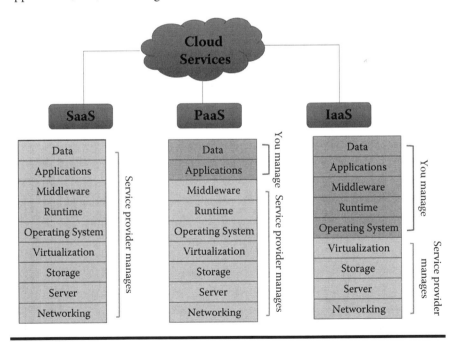

Figure 1.2 Cloud Service Models (SaaS, PaaS, IaaS).

The review in this chapter was conducted using papers published in highly ranked journals, i.e., *Sensors, Scientific Reports, Diagnostics, Medical Physics, IEEE Transactions on Biomedical Engineering,* and *Journal of Medical Systems.* We used the following keywords: cloud, cloud computing, healthcare cloud-based, medical cloud, IaaS, PaaS, SaaS, and medical data, and used combinations of them. The remainder of this chapter is organized as follows: Section 1.2 provides an overview of adopting cloud computing in healthcare and the pressing challenges. Section 1.3 provides the rationale for cloud solutions in healthcare. Lastly, we provide our concluding remarks in Section 1.4.

1.2 Adopting Cloud for Healthcare

The current push for personalized treatment of diseases encourages seamless integration of data obtained from many sources of investigation. To achieve this goal, a collaboration between hospitals and health centers is required for sharing data of the patients and imaging informatics [21–25]. The advantages of adopting cloud computing in healthcare include scalability, reliability, environmental sustainability, data migration, cost-saving, and connected systems that focus on the patient [13,17]. Hence, hospitals, doctor's clinics, insurance companies, pharmacies, and imaging centers can store and share patient's medical records, pharmaceutical diagnostics, patient's scans, test results, doctor's references, data analytics, etc., which can be accessed everywhere and anywhere by authorized people [26].

Nevertheless, cloud computing provides valuable advantages, and the large volume and high dimensionality of data posed clear challenges [19,21,27]. Some of the challenges relate to data privacy and security and can be considered as the main issue to cloud computing in the field of healthcare data analytics [19]. They are considered the basis for determining the right solution for any service provider [28]. Generally, ownership of data in the healthcare industry is another challenge without clear guidelines [14]. The patient record can, for example, be the private property of the patient. However, the physicians also claim ownership. This idea relates to establishing policies and guidelines that delineate clear ownership limits [14]. A further concern in building healthcare services in the cloud is the data availability [15,29]. Any healthcare service on the cloud must be continuously available without interruptions or performance degradation. Moreover, a cloud-based ecosystem needs the capability to interoperate between clouds and develop tools that can operate in many cloud environments [30].

1.3 Related Work

Our goal of this chapter is to review and study the rationale of healthcare services and solutions in the cloud. They are many studies and commentaries that have developed as cloud-computing systems that deal with many of the challenges mentioned before. For example, authors in [31] proposed a new hybrid computing platform between grid computing and cloud computing, called "Acigna-G." The medical images cloud service is offered at MapReduce PaaS and integrates existing grid applications. They also developed a segmentation algorithm for images on their platform. In the same year, another study [32], focused on home healthcare. Authors introduced a number of use cases and drew an architecture that addressed two of the main challenges of cloud systems, security and privacy. In addition, they studied a mitigation solution that focuses on facilitating patients and data protection for electronic data.

In [33], the authors designed a healthcare framework called "UbeHealth," that consists of four stages; namely (i) mobile stage, (ii) cloudlet stage, (iii) network stage, and (iv) cloud stage. This framework allows network quality of service to be improved by using three key elements and the four stages mentioned above. In [34], authors introduced a standard mutual authentication protocol to work in healthcare-based cloud systems. Their protocol focused on reinforcing security. They also enhanced computation overhead. However, they did not consider some of the security issues of cloud computing. Accordingly, authors in [35] proposed a new mutual authentication framework that is based on the standard one for the healthcare system. Authors first discussed the standard mutual authentication scheme. Then they introduced their framework that fixed the mentioned security weaknesses efficiently.

All modalities in radiology practice must consider DICOM images, which is abbreviated for "digital imaging and communications in medicine" [36–40]. DICOM format is different from other formats in that it stores many details about the images and patient into the dataset. In [41], authors implemented a prototype cloud system for DICOM images archive solution. Their system was evaluated using many DICOM images in different modalities. The system proved as a long-term offline medical-imagery solution for archive with lower cost.

Over recent years, mobile healthcare investments have grown dramatically, leading to better patient care [42–46]. In [42], authors proposed a new technique for diagnosis of stroke subtypes. They attained an accuracy of 85.3% using a three-layered multilayer perceptron algorithm with a user-friendly service available for patients. A more recent study for mobile healthcare to diagnose COVID is proposed in [46], where authors ensured the appropriate level of security, privacy, and integrity for patient's data. This is achieved through using white-box cryptography for the first time in mobile applications.

Cloud applications for preventive healthcare are rapidly improving and expanding. They can be applied for various chronic diseases, i.e., such as the prostate [47–51], the kidney [52–75], the heart [76–92], the lung [93–141], the brain [142–163], the vascular system [164–174], the retina [173–182], the bladder [183–187], the liver [188,189], head and neck [190–192], and injury prediction [193], as well as several nonmedical applications [194–200].

1.4 Conclusion

Cloud computing is transforming many healthcare solutions into virtual public services. This transformation can enhance and solve many collaborative information problems in healthcare organizations through improved costs. In this chapter, we reviewed cloud-based healthcare applications and analyzed the different issues associated with these applications. In addition, we examined the current challenges when building healthcare systems in the cloud.

References

[1] A. El-Baz, G. Gimel'farb, R. Falk, and M. A. El-Ghar, (2009) "Automatic analysis of 3D low dose CT images for early diagnosis of lung cancer," *Pattern Recognition*, vol. 42, no. 6, pp. 1041–1051.

[2] F. Khalifa, A. Elnakib, G. M. Beache, G. Gimel'farb, M. A. El-Ghar, G. Sokhadze, S. Manning, P. McClure, and A. El-Baz, (2011) "3D kidney segmentation from CT images using a level set approach guided by a novel stochastic speed function," in *Proceedings of International Conference Medical Image Computing and Computer-Assisted Intervention, (MICCAI'11)*, Toronto, Canada, September 18–22, pp. 587–594.

[3] F. Khalifa, G. Gimel'farb, M. A. El-Ghar, G. Sokhadze, S. Manning, P. McClure, R. Ouseph, and A. El-Baz, (2011) "A new deformable model-based segmentation approach for accurate extraction of the kidney from abdominal CT images," in *2011 18th IEEE International Conference on Image Processing (ICIP'11)*, pp. 3393–3396.

[4] A. Soliman, F. Khalifa, A. Elnakib, M. Abou El-Ghar, N. Dunlap, B. Wang, ... and A. El-Baz, (2016) Accurate lungs segmentation on CT chest images by adaptive appearance-guided shape modeling. *IEEE Transactions on Medical Imaging*, vol. 36, no. 1, 263–276.

[5] H. Abdeltawab, M. Shehatal, A. Shalaby, S. Mesbah, M. El-Baz, M. Ghazal, Y. AlKhali, M. AbouEl-Ghar, A. C. Dwyer, M. El-Melegy et al., (2018) "A new 3D CNN-based CAD system for early detection of acute renal transplant rejection," in *2018 24th International Conference on Pattern Recognition (ICPR)*. IEEE Computer Society, pp. 3898–3903.

[6] M. Shehata, F. Khalifa, A. Soliman, R. Alrefai, M. Abou El-Ghar, A. C. Dwyer, R. Ouseph, and A. El-Baz, (2015) "A novel framework for automatic segmentation of kidney from DW-MRI," in *2015 IEEE 12th International Symposium on Biomedical Imaging (ISBI)*. IEEE, pp. 951–954.

[7] M. Shehata, F. Khalifa, A. Soliman, A. T. Eldeen, M. Abou El-Ghar, T. El-Diasty, A. El-Baz, and R. Keynton, (2016) "An appearance-guided deformable model for 4D kidney segmentation using diffusion MRI," in *Biomedical Image Segmentation*. CRC Press, pp. 291–312.

[8] F. Khalifa, M. Shehata, A.. Soliman, M. Abou El-Ghar, T. El-Diasty, A. C. Dwyer, M. El-Melegy, G. Gimel'farb, R. Keynton, and A. El-Baz, (2017) "A generalized MRI-based CAD system for functional assessment of renal transplant," in *2017 IEEE 14th International Symposium on Biomedical Imaging (ISBI 2017)*. IEEE, pp. 758–761.

[9] N. Eladawi, M. Elmogy, M. Ghazal, O. Helmy, A. Aboelfetouh, A. Riad, S. Schaal, and A. El-Baz, (2018) "Classification of retinal diseases based on OCT images," *Frontiers in Bioscience (Landmark Ed)*, vol. 23, pp. 247–264.

[10] M. Elsharkawy, A. Sharafeldeen, A. Soliman, F. Khalifa, M. Ghazal, E. El-Daydamony, A. Atwan, H. S. Sandhu, and A. El-Baz, (2022) "A novel computer-aided diagnostic system for early detection of diabetic retinopathy using 3D-OCT higher-order spatial appearance model," *Diagnostics*, vol. 12, no. 2, p. 461.

[11] A. ElTanboly, M. Ismail, A. Switala, M. Mahmoud, A. Soliman, T. Neyer, … and A. El-Baz, (2016, September) "A novel automatic segmentation of healthy and diseased retinal layers from OCT scans," in *2016 IEEE International Conference on Image Processing (ICIP)* (pp. 116–120). IEEE.

[12] A. ElTanboly, M. Ismail, A. Shalaby, A. Switala, A. El-Baz, S. Schaal, … and M. El-Azab, (2017) "A computer-aided diagnostic system for detecting diabetic retinopathy in optical coherence tomography images," *Medical Physics*, vol. 44, no. 3, pp.914–923.

[13] S. G. Shini, T. Thomas, and K. Chithraranjan, (2012) "Cloud based medical image exchange-security challenges," *Procedia Engineering*, vol. 38, pp. 3454–3461.

[14] E. AbuKhousa, N. Mohamed, and J. Al-Jaroodi, (2012) "e-Health cloud: Opportunities and challenges," *Future Internet*, vol. 4, no. 3, pp. 621–645.

[15] M. Rahimi, N. J. Navimipour, M. Hosseinzadeh, M. H. Moattar, and A. Darwesh, (2022) "Cloud healthcare services: A comprehensive and systematic literature review," *Transactions on Emerging Telecommunications Technologies*, vol. 40, no. 7, p. e4473.

[16] G. C. Kagadis, C. Kloukinas, K. Moore, J. Philbin, P. Papadimitroulas, C. Alexakos, … and W. R. Hendee, (2013) "Cloud computing in medical imaging," *Medical Physics*, vol. 40, no. 7, p. 070901.

[17] S. B. Nalawade, (2015) "Cloud Computing in Healthcare and Biomedical research: Exchanging data at the speed of thought," *Biology, Engineering, Medicine and Science Reports*, vol. 1, no. 1, pp. 07–10.

[18] M. Ghazal, T. Basmaji, M. Yaghi, M. Alkhedher, M. Mahmoud, and A. S. El-Baz, (2020) "Cloud-based monitoring of thermal anomalies in industrial environments using AI and the internet of robotic things," *Sensors*, vol. 20, no. 21, pp. 6348.

[19] S. Koppad, G. V. Gkoutos, and A. Acharjee, (2021) "Cloud Computing Enabled Big Multi-Omics Data Analytics," *Bioinformatics and Biology Insights*, vol. 15, 11779322211035921.

[20] C. M. Mohammed, and S. R. Zeebaree, (2021) "Sufficient comparison among cloud computing services: IaaS, PaaS, and SaaS: A review," *International Journal of Science and Business*, vol. 5, no. 2, pp. 17–30.

[21] J. Chen, F. Qian, W. Yan, and B. Shen, (2013) "Translational biomedical informatics in the cloud: Present and future," *BioMed Research International*, vol. 2013, pp. 1–8.

[22] E. Hollis, M. Shehata, F. Khalifa, M. A. El-Ghar, T. El-Diasty, and A. El-Baz, (2016) "Towards non-invasive diagnostic techniques for early detection of acute renal transplant rejection: A review," *The Egyptian Journal of Radiology and Nuclear Medicine*, vol. 48, no. 1, pp. 257–269.

[23] M. Shehata, F. Khalifa, A. Soliman, M. A. El-Ghar, A. Dwyer, G. Gimel'farb, … and A. El-Baz, (2016, October) "A promising non-invasive cad system for kidney

function assessment," in *International Conference on Medical Image Computing and Computer-Assisted Intervention* (pp. 613–621). Springer, Cham.

[24] A. A. K. Abdel Razek, A. Alksas, M. Shehata, A. AbdelKhalek, K. Abdel Baky, A. El-Baz, and E. Helmy, (2021) "Clinical applications of artificial intelligence and radiomics in neuro-oncology imaging," *Insights into Imaging*, vol. 12, no. 1, pp. 1–17.

[25] M. Shehata, F. Khalifa, A. Soliman, S. Shaker, A. Shalaby, M. El-Baz, A. Mahmoud, A. C. Dwyer, M. Abou El-Ghar, M. Ghazal et al., (2021) "Early classification of renal rejection types: A deep learning approach," in *Machine Learning in Medicine* (pp. 257–280). CRC Press.

[26] S. P. Ahuja, S. Mani, and J. Zambrano, (2012) "A survey of the state of cloud computing in healthcare," *Network and Communication Technologies*, vol. 1, no. 2, p. 12.

[27] M. Shehata, A. Shalaby, A. Mahmoud, M. Ghazal, H. Hajjdiab, M. A. Badawy, M. Abou El-Ghar, A. M. Bakr, A. C. Dwyer, R. Keynton et al., (2019) *Towards Big Data in Acute Renal Rejection*. Chapman and Hall/CRC.

[28] Hucíková, A., and Babic, A., (2016) "Overcoming constraints in healthcare with cloud technology," *ICIMTH* vol. 226, pp. 165–168.

[29] V. K. Nigam, and S. Bhatia, (2016) "Impact of cloud computing on health care," *International Research Journal of Engineering and Technology*, vol. 3, no. 5, pp. 2804–2810.

[30] V. Navale, and P. E. Bourne, (2018) "Cloud computing applications for bio-medical science: A perspective," *PLoS Computational Biology*, vol. 14, no. 6, p. e1006144.

[31] T. Z. Benmerar, and F. O. Boumghar, (2011, April) "Toward a cloud architecture for medical imagery grid applications: The acigna-g project," in *2011 10th International Symposium on Programming and Systems* (pp. 134–139). IEEE.

[32] M. Deng, M. Petkovic, M. Nalin, and I. Baroni, (2011, July) "A Home Healthcare System in the Cloud-Addressing Security and Privacy Challenges," In *2011 IEEE 4th International Conference on Cloud Computing* (pp. 549–556). IEEE.

[33] T. Muhammed, R. Mehmood, A. Albeshri, and I. Katib, (2018) "UbeHealth: A personalized ubiquitous cloud and edge-enabled networked healthcare system for smart cities," *IEEE Access*, vol. 6, pp. 32258–32285.

[34] P. Mohit, R. Amin, A. Karati, G. P. Biswas, and M. K. Khan, (2017) "A standard mutual authentication protocol for cloud computing based health care system," *Journal of Medical Systems*, vol. 41, no. 4, pp. 1–13.

[35] V. Abeer Kumar, S. Jangirala, and M. Ahmad, (2018) "An efficient mutual authentication framework for healthcare system in cloud computing," *Journal of Medical Systems*, vol. 42, no. 8, pp. 1–25.

[36] D. R. Varma, (2012) "Managing DICOM images: Tips and tricks for the radiologist," *Indian Journal of Radiology and Imaging*, vol. 22, no. 01, pp. 4–13.

[37] A. Elnakib, G. Gimel'farb, J. S. Suri, and A. El-Baz, (2011) "Medical image segmentation: A brief survey," *Multi-Modality State-of-the-Art Medical Image Segmentation and Registration Methodologies* vol. 2, no. 1, pp. 1–39.

[38] A. A. Farag, A. S. El-Baz, and G. Gimel'farb, (2006) "Precise segmentation of multimodal images," *IEEE Transactions on Image Processing*, vol. 15, no. 4, pp. 952–968.

[39] F. Khalifa, G. M. Beache, G. Gimel'farb, G. A. Giridharan, and A. El-Baz, (2011) "A new image-based framework for analyzing cine images," in *Handbook of Multi-Modality State-of-the-Art Medical Image Segmentation and Registration Methodologies*, A. El-Baz, U. R. Acharya, M. Mirmedhdi, and J. S. Suri, Eds. (pp. 69–98). Springer, vol. 2, ch. 3.

[40] H. Sliman, F. Khalifa, A. Elnakib, A. Soliman, A. El-Baz, G. M. Beache, … and G. Gimel'farb, (2013) "Myocardial borders segmentation from cine MR images using bidirectional coupled parametric deformable models," *Medical Physics*, vol. 40, no. 9, pp. 092302.

[41] C. C. Teng, J. Mitchell, C. Walker, A. Swan, C. Davila, D. Howard, and T. Needham (2010, July). "A medical image archive solution in the cloud," in *2010 IEEE International Conference on Software Engineering and Service Sciences* (pp. 431–434). IEEE.

[42] Y. Karaca, M. Moonis, Y. D. Zhang, and C. Gezgez, (2019) "Mobile cloud computing based stroke healthcare system," *International Journal of Information Management*, vol. 45, pp. 250–261.

[43] E. M. Fong, and W. Y. Chung, (2013) "Mobile cloud-computing-based healthcare service by noncontact ECG monitoring," *Sensors*, vol. 13, no. 12, pp. 16451–16473.

[44] I. Mehmood, Z. Lv, Y. Zhang, K. Ota, M. Sajjad, and A. K. Singh, (2019) "Mobile cloud-assisted paradigms for management of multimedia big data in healthcare systems: Research challenges and opportunities," *International Journal of Information Management*, vol. 45, pp. 246–249.

[45] S. L. Wang, and H. I. Lin, (2019) "Integrating TTF and IDT to evaluate user intention of big data analytics in mobile cloud healthcare system," *Behaviour & Information Technology*, vol. 38, no. 9, pp. 974–985.

[46] S. S. Ahamad, and A. S. Khan Pathan, (2021) "A formally verified authentication protocol in secure framework for mobile healthcare during COVID-19-like pandemic," *Connection Science*, vol. 33, no. 3, pp. 532–554.

[47] I. Reda, M. Ghazal, A. Shalaby, M. Elmogy, A. AbouEl-Fetouh, B. O. Ayinde, M. AbouEl-Ghar, A. Elmaghraby, R. Keynton, and A. El-Baz, (2018) "A novel adcs-based cnn classification system for precise diagnosis of prostate cancer," in *2018 24th International Conference on Pattern Recognition (ICPR)*. IEEE, pp. 3923–3928.

[48] I. Reda, A. Khalil, M. Elmogy, A. Abou El-Fetouh, A. Shalaby, M. Abou El-Ghar, A. Elmaghraby, M. Ghazal, and A. El-Baz, (2018) "Deep learning role in early diagnosis of prostate cancer," *Technology in Cancer Research & Treatment*, vol. 17, p. 1533034618775530.

[49] I. Reda, B. O. Ayinde, M. Elmogy, A. Shalaby, M. El-Melegy, M. A. El-Ghar, A. A. El-Fetouh, M. Ghazal, and A. El-Baz, (2018) "A new cnn-based system for early diagnosis of prostate cancer," in *2018 IEEE 15th International Symposium on Biomedical Imaging (ISBI 2018)*. IEEE, pp. 207–210.

[50] S. M. Ayyad, M. A. Badawy, M. Shehata, A. Alksas, A. Mahmoud, M. Abou El-Ghar, M. Ghazal, M. El-Melegy, N. B. Abdel-Hamid, L. M. Labib, H. A. Ali, and A. El-Baz, (2022) "A new framework for precise identification of prostatic adenocarcinoma," *Sensors*, vol. 22, no. 5. [Online]. Available: https://www.mdpi.com/1424-8220/22/5/1848

[51] K. Hammouda, F. Khalifa, M. El-Melegy, M. Ghazal, H. E. Darwish, M. A. El-Ghar, and A. El-Baz, (2021) "A deep learning pipeline for grade groups classification using digitized prostate biopsy specimens," *Sensors*, vol. 21, no. 20, p. 6708.

[52] M. Shehata, A. Shalaby, A. E. Switala, M. El-Baz, M. Ghazal, L. Fraiwan, A. Khalil, M. A. El-Ghar, M. Badawy, A. M. Bakr et al., (2020) "A multimodal computer-aided diagnostic system for precise identification of renal allograft rejection: Preliminary results," *Medical Physics*, vol. 47, no. 6, pp. 2427–2440.

[53] M. Shehata, F. Khalifa, A. Soliman, M. Ghazal, F. Taher, M. Abou El-Ghar, A. C. Dwyer, G. Gimel'farb, R. S. Keynton, and A. El-Baz, (2018) "Computer-aided diagnostic system for early detection of acute renal transplant rejection using diffusion-weighted mri," *IEEE Transactions on Biomedical Engineering*, vol. 66, no. 2, pp. 539–552.

[54] E. Hollis, M. Shehata, M. Abou El-Ghar, M. Ghazal, T. El-Diasty, M. Merchant, A. E. Switala, and A. El-Baz, (2017) "Statistical analysis of adcs and clinical biomarkers in detecting acute renal transplant rejection," *The British Journal of Radiology*, vol. 90, no. 1080, p. 20170125.

[55] M. Shehata, A. Alksas, R. T. Abouelkheir, A. Elmahdy, A. Shaffie, A. Soliman, M. Ghazal, H. Abu Khalifeh, R. Salim, A. A. K. Abdel Razek et al., (2021) "A comprehensive computer-assisted diagnosis system for early assessment of renal cancer tumors," *Sensors*, vol. 21, no. 14, p. 4928.

[56] F. Khalifa, G. M. Beache, M. A. El-Ghar, T. El-Diasty, G. Gimel'farb, M. Kong, and A. El-Baz, (2013) "Dynamic contrast-enhanced MRI based early detection of acute renal transplant rejection," *IEEE Transactions on Medical Imaging*, vol. 32, no. 10, pp. 1910–1927.

[57] F. Khalifa, M. A. El-Ghar, B. Abdollahi, H. Frieboes, T. El-Diasty, and A. El-Baz, (2013) "A comprehensive non-invasive framework for automated evaluation of acute renal transplant rejection using DCE-MRI," *NMR in Biomedicine*, vol. 26, no. 11, pp. 1460–1470.

[58] M. Shehata, M. Ghazal, G. Beache, M. Abou EI-Ghar, A. Dwyer, H. Hajjdiab, A. Khalil, and A. El-Baz, (2018) "Role of integrating diffusion MR image-markers with clinical-biomarkers for early assessment of renal transplants," in *2018 25th IEEE International Conference on Image Processing (ICIP)*. IEEE, pp. 146–150.

[59] M. Shehata, F. Khalifa, E. Hollis, A. Soliman, E. Hosseini-Asl, M. A. El-Ghar, M. El-Baz, A. C. Dwyer, A. El-Baz, and R. Keynton, (2016) "A new non-invasive approach for early classification of renal rejection types using diffusion-weighted mri," in *IEEE International Conference on Image Processing (ICIP), 2016*. IEEE, pp. 136–140.

[60] F. Khalifa, A. Soliman, A. Takieldeen, M. Shehata, M. Mostapha, A. Shaffie, R. Ouseph, A. Elmaghraby, and A. El-Baz, (2016) "Kidney segmentation from CT images using a 3D NMF-guided active contour model," in *IEEE 13th International Symposium on Biomedical Imaging (ISBI), 2016*. IEEE, pp. 432–435.

[61] M. Shehata, F. Khalifa, A. Soliman, A. Takieldeen, M. A. El-Ghar, A. Shaffie, A. C. Dwyer, R. Ouseph, A. El-Baz, and R. Keynton, (2016) "3d diffusion mri-based cad system for early diagnosis of acute renal rejection," in *2016 IEEE 13th International Symposium on Biomedical Imaging (ISBI)*. IEEE, pp. 1177–1180.

[62] M. Shehata, F. Khalifa, A. Soliman, R. Alrefai, M. A. El-Ghar, A. C. Dwyer, R. Ouseph, and A. El-Baz, (2015) "A level set-based framework for 3d kidney segmentation from diffusion mr images," in *IEEE International Conference on Image Processing (ICIP), 2015 IEEE*, pp. 4441–4445.

[63] M. Shehata, F. Khalifa, A. Soliman, M. A. El-Ghar, A. C. Dwyer, G. Gimel'farb, R. Keynton, and A. El-Baz, (2016) "A promising noninvasive cad system for kidney function assessment," in *International Conference on Medical Image Computing and Computer-Assisted Intervention*. Springer, pp. 613–621.

[64] F. Khalifa, A. Soliman, A. Elmaghraby, G. Gimel'farb, and A. El-Baz, (2017) "3d kidney segmentation from abdominal images using spatial-appearance models," *Computational and Mathematical Methods in Medicine*, vol. 2017, pp. 1–10.

[65] M. Shehata, M. Ghazal, F. Khalifa, M. Abou El-Ghar, A. Khalil, A. C. Dwyer, A. El-Giziri, M. El-Melegy, and A. El-Baz, (2018) "A novel CAD system for detecting acute rejection of renal allografts based on integrating imaging-markers and laboratory biomarkers," in *2018 IEEE International Conference on Imaging Systems and Techniques (IST)*. IEEE, pp. 1–6.

[66] M. Shehata, F. Khalifa, A. Soliman, M. A. El-Ghar, A. C. Dwyer, and A. El-Baz, (2017) "Assessment of renal transplant using image and clinical-based biomarkers," in *Proceedings of 13th Annual Scientific Meeting of American Society for Diagnostics and Interventional Nephrology (ASDIN'17)*, New Orleans, LA, USA, February 10–12, 2017.

[67] M. Shehata, F. Khalifa, A. Soliman, M. A. El-Ghar, A. C. Dwyer, and A. El-Baz, (2016) "Early assessment of acute renal rejection," in *Proceedings of 12th Annual Scientific Meeting of American Society for Diagnostics and Interventional Nephrology (ASDIN'16)*, Pheonix, AZ, USA, February 19–21, 2016.

[68] A. Eltanboly, M. Ghazal, H. Hajjdiab, A. Shalaby, A. Switala, A. Mahmoud, P. Sahoo, M. El-Azab, and A. El-Baz, (2019) "Level sets-based image segmentation approach using statistical shape priors," *Applied Mathematics and Computation*, vol. 340, pp. 164–179.

[69] M. Shehata, A. Mahmoud, A. Soliman, F. Khalifa, M. Ghazal, M. A. El-Ghar, M. El-Melegy, and A. El-Baz, (2018) "3D kidney segmentation from abdominal diffusion MRI using an appearance-guided deformable boundary," *PLOS One*, vol. 13, no. 7, p. e0200082.

[70] H. Abdeltawab, M. Shehata, A. Shalaby, F. Khalifa, A. Mahmoud, M. A. El-Ghar, A. C. Dwyer, M. Ghazal, H. Hajjdiab, R. Keynton et al., (2019) "A novel CNN-based CAD system for early assessment of transplanted kidney dysfunction," *Scientific Reports*, vol. 9, no. 1, p. 5948.

[71] M. Shehata, F. Taher, M. Ghazal, A. Mahmoud, G. Beache, M. Abou El-Ghar, A. C. Dwyer, A. Elmaghraby, and A. El-Baz, (2018) "Early assessment of acute renal rejection post-transplantation: A combined imaging and clinical biomarkers protocol," in *2018 IEEE International Symposium on Signal Processing and Information Technology (ISSPIT)*. IEEE, pp. 297–302.

[72] M. Shehata, F. Taher, M. Ghazal, S. Shaker, M. Abou El-Ghar, M. Badawy, A. Shalaby, M. El-Baz, A. Mahmoud, A. C. Dwyer et al., (2021) "Early identification of acute rejection for renal allografts: a machine learning approach," in *State of the Art in Neural Networks and Their Applications* (pp. 197–218). Elsevier.

[73] M. Shehata, A. Shalaby, M. Ghazal, M. Abou El-Ghar, M. Badawy, G. Beache, A. Dwyer, M. El-Melegy, G. Giridharan, R. Keynton et al., (2019) "Early assessment of renal transplants using BOLD-MRI: Promising results," in *2019 IEEE International Conference on Image Processing (ICIP)*. IEEE, pp. 1395–1399.

[74] M. Shehata, M. Ghazal, H. A. Khalifeh, A. Khalil, A. Shalaby, A. C. Dwyer, A. M. Bakr, R. Keynton, and A. El-Baz, (2020) "A deep learning based CAD system for renal allograft assessment: Diffusion, BOLD, and clinical biomarkers," in *2020 IEEE International Conference on Image Processing (ICIP)*. IEEE, pp. 355–359.

[75] M. Shehata, H. Abdeltawab, M. Ghazal, A. Khalil, S. Shaker, A. Shalaby, A. Mahmoud, M. Abou El-Ghar, A. C. Dwyer, M. El-Melegy et al., (2021) "Accurate identification of renal transplant rejection: convolutional neural networks and diffusion MRI," in *State of the Art in Neural Networks and Their Applications* (pp. 91–115). Elsevier.

[76] K. Hammouda, F. Khalifa, H. Abdeltawab, A. Elnakib, G. Giridharan, M. Zhu, C. Ng, S. Dassanayaka, M. Kong, H. Darwish et al., (2020) "A new framework for performing cardiac strain analysis from cine mri imaging in mice," *Scientific Reports*, vol. 10, no. 1, pp. 1–15.

[77] H. Abdeltawab, F. Khalifa, K. Hammouda, J. M. Miller, M. M. Meki, Q. Ou, A. El-Baz, and T. Mohamed, (2021) "Artificial intelligence based framework to quantify the cardiomyocyte structural integrity in heart slices," *Cardiovascular Engineering and Technology* vol. 13, pp. 1–11.

[78] F. Khalifa, G. M. Beache, A. Elnakib, H. Sliman, G. Gimel'farb, K. C. Welch, and A. El-Baz, (2013) "A new shape-based framework for the left ventricle wall segmentation from cardiac first-pass perfusion MRI," in *Proceedings of IEEE International Symposium on Biomedical Imaging: From Nano to Macro, (ISBI'13)*, San Francisco, CA, April 7–11, pp. 41–44.

[79] F. Khalifa, G. M. Beache, A. Elnakib, H. Sliman, G. Gimel'farb, K. C. Welch, and A. El-Baz, (2012) "A new nonrigid registration framework for improved visualization of transmural perfusion gradients on cardiac first–pass perfusion MRI," in *Proceedings of IEEE International Symposium on Biomedical Imaging: From Nano to Macro, (ISBI'12)*, Barcelona, Spain, May 2–5, pp. 828–831.

[80] F. Khalifa, G. M. Beache, A. Firjani, K. C. Welch, G. Gimel'farb, and A. El-Baz, (2012) "A new nonrigid registration approach for motion correction of cardiac first-pass perfusion MRI," in *Proceedings of IEEE International Conference on Image Processing, (ICIP'12)*, Lake Buena Vista, Florida, September 30–October 3, pp. 1665–1668.

[81] F. Khalifa, G. M. Beache, G. Gimel'farb, and A. El-Baz, (2012) "A novel CAD system for analyzing cardiac first-pass MR images," in *Proceedings of IAPR International Conference on Pattern Recognition (ICPR'12)*, Tsukuba Science City, Japan, November 11–15, pp. 77–80.

[82] F. Khalifa, G. M. Beache, G. Gimel'farb, and A. El-Baz, (2011) "A novel approach for accurate estimation of left ventricle global indexes from short-axis cine MRI," in *Proceedings of IEEE International Conference on Image Processing, (ICIP'11)*, Brussels, Belgium, September 11–14, pp. 2645–2649.

[83] F. Khalifa, G. M. Beache, G. Gimel'farb, and A. El-Baz, (2012) "Accurate automatic analysis of cardiac cine images," *IEEE Transactions on Biomedical Engineering*, vol. 59, no. 2, pp. 445–455.

[84] F. Khalifa, G. M. Beache, M. Nitzken, G. Gimel'farb, G. A. Giridharan, and A. El-Baz, (2011) "Automatic analysis of left ventricle wall thickness using short-axis cine CMR images," in *Proceedings of IEEE International Symposium on Biomedical Imaging: From Nano to Macro, (ISBI'11)*, Chicago, Illinois, March 30 April 2, pp. 1306–1309.

[85] M. Nitzken, G. Beache, A. Elnakib, F. Khalifa, G. Gimel'farb, and A. El-Baz, (Sep. 2012) "Accurate modeling of tagged CMR 3D image appearance characteristics to improve cardiac cycle strain estimation," in *2012 19th IEEE International Conference on Image Processing (ICIP)*, Orlando, Florida, USA: IEEE, pp. 521–524.

[86] M. Nitzken, G. Beache, A. Elnakib, F. Khalifa, G. Gimel'farb, and A. El-Baz, (May 2012) "Improving full-cardiac cycle strain estimation from tagged cmr by accurate modeling of 3D image appearance characteristics," in *International Symposium on Biomedical Imaging (ISBI), 2012 9th IEEE*. Barcelona, Spain: IEEE, pp. 462–465.

[87] M. J. Nitzken, A. S. El-Baz, and G. M. Beache, (2012) "Markov-gibbs random field model for improved full-cardiac cycle strain estimation from tagged CMR," *Journal of Cardiovascular Magnetic Resonance*, vol. 14, no. 1, pp. 1–2.

[88] H. Sliman, A. Elnakib, G. Beache, A. Elmaghraby, and A. El-Baz, (2014) "Assessment of myocardial function from cine cardiac MRI using a novel 4D tracking approach," *J Comput Sci Syst Biol*, vol. 7, pp. 169–173.

[89] H. Sliman, A. Elnakib, G. M. Beache, A. Soliman, F. Khalifa, G. Gimel'farb, A. Elmaghraby, and A. El-Baz, (2014) "A novel 4D PDE-based approach for accurate assessment of myocardium function using cine cardiac magnetic resonance images," in *Proceedings of IEEE International Conference on Image Processing (ICIP'14)*, Paris, France, October 27–30, pp. 3537–3541.

[90] H. Sliman, F. Khalifa, A. Elnakib, G. M. Beache, A. Elmaghraby, and A. El-Baz, (2013) "A new segmentation-based tracking framework for extracting the left ventricle cavity from cine cardiac MRI," in *Proceedings of IEEE International Conference on Image Processing, (ICIP'13)*, Melbourne, Australia, September 15–18, pp. 685–689.

[91] H. Sliman, F. Khalifa, A. Elnakib, A. Soliman, G. M. Beache, A. Elmaghraby, G. Gimel'farb, and A. El-Baz, (2013) "Myocardial borders segmentation from cine MR images using bi-directional coupled parametric deformable models," *Medical Physics*, vol. 40, no. 9, pp. 1–13.

[92] H. Sliman, F. Khalifa, A. Elnakib, A. Soliman, G. M. Beache, G. Gimel'farb, A. Emam, A. Elmaghraby, and A. El-Baz, (2013) "Accurate segmentation framework for the left ventricle wall from cardiac cine MRI," in *Proceedings of International Symposium on Computational Models for Life Science, (CMLS'13)*, vol. 1559, Sydney, Australia, November 27–29, pp. 287–296.

[93] A. Sharafeldeen, M. Elsharkawy, N. S. Alghamdi, A. Soliman, and A. El-Baz, (2021) "Precise segmentation of covid-19 infected lung from ct images based on adaptive first-order appearance model with morphological/anatomical constraints," *Sensors*, vol. 21, no. 16, p. 5482.

[94] M. Elsharkawy, A. Sharafeldeen, F. Taher, A. Shalaby, A. Soliman, A. Mahmoud, M. Ghazal, A. Khalil, N. S. Alghamdi, A. A. K. A. Razek et al., (2021) "Early assessment of lung function in coronavirus patients using invariant markers from chest x-rays images," *Scientific Reports*, vol. 11, no. 1, pp. 1–11.

[95] B. Abdollahi, A. C. Civelek, X.-F. Li, J. Suri, and A. El-Baz, (2014) "PET/CT nodule segmentation and diagnosis: A survey," in *Multi Detector CT Imaging*, L. Saba and J. S. Suri, Eds. (pp. 639–651). Taylor, Francis, ch. 30.

[96] B. Abdollahi, A. El-Baz, and A. A. Amini, (2011) "A multi-scale non-linear vessel enhancement technique," in *Engineering in Medicine and Biology Society, EMBC, 2011 Annual International Conference of the IEEE*. IEEE, pp. 3925–3929.

[97] B. Abdollahi, A. Soliman, A. Civelek, X.-F. Li, G. Gimel'farb, and A. El-Baz, (2012) "A novel gaussian scale space-based joint MGRF framework for precise lung segmentation," in *Proceedings of IEEE International Conference on Image Processing, (ICIP'12)*. IEEE, pp. 2029–2032.

[98] B. Abdollahi, A. Soliman, A. Civelek, X.-F. Li, G. Gimel'farb, and A. El-Baz, (2012) "A novel 3D joint MGRF framework for precise lung segmentation," in *Machine Learning in Medical Imaging*. Springer, pp. 86–93.

[99] A. M. Ali, A. S. El-Baz, and A. A. Farag, (2007) "A novel framework for accurate lung segmentation using graph cuts," in *Proceedings of IEEE International Symposium on Biomedical Imaging: From Nano to Macro, (ISBI'07)*. IEEE, pp. 908–911.

[100] A. El-Baz, G. M. Beache, G. Gimel'farb, K. Suzuki, and K. Okada, (2013) "Lung imaging data analysis," *International Journal of Biomedical Imaging*, vol. 2013, pp. 1–2.

[101] A. El-Baz, G. M. Beache, G. Gimel'farb, K. Suzuki, K. Okada, A. Elnakib, A. Soliman, and B. Abdollahi, (2013) "Computer-aided diagnosis systems for lung cancer: Challenges and methodologies," *International Journal of Biomedical Imaging*, vol. 2013, pp. 1–46.

[102] A. El-Baz, A. Elnakib, M. Abou El-Ghar, G. Gimel'farb, R. Falk, and A. Farag, (2013) "Automatic detection of 2D and 3D lung nodules in chest spiral CT scans," *International Journal of Biomedical Imaging*, vol. 2013, pp. 1–11.

[103] A. El-Baz, A. A. Farag, R. Falk, and R. La Rocca, (2003) "A unified approach for detection, visualization, and identification of lung abnormalities in chest spiral CT scans," in *International Congress Series*, vol. 1256. Elsevier, pp. 998–1004.

[104] A. El-Baz, A. A. Farag, R. Falk, and R. La Rocca, (2002) "Detection, visualization and identification of lung abnormalities in chest spiral CT scan: Phase-I," in *Proceedings of International conference on Biomedical Engineering*, Cairo, Egypt, vol. 12, no. 1.

[105] A. El-Baz, A. Farag, G. Gimel'farb, R. Falk, M. A. El-Ghar, and T. Eldiasty, (2006) "A framework for automatic segmentation of lung nodules from low dose chest CT scans," in *Proceedings of International Conference on Pattern Recognition, (ICPR'06)*, vol. 3. IEEE, pp. 611–614.

[106] A. El-Baz, A. Farag, G. Gimel'farb, R. Falk, and M. A. El-Ghar, (2011) "A novel level set-based computer-aided detection system for automatic detection of lung nodules in low dose chest computed tomography scans," *Lung Imaging and Computer Aided Diagnosis*, vol. 10, pp. 221–238.

[107] A. El-Baz, G. Gimel'farb, M. Abou El-Ghar, and R. Falk, (2012) "Appearance-based diagnostic system for early assessment of malignant lung nodules," in *Proceedings of IEEE International Conference on Image Processing, (ICIP'12)*. IEEE, pp. 533–536.

[108] A. El-Baz, G. Gimel'farb, and R. Falk, (2011) "A novel 3D framework for automatic lung segmentation from low dose CT images," in *Lung Imaging and Computer Aided Diagnosis*, A. El-Baz and J. S. Suri, Eds. (pp. 1–16). Taylor, Francis, ch. 1.

[109] A. El-Baz, G. Gimel'farb, R. Falk, and M. El-Ghar, (2010) "Appearance analysis for diagnosing malignant lung nodules," in *Proceedings of IEEE International Symposium on Biomedical Imaging: From Nano to Macro (ISBI'10).* IEEE, pp. 193 196.

[110] A. El-Baz, G. Gimel'farb, R. Falk, and M. A. El-Ghar, (2011) "A novel level set-based CAD system for automatic detection of lung nodules in low dose chest CT scans," in *Lung Imaging and Computer Aided Diagnosis*, A. El-Baz and J. S. Suri, Eds. (pp. 221–238). Taylor, Francis, vol. 1, ch. 10.

[111] A. El-Baz, G. Gimel'farb, R. Falk, and M. A. El-Ghar, (2008) "A new approach for automatic analysis of 3D low dose CT images for accurate monitoring the detected lung nodules," in *Proceedings of International Conference on Pattern Recognition, (ICPR'08).* IEEE, pp. 1–4.

[112] A. El-Baz, G. Gimel'farb, R. Falk, and M. A. El-Ghar, (2007) "A novel approach for automatic follow-up of detected lung nodules," in *Proceedings of IEEE International Conference on Image Processing, (ICIP'07)*, vol. 5. IEEE, pp. V–501.

[113] A. El-Baz, G. Gimel'farb, R. Falk, and M. A. El-Ghar, (2007) "A new CAD system for early diagnosis of detected lung nodules," in *IEEE International Conference on Image Processing, 2007, ICIP 2007*, vol. 2. IEEE, pp. II–461.

[114] A. El-Baz, G. Gimel'farb, R. Falk, M. A. El-Ghar, and H. Refaie, (2008) "Promising results for early diagnosis of lung cancer," in *Proceedings of IEEE International Symposium on Biomedical Imaging: From Nano to Macro, (ISBI'08).* IEEE, pp. 1151–1154.

[115] A. El-Baz, G. L. Gimel'farb, R. Falk, M. Abou El-Ghar, T. Holland, and T. Shaffer, (2008) "A new stochastic framework for accurate lung segmentation," in *Proceedings of Medical Image Computing and Computer-Assisted Intervention, (MICCAI'08)*, pp. 322–330.

[116] A. El-Baz, G. L. Gimel'farb, R. Falk, D. Heredis, and M. Abou El-Ghar, (2008) "A novel approach for accurate estimation of the growth rate of the detected lung nodules," in *Proceedings of International Workshop on Pulmonary Image Analysis*, pp. 33–42.

[117] A. El-Baz, G. L. Gimel'farb, R. Falk, T. Holland, and T. Shaffer, (2008) "A framework for unsupervised segmentation of lung tissues from low dose computed tomography images," in *Proceedings of British Machine Vision, (BMVC'08)*, pp. 1–10.

[118] A. El-Baz, G. Gimel'farb, R. Falk, and M. A. El-Ghar, (2011) "3D MGRF-based appearance modeling for robust segmentation of pulmonary nodules in 3D LDCT chest images," in Ayman El-Baz and Jasjit S. Suri (eds.), *Lung Imaging and Computer Aided Diagnosis.* CRC Press. pp. 51–63.

[119] A. El-Baz, G. Gimel'farb, R. Falk, M. A. El-Ghar, S. Rainey, D. Heredia, and T. Shaffer, (2009) "Toward early diagnosis of lung cancer," in *Proceedings of Medical Image Computing and Computer-Assisted Intervention, (MICCAI'09).* Springer, pp. 682–689.

[120] A. El-Baz, G. Gimel'farb, R. Falk, M. A. El-Ghar, and J. Suri, (2011) "Appearance analysis for the early assessment of detected lung nodules," in Ayman El-Baz and Jasjit S. Suri (eds.), *Lung Imaging and Computer Aided Diagnosis.* CRC Press, pp. 395–404.

[121] A. El-Baz, F. Khalifa, A. Elnakib, M. Nitkzen, A. Soliman, P. McClure, G. Gimel'farb, and M. A. El-Ghar, (2012) "A novel approach for global lung registration using 3D Markov Gibbs appearance model," in *Proceedings of International Conference Medical Image Computing and Computer-Assisted Intervention, (MICCAI'12)*, Nice, France, October 1–5, pp. 114–121.

[122] A. El-Baz, M. Nitzken, A. Elnakib, F. Khalifa, G. Gimel'farb, R. Falk, and M. A. El-Ghar, (2011) "3D shape analysis for early diagnosis of malignant lung nodules," in *Proceedings of International Conference Medical Image Computing and Computer-Assisted Intervention, (MICCAI'11)*, Toronto, Canada, September 18–22, pp. 175–182.

[123] A. El-Baz, M. Nitzken, G. Gimel'farb, E. Van Bogaert, R. Falk, M. A. El-Ghar, and J. Suri, (2011) "Three-dimensional shape analysis using spherical harmonics for early assessment of detected lung nodules," in Ayman El-Baz and Jasjit S. Suri (eds.), *Lung Imaging and Computer Aided Diagnosis*. CRC Press, pp. 421–438.

[124] A. El-Baz, M. Nitzken, F. Khalifa, A. Elnakib, G. Gimel'farb, R. Falk, and M. A. El-Ghar, (2011) "3D shape analysis for early diagnosis of malignant lung nodules," in *Proceedings of International Conference on Information Processing in Medical Imaging, (IPMI'11)*, Monastery Irsee, Germany (Bavaria), July 3–8, pp. 772–783.

[125] A. El-Baz, M. Nitzken, E. Vanbogaert, G. Gimel'Farb, R. Falk, and M. Abo, (2011) El-Ghar, "A novel shape-based diagnostic approach for early diagnosis of lung nodules," in *2011 IEEE International Symposium on Biomedical Imaging: From Nano to Macro*. IEEE, pp. 137–140.

[126] A. El-Baz, P. Sethu, G. Gimel'farb, F. Khalifa, A. Elnakib, R. Falk, and M. A. El-Ghar, (2011) "Elastic phantoms generated by microfluidics technology: Validation of an imaged-based approach for accurate measurement of the growth rate of lung nodules," *Biotechnology Journal*, vol. 6, no. 2, pp. 195–203.

[127] A. El-Baz, P. Sethu, G. Gimel'farb, F. Khalifa, A. Elnakib, R. Falk, and M. A. El-Ghar, (2010) "A new validation approach for the growth rate measurement using elastic phantoms generated by state-of-the-art microfluidics technology," in *Proceedings of IEEE International Conference on Image Processing, (ICIP'10)*, Hong Kong, September 26–29, pp. 4381–4383.

[128] A. El-Baz, P. Sethu, G. Gimel'farb, F. Khalifa, A. Elnakib, R. Falk, and M. A. E.-G. J. Suri, (2011) "Validation of a new imaged-based approach for the accurate estimating of the growth rate of detected lung nodules using real CT images and elastic phantoms generated by state-of-the-art microfluidics technology," in *Handbook of Lung Imaging and Computer Aided Diagnosis*, A. El-Baz and J. S. Suri, Eds. (pp. 405–420). Taylor & Francis, vol. 1.

[129] A. El-Baz, A. Soliman, P. McClure, G. Gimel'farb, M. A. El-Ghar, and R. Falk, (2012) "Early assessment of malignant lung nodules based on the spatial analysis of detected lung nodules," in *Proceedings of IEEE International Symposium on Biomedical Imaging: From Nano to Macro, (ISBI'12)*. IEEE, pp. 1463–1466.

[130] A. El-Baz, S. E. Yuksel, S. Elshazly, and A. A. Farag, (2005) "Non-rigid registration techniques for automatic follow-up of lung nodules," in *Proceedings of Computer Assisted Radiology and Surgery, (CARS'05)*, vol. 1281. Elsevier, pp. 1115–1120.

[131] A. S. El-Baz and J. S. Suri, (2011) *Lung Imaging and Computer Aided Diagnosis*. CRC Press.

[132] A. Soliman, F. Khalifa, N. Dunlap, B. Wang, M. El-Ghar, and A. El-Baz, (2016) "An iso-surfaces based local deformation handling framework of lung tissues," in *2016 IEEE 13th International Symposium on Biomedical Imaging (ISBI)*. IEEE, pp. 1253–1259.

[133] A. Soliman, F. Khalifa, A. Shaffie, N. Dunlap, B. Wang, A. Elmaghraby, and A. El-Baz, (2016) "Detection of lung injury using 4d-ct chest images," in *2016 IEEE 13th International Symposium on Biomedical Imaging (ISBI)*. IEEE, pp. 1274–1277.

[134] A. Soliman, F. Khalifa, A. Shaffie, N. Dunlap, B. Wang, A. Elmaghraby, G. Gimel'farb, M. Ghazal, and A. El-Baz, (2017) "A comprehensive framework for early assessment of lung injury," in *2017 IEEE International Conference on Image Processing (ICIP)*. IEEE, pp. 3275–3279.

[135] A. Shaffie, A. Soliman, M. Ghazal, F. Taher, N. Dunlap, B. Wang, A. Elmaghraby, G. Gimel'farb, and A. El-Baz, (2017) "A new framework for incorporating appearance and shape features of lung nodules for precise diagnosis of lung cancer," in *2017 IEEE International Conference on Image Processing (ICIP)*. IEEE, pp. 1372–1376.

[136] A. Soliman, F. Khalifa, A. Shaffie, N. Liu, N. Dunlap, B. Wang, A. Elmaghraby, G. Gimel'farb, and A. El-Baz, (2016) "Image-based cad system for accurate identification of lung injury," in *2016 IEEE International Conference on Image Processing (ICIP)*. IEEE, pp. 121–125.

[137] A. Soliman, A. Shaffie, M. Ghazal, G. Gimel'farb, R. Keynton, and A. El-Baz, (2018) "A novel cnn segmentation framework based on using new shape and appearance features," in *2018 25th IEEE International Conference on Image Processing (ICIP)*. IEEE, pp. 3488–3492.

[138] A. Shaffie, A. Soliman, H. A. Khalifeh, M. Ghazal, F. Taher, R. Keynton, A. Elmaghraby, and A. El-Baz, (2018) "On the integration of ct derived features for accurate detection of lung cancer," in *2018 IEEE International Symposium on Signal Processing and Information Technology (ISSPIT)*. IEEE, pp. 435–440.

[139] A. Shaffie, A. Soliman, H. A. Khalifeh, M. Ghazal, F. Taher, A. Elmaghraby, R. Keynton, and A. El-Baz, (2019) "Radiomic-based framework for early diagnosis of lung cancer," in *2019 IEEE 16th International Symposium on Biomedical Imaging (ISBI 2019)*. IEEE, pp. 1293–1297.

[140] A. Shaffie, A. Soliman, M. Ghazal, F. Taher, N. Dunlap, B. Wang, V. Van Berkel, G. Gimelfarb, A. Elmaghraby, and A. El-Baz, (2018) "A novel autoencoder-based diagnostic system for early assessment of lung cancer," in *2018 25th IEEE International Conference on Image Processing (ICIP)*. IEEE, pp. 1393–1397.

[141] A. Shaffie, A. Soliman, L. Fraiwan, M. Ghazal, F. Taher, N. Dunlap, B. Wang, V. van Berkel, R. Keynton, A. Elmaghraby et al., (2018) "A generalized deep learning-based diagnostic system for early diagnosis of various types of pulmonary nodules," *Technology in Cancer Research & Treatment*, vol. 17, p. 1533033818798800

[142] Y. ElNakieb, M. T. Ali, O. Dekhil, M. E. Khalefa, A. Soliman, A. Shalaby, A. Mahmoud, M. Ghazal, H. Hajjdiab, A. Elmaghraby et al., (2018) "Towards accurate personalized autism diagnosis using different imaging modalities: SMRI, FMRI, and DTI," in *2018 IEEE International Symposium on Signal Processing and Information Technology (ISSPIT)*. IEEE, pp. 447–452.

[143] Y. ElNakieb, A. Soliman, A. Mahmoud, O. Dekhil, A. Shalaby, M. Ghazal, A. Khalil, A. Switala, R. S. Keynton, G. N. Barnes et al., (2019) "Autism spectrum disorder diagnosis framework using diffusion tensor imaging," in *2019 IEEE International Conference on Imaging Systems and Techniques (IST)*. IEEE, pp. 1–5.

[144] R. Haweel, O. Dekhil, A. Shalaby, A. Mahmoud, M. Ghazal, R. Keynton, G. Barnes, and A. El-Baz, (2019) "A machine learning approach for grading autism severity levels using task-based functional mri," in *2019 IEEE International Conference on Imaging Systems and Techniques (IST)*. IEEE, pp. 1–5.

[145] O. Dekhil, M. Ali, R. Haweel, Y. Elnakib, M. Ghazal, H. Hajjdiab, L. Fraiwan, A. Shalaby, A. Soliman, A. Mahmoud et al., (2020) "A comprehensive framework for differentiating autism spectrum disorder from neurotypicals by fusing structural mri and resting state functional mri," in *Seminars in Pediatric Neurology*. Elsevier, p. 100805.

[146] R. Haweel, O. Dekhil, A. Shalaby, A. Mahmoud, M. Ghazal, A. Khalil, R. Keynton, G. Barnes, and A. El-Baz, (2020) "A novel framework for grading autism severity using task-based fmri," in *2020 IEEE 17th International Symposium on Biomedical Imaging (ISBI)*. IEEE, pp. 1404–1407.

[147] A. El-Baz, A. Elnakib, F. Khalifa, M. A. El-Ghar, P. McClure, (2012) A. Soliman, and G. Gimel'farb, "Precise segmentation of 3-D magnetic resonance angiography," *IEEE Transactions on Biomedical Engineering*, vol. 59, no. 7, pp. 2019–2029.

[148] A. El-Baz, A. Farag, A. Elnakib, M. F. Casanova, G. Gimel'farb, A. E. Switala, D. Jordan, and S. Rainey, (2011) "Accurate automated detection of autism related corpus callosum abnormalities," *Journal of Medical Systems*, vol. 35, no. 5, pp. 929–939.

[149] A. El-Baz, G. Gimel'farb, R. Falk, M. A. El-Ghar, V. Kumar, and D. Heredia, (2009) "A novel 3D joint Markov-gibbs model for extracting blood vessels from PC–mra images," in *Medical Image Computing and Computer-Assisted Intervention–MICCAI 2009*, vol. 5762. Springer, pp. 943–950.

[150] A. Elnakib, A. El-Baz, M. F. Casanova, G. Gimel'farb, and A. E. Switala, (2010) "Image-based detection of corpus callosum variability for more accurate discrimination between dyslexic and normal brains," in *Proceedings of IEEE International Symposium on Biomedical Imaging: From Nano to Macro (ISBI'2010)*. IEEE, pp. 109–112.

[151] A. Elnakib, M. F. Casanova, G. Gimel'farb, A. E. Switala, and A. El-Baz, (2011) "Autism diagnostics by centerline-based shape analysis of the corpus callosum," in *Proceedings of IEEE International Symposium on Biomedical Imaging: From Nano to Macro (ISBI'2011)*. IEEE, pp. 1843–1846.

[152] A. Elnakib, M. Nitzken, M. Casanova, H. Park, G. Gimel'farb, and A. El-Baz, (2012) "Quantification of age-related brain cortex change using 3D shape analysis," in *2012 21st International Conference on Pattern Recognition (ICPR)*. IEEE, pp. 41–44.

[153] M. Nitzken, M. Casanova, G. Gimel'farb, A. Elnakib, F. Khalifa, A. Switala, and A. El-Baz, (2011) "3D shape analysis of the brain cortex with application to dyslexia," in *2011 18th IEEE International Conference on Image Processing (ICIP)*. Brussels, Belgium: IEEE, Sep. pp. 2657–2660.

[154] F. E.-Z. A. El-Gamal, M. M. Elmogy, M. Ghazal, A. Atwan, G. N. Barnes, M. F. Casanova, R. Keynton, and A. S. El-Baz, (2017) "A novel cad system for local and global early diagnosis of alzheimer's disease based on pib-pet scans," in *2017 IEEE International Conference on Image Processing (ICIP)*. IEEE, pp. 3270–3274.

[155] M. M. Ismail, R. S. Keynton, M. M. Mostapha, A. H. ElTanboly, M. F. Casanova, G. L. Gimel'farb, and A. El-Baz, (2016) "Studying autism spectrum disorder with structural and diffusion magnetic resonance imaging: A survey," *Frontiers in Human Neuroscience*, vol. 10, p. 211.

[156] A. Alansary, M. Ismail, A. Soliman, F. Khalifa, M. Nitzken, A. Elnakib, M. Mostapha, A. Black, K. Stinebruner, M. F. Casanova et al., (2016) "Infant brain extraction in t1-weighted mr images using bet and refinement using lcdg and mgrf models," *IEEE Journal of Biomedical and Health Informatics*, vol. 20, no. 3, pp. 925–935.

[157] E. H. Asl, M. Ghazal, A. Mahmoud, A. Aslantas, A. Shalaby, M. Casanova, G. Barnes, G. Gimel'farb, R. Keynton, and A. El-Baz, (2018) "Alzheimer's disease diagnostics by a 3d deeply supervised adaptable convolutional network," *Frontiers in Bioscience (Landmark edition)*, vol. 23, pp. 584–596.

[158] O. Dekhil, M. Ali, Y. El-Nakieb, A. Shalaby, A. Soliman, A. Switala, A. Mahmoud, M. Ghazal, H. Hajjdiab, M. F. Casanova, A. Elmaghraby, R. Keynton, A. El-Baz, and G. Barnes, (2019) "A personalized autism diagnosis cad system using a fusion of structural mri and resting-state functional mri data," *Frontiers in Psychiatry*, vol. 10, p. 392. [Online]. Available: https://www.frontiersin.org/article/10.3389/fpsyt.2019.00392

[159] O. Dekhil, A. Shalaby, A. Soliman, A. Mahmoud, M. Kong, G. Barnes, A. Elmaghraby, and A. El-Baz, (2021) "Identifying brain areas correlated with ados raw scores by studying altered dynamic functional connectivity patterns," *Medical Image Analysis*, vol. 68, p. 101899.

[160] Y. A. Elnakieb, M. T. Ali, A. Soliman, A. H. Mahmoud, A. M. Shalaby, N. S. Alghamdi, M. Ghazal, A. Khalil, A. Switala, R. S. Keynton et al., (2020) "Computer aided autism diagnosis using diffusion tensor imaging," *IEEE Access*, vol. 8, pp. 191298–191308.

[161] M. T. Ali, Y. A. Elnakieb, A. Shalaby, A. Mahmoud, A. Switala, M. Ghazal, A. Khelifi, L. Fraiwan, G. Barnes, and A. El-Baz, (2021) "Autism classification using smri: A recursive features selection based on sampling from multi-level high dimensional spaces," in *2021 IEEE 18th International Symposium on Biomedical Imaging (ISBI)*. IEEE, pp. 267–270.

[162] M. T. Ali, Y. ElNakieb, A. Elnakib, A. Shalaby, A. Mahmoud, M. Ghazal, J. Yousaf, H. Abu Khalifeh, M. Casanova, G. Barnes et al., (2022) "The role of structure MRI in diagnosing autism," *Diagnostics*, vol. 12, no. 1, p. 165.

[163] Y. ElNakieb, M. T. Ali, A. Elnakib, A. Shalaby, A. Soliman, A. Mahmoud, M. Ghazal, G. N. Barnes, and A. El-Baz, (2021) "The role of diffusion tensor mr imaging (dti) of the brain in diagnosing autism spectrum disorder: Promising results," *Sensors*, vol. 21, no. 24, p. 8171.

[164] A. Mahmoud, A. El-Barkouky, H. Farag, J. Graham, and A. Farag, (2013) "A non-invasive method for measuring blood flow rate in superficial veins from a single thermal image," in *Proceedings of the IEEE Conference on Computer Vision and Pattern Recognition Workshops*, pp. 354–359.

[165] N. Elsaid, A. Saied, H. Kandil, A. Soliman, F. Taher, M. Hadi, G. Giridharan, R. Jennings, M. Casanova, R. Keynton et al., (2021) "Impact of stress and hypertension on the cerebrovasculature," *Frontiers in Bioscience-Landmark*, vol. 26, no. 12, p. 1643.

[166] F. Taher, H. Kandil, Y. Gebru, A. Mahmoud, A. Shalaby, S. El-Mashad, and A. El-Baz, (2021) "A novel mra-based framework for segmenting the cerebrovascular system and correlating cerebral vascular changes to mean arterial pressure," *Applied Sciences*, vol. 11, no. 9, p. 4022.

[167] H. Kandil, A. Soliman, F. Taher, M. Ghazal, A. Khalil, G. Giridharan, R. Keynton, J. R. Jennings, and A. El-Baz, (2020) "A novel computer aided diagnosis system for the early detection of hypertension based on cerebrovascular alterations," *NeuroImage: Clinical*, vol. 25, p. 102107.

[168] H. Kandil, A. Soliman, M. Ghazal, A. Mahmoud, A. Shalaby, R. Keynton, A. Elmaghraby, G. Giridharan, and A. El-Baz, (2019) "A novel framework for early detection of hypertension using magnetic resonance angiography," *Scientific Reports*, vol. 9, no. 1, pp. 1–12.

[169] Y. Gebru, G. Giridharan, M. Ghazal, A. Mahmoud, A. Shalaby, and A. El-Baz, (2018) "Detection of cerebrovascular changes using magnetic resonance angiography," in *Cardiovascular Imaging and Image Analysis* (pp. 1–22). CRC Press.

[170] A. Mahmoud, A. Shalaby, F. Taher, M. El-Baz, J. S. Suri, and A. El-Baz, (2018) "Vascular tree segmentation from different image modalities," in Ayman El-Baz and Jasjit S. Suri (eds.), *Cardiovascular Imaging and Image Analysis* (pp. 43–70). CRC Press.

[171] F. Taher, A. Mahmoud, A. Shalaby, and A. El-Baz, (2018) "A review on the cerebrovascular segmentation methods," in *2018 IEEE International Symposium on Signal Processing and Information Technology (ISSPIT)*. IEEE, pp. 359–364.

[172] H. Kandil, A. Soliman, L. Fraiwan, A. Shalaby, A. Mahmoud, A. ElTanboly, A. Elmaghraby, G. Giridharan, and A. El-Baz, (2018) "A novel mra framework based on integrated global and local analysis for accurate segmentation of the cerebral vascular system," in *2018 IEEE 15th International Symposium on Biomedical Imaging (ISBI 2018)*. IEEE, pp. 1365–1368.

[173] F. Taher, A. Soliman, H. Kandil, A. Mahmoud, A. Shalaby, G. Gimel'farb, and A. El-Baz, (2020) "Accurate segmentation of cerebrovasculature from tof-mra images using appearance descriptors," *IEEE Access* vol. 8, pp. 96139–96149.

[174] F. Taher, A. Soliman, H. Kandil, A. Mahmoud, A. Shalaby, G. Gimel'farb, and A. El-Baz, (2020) "Precise cerebrovascular segmentation," in *2020 IEEE International Conference on Image Processing (ICIP)*. IEEE, pp. 394–397.

[175] M. Elsharkawy, M. Elrazzaz, M. Ghazal, M. Alhalabi, A. Soliman, A. Mahmoud, E. El-Daydamony, A. Atwan, A. Thanos, H. S. Sandhu et al., (2021) "Role of optical coherence tomography imaging in predicting progression of age-related macular disease: A survey," *Diagnostics*, vol. 11, no. 12, p. 2313.

[176] H. S. Sandhu, M. Elmogy, A. T. Sharafeldeen, M. Elsharkawy, N. El-Adawy, A. Eltanboly, A. Shalaby, R. Keynton, and A. El-Baz, (2020) "Automated diagnosis of diabetic retinopathy using clinical biomarkers, optical coherence tomography, and optical coherence tomography angiography," *American Journal of Ophthalmology*, vol. 216, pp. 201–206.

[177] A. Sharafeldeen, M. Elsharkawy, F. Khalifa, A. Soliman, M. Ghazal, M. AlHalabi, M. Yaghi, M. Alrahmawy, S. Elmougy, H. Sandhu et al., (2021) "Precise higher-order reflectivity and morphology models for early diagnosis of diabetic retinopathy using oct images," *Scientific Reports*, vol. 11, no. 1, pp. 1–16.

[178] A. A. Sleman, A. Soliman, M. Elsharkawy, G. Giridharan, M. Ghazal, H. Sandhu, S. Schaal, R. Keynton, A. Elmaghraby, and A. El-Baz, (2021) "A novel 3d segmentation approach for extracting retinal layers from optical coherence tomography images," *Medical Physics*, vol. 48, no. 4, pp. 1584–1595.

[179] A. A. Sleman, A. Soliman, M. Ghazal, H. Sandhu, S. Schaal, A. Elmaghraby, and A. El-Baz, (2019) "Retinal layers OCT scans 3-D segmentation," in *2019 IEEE International Conference on Imaging Systems and Techniques (IST)*. IEEE, pp. 1–6.

[180] A. ElTanboly, M. Ismail, A. Shalaby, A. Switala, A. El-Baz, S. Schaal, G. Gimel'farb, and M. El-Azab, (2017) "A computer-aided diagnostic system for detecting diabetic retinopathy in optical coherence tomography images," *Medical Physics*, vol. 44, no. 3, pp. 914–923.

[181] H. S. Sandhu, A. El-Baz, and J. M. Seddon, (2018) "Progress in automated deep learning for macular degeneration," *JAMA Ophthalmology* vol. 136, no. 12, pp. 1366–1367.

[182] M. Ghazal, S. S. Ali, A. H. Mahmoud, A. M. Shalaby, and A. El-Baz, (2020) "Accurate detection of non-proliferative diabetic retinopathy in optical coherence tomography images using convolutional neural networks," *IEEE Access*, vol. 8, pp. 34 387–34 397.

[183] K. Hammouda, F. Khalifa, A. Soliman, M. Ghazal, M. Abou El-Ghar, A. Haddad, M. Elmogy, H. Darwish, A. Khalil, A. Elmaghraby et al., (2019) "A CNN-based framework for bladder wall segmentation using MRI," in *2019 Fifth International Conference on Advances in Biomedical Engineering (ICABME)*. IEEE, pp. 1–4.

[184] K. Hammouda, F. Khalifa, A. Soliman, M. Ghazal, M. Abou El-Ghar, A. Haddad, M. Elmogy, H. Darwish, R. Keynton, and A. El-Baz, (2019) "A deep learning-based approach for accurate segmentation of bladder wall using mr images," in *2019 IEEE International Conference on Imaging Systems and Techniques (IST)*. IEEE, pp. 1–6.

[185] K. Hammouda, F. Khalifa, A. Soliman, H. Abdeltawab, M. Ghazal, M. Abou El-Ghar, A. Haddad, H. E. Darwish, R. Keynton, and A. El-Baz, (2020) "A 3d cnn with a learnable adaptive shape prior for accurate segmentation of bladder wall using mr images," in *2020 IEEE 17th International Symposium on Biomedical Imaging (ISBI)*. IEEE, pp. 935–938.

[186] K. Hammouda, F. Khalifa, A. Soliman, M. Ghazal, M. Abou El-Ghar, M. Badawy, H. Darwish, A. Khelifi, and A. El-Baz, (2021) "A multiparametric mri-based cad system for accurate diagnosis of bladder cancer staging," *Computerized Medical Imaging and Graphics*, vol. 90, p. 101911.

[187] K. Hammouda, F. Khalifa, A. Soliman, M. Ghazal, M. Abou El-Ghar, M. Badawy, H. Darwish, and A. El-Baz, (2021) "A cad system for accurate diagnosis of bladder cancer staging using a multiparametric mri," in *2021 IEEE 18th International Symposium on Biomedical Imaging (ISBI)*. IEEE, pp. 1718–1721.

[188] A. Alksas, M. Shehata, G. A. Saleh, A. Shaffie, A. Soliman, M. Ghazal, H. A. Khalifeh, A. A. Razek, and A. El-Baz, (2021) "A novel computer-aided diagnostic system for early assessment of hepatocellular carcinoma," in *2020 25th International Conference on Pattern Recognition (ICPR)*. IEEE, pp. 10 375–10 382.

[189] A. Alksas, M. Shehata, G. A. Saleh, A. Shaffie, A. Soliman, M. Ghazal, A. Khelifi, H. A. Khalifeh, A. A. Razek, G. A. Giridharan et al., (2021) "A novel computer-aided diagnostic system for accurate detection and grading of liver tumors," *Scientific Reports*, vol. 11, no. 1, pp. 1–18.

[190] A. A. K. A. Razek, R. Khaled, E. Helmy, A. Naglah, A. AbdelKhalek, and A. El-Baz, (2022) "Artificial intelligence and deep learning of head and neck cancer," *Magnetic Resonance Imaging Clinics*, vol. 30, no. 1, pp. 81–94.

[191] A. Sharafeldeen, M. Elsharkawy, R. Khaled, A. Shaffie, F. Khalifa, A. Soliman, A. A. k. Abdel Razek, M. M. Hussein, S. Taman, A. Naglah et al., (2021) "Texture and shape analysis of diffusion-weighted imaging for thyroid nodules classification using machine learning," *Medical Physics* vol. 49, no. 2, pp. 988–999.

[192] A. Naglah, F. Khalifa, R. Khaled, A. A. K. Abdel Razek, M. Ghazal, G. Giridharan, and A. El-Baz, (2021) "Novel mri-based cad system for early detection of thyroid cancer using multi-input cnn," *Sensors*, vol. 21, no. 11, p. 3878.

[193] A. Naglah, F. Khalifa, A. Mahmoud, M. Ghazal, P. Jones, T. Murray, A. S. Elmaghraby, and A. El-Baz, (2018) "Athlete-customized injury prediction using training load statistical records and machine learning," in *2018 IEEE International Symposium on Signal Processing and Information Technology (ISSPIT)*. IEEE, pp. 459–464.

[194] A. H. Mahmoud, (2014) "Utilizing radiation for smart robotic applications using visible, thermal, and polarization images." Ph.D. dissertation, University of Louisville.

[195] A. Mahmoud, A. El-Barkouky, J. Graham, and A. Farag, (2014) "Pedestrian detection using mixed partial derivative based histogram of oriented gradients," in *2014 IEEE International Conference on Image Processing (ICIP)*. IEEE, pp. 2334–2337.

[196] A. El-Barkouky, A. Mahmoud, J. Graham, and A. Farag, (2013) "An interactive educational drawing system using a humanoid robot and light polarization," in *2013 IEEE International Conference on Image Processing*. IEEE, pp. 3407–3411.

[197] A. H. Mahmoud, M. T. El-Melegy, and A. A. Farag, (2012) "Direct method for shape recovery from polarization and shading," in *2012 19th IEEE International Conference on Image Processing*. IEEE, pp. 1769–1772.

[198] M. A. Ghazal, A. Mahmoud, A. Aslantas, A. Soliman, A. Shalaby, J. A. Benediktsson, and A. El-Baz, (2019) "Vegetation cover estimation using convolutional neural networks," *IEEE Access*, vol. 7, pp. 132 563–132 576.

[199] M. Ghazal, A. Mahmoud, A. Shalaby, and A. El-Baz, (2019) "Automated framework for accurate segmentation of leaf images for plant health assessment," *Environmental Monitoring and Assessment*, vol. 191, no. 8, p. 491.

[200] M. Ghazal, A. Mahmoud, A. Shalaby, S. Shaker, A. Khelifi, and A. El-Baz, (2020) "Precise statistical approach for leaf segmentation," in *2020 IEEE International Conference on Image Processing (ICIP)*. IEEE, pp. 2985–2989.

Chapter 2

ISM and DEMATEL Analysis of H4.0 Enablers in the Indian Healthcare Industry

Padmakali Banerjee[1], Vineet Jain[2], and Puneeta Ajmera[3]

[1]Vice Chancellor, Sir Padampat Singhania University, Udaipur, India
[2]Department of Mechanical Engineering, Mewat Engineering College, Nuh, Haryana, India
[3]Department of Public Health, Delhi Pharmaceutical Sciences and Research University, New Delhi, India

Contents

2.1 Introduction 24
2.2 Review of Literature 25
    2.2.1 Enablers of Health 4.0 25
2.3 Research Methodology 29
    2.3.1 ISM Methodology 29
    2.3.2 DEMATEL Methodology 30
2.4 Modeling the Enablers of the Indian Healthcare Industry by ISM Methodology 31
2.5 MICMAC Analysis of the Enablers 32
2.6 DEMATEL Analysis of the Enablers 39

DOI: 10.1201/9781003145189-2

2.7 Discussion and Conclusion... 39

2.8 Implications of Research 45

2.9 Limitations and Future Prospects of Research......................... 46

References 46

2.1 Introduction

Industry 4.0 (I4.0) is an astonishing phenomenon that includes the latest digital technologies and concepts of smart factories where the physical processes are managed by cyber physical based upon the data obtained from the virtual and physical worlds. "Cyber-physical system" (CPS) blends the tangible world and the digital world for sustainable industrial growth. Devices using artificial intelligence like robots, 3D printers, and drones, etc., are used for value-added services. I4.0 automated systems integrate all supply-chain processes and facilitate data convergence. Industry 4.0 seeks to turn traditional manufacturing processes into an incredibly versatile production system with digital goods and intercommunicating person, product, and computer in real time.

In healthcare, Industry 4.0 is popularly known as Health 4.0 (H4.0) and smart factories as smart medical factories where individualized and personalized services are provided to the patients through hospital information systems (Thuemmler and Bai 2017). Technologies of H4.0 have the potential to make the healthcare industry more participative, confluent, and predictive. For example, smart pharmaceuticals embedded with biosensors are being used in pharmaceutical industries. These biosensors continuously generate tremendous data known as big data. Jee and Kim (2013) have elaborated ways to revolutionize the healthcare industry by choosing suitable treatment design and improving clinical outcomes and healthcare delivery systems using big data analytics. A new concept of Health 4.0 called precision medicine has emerged; it uses information from the physical world (patients) and virtual world (cloud-computing algorithms) where treatment is selected based on an individual variance in the genetic composition of each patient. This will help the healthcare professionals to identify more precisely the diagnostic, preventive, and therapeutic strategies for a specific disease in a specific group of people (Wei and Denny 2015).

Industry 4.0 can create mobility in healthcare systems by meeting individual patient requirements and optimizing clinical decision making. The United States has aimed to convert 90% of Medicare into a value-based framework by using Health 4.0 technologies. The Indian healthcare industry is growing swiftly and is projected to reach 280 billion US $ by 2020 (Raghupathi and Raghupathi 2014). H4.0 is the most innovative phenomenon that can bring revolution in the Indian healthcare industry, if executed cautiously and vigilantly. Only some of the tertiary care hospitals are trying to adopt H4.0 technologies. Numerous healthcare units are still uncertain about its employment because of excessive initial investments for creating proper infrastructure and organizing training sessions (Kagermann 2015).

Industry 4.0 is explored in nine technologies (Rüßmann et al. 2015, Ajmera and Jain 2019c).

H4.0 can pinpoint the areas that require improvements, making healthcare processes more edifying and innovative. H4.0 is the most innovative phenomenon that can bring revolution in the Indian healthcare industry if executed cautiously and vigilantly. Only some of the tertiary care hospitals are trying to adopt H4.0 technologies. Many healthcare units are still uncertain about its employment because of excessive initial investments for creating proper infrastructure and organizing training sessions (Kagermann 2015); therefore, it is important to identify the enablers of H4.0 application in healthcare. The aims of the present paper are to:

1. identify the enablers of Health 4.0 and to find out interrelationships among them.
2. establish a comprehensive structured model using the ISM approach to strengthen these enablers.
3. quantify these enablers using MICMAC analysis to prioritize them so that they can be handled appropriately.
4. analyze the enablers through a casual diagram by using the DEMATEL approach.

2.2 Review of Literature

Kamble, Gunasekaran, and Sharma (2018) have used I4.0 technologies in the manufacturing sector. Thuemmler and Bai (2017) described the impact of big data and innovative digital services on the healthcare industry. Harrison, Vera, and Ahmad (2016) reviewed the role of cyber-physical system toolkit in supporting automation systems. Bahrin et al. (2016) discussed the role of robotics and other automated technologies in accomplishing I4.0. Bagheri et al. (2015) developed a model for the integration of the manufacturing sector. Lasi et al. (2014) discussed various crucial technologies and driving forces for the I4.0 concept. Kagerman laid down the basis of the I4.0 phenomenon and stated that Germany was the first country to implement I4.0 in its manufacturing organizations (Kagermann 2015). Bates et al. (2014) discussed how different data analysis techniques can decrease costs and improve clinical outcomes. Chawla and Davis (2013) developed a framework to reduce patient readmission rates. Jee and Kim explored the role of big data in reforming the healthcare industry (Jee and Kim 2013). Kumar and Lee (2011) surveyed perilous issues such as data security in healthcare digital programs. Lorincz et al. (2004) discussed the use of sensor networking technologies in clinical emergency responses.

2.2.1 Enablers of Health 4.0

There is a wide digital divide between rural and urban areas in India. Some areas are devoid of even basic health facilities. H4.0 technologies such as telemedicine and robotics can help resolve this issue to a great extent. But this revolution is still in its nascent stage in India. Initially, we identified 21 enablers of H4.0 in India through extensive literature review and expert opinions from the healthcare sector. The Delphi technique was then carried out by asking 15 experts from appropriate areas to validate the enablers; after some rounds of Delphi, 17 enablers were chosen.

These enablers are explained in Table 2.1:

Table 2.1 Health 4.0 Enablers

Sl. no.	Enabler	Description
1	Clinical information confidentiality and security	Confidential data is available on cloud. There may be issues for data security. So, employees should be aware of this possibility (Kamble, Gunasekaran, and Sharma 2018).
2	Adequate IT infrastructure	Proper IT infrastructure is required for the use of IoT for reinforcing H4.0 technologies (Hecklau et al. 2016).
	Financial support	IoT required heavy investment for properly implementation. So, implementation of H4.0 requires financial support (Kamigaki 2017).
	Continuous training of employees	Proper training is required to handle smart technologies and use IoT and digitization (Hung 2016).
	Leadership	Ideally, Industry 4.0 deployment requires collaboration from all agencies to improve productivity. However, managers and supervisors should motivate staff to do more so that their organisations' outcomes are optimal (Gilchrist 2016, Kamigaki 2017).
	Qualified team of experts	For the successful implementation of H4.0 technologies, a well-qualified team of experts is required. The team members should be well versed in the latest technology and actively engage in all the activities relevant to their implementation (Willcocks and Sykes 2000, Chen 2001).

(*Continued*)

Table 2.1 (Continued)   Health 4.0 Enablers

Sl. no.	Enabler	Description
	Standardization of clinical data	India's healthcare sector is highly fragmented and scarcely standardised. A general description of the various facets of treatment is hard for physicians, patients, and administrators to retain. Therefore, sufficient steps toward standardization of clinical data can prove beneficial for Health 4.0 implementation (Raghupathi and Raghupathi 2014).
	Technological support from the government	The absence of a reliable communication network and weak signal quality would hamper the whole process as it is essential to have continuous horizontal and vertical access to information. The government can provide technical assistance by offering Internet access at subsidised rates for health industries that plan to incorporate Health 4.0 technology to boost digitisation of the health sector (Bonczek, Holsapple, and Whinston 2014).
	Confidence of patients in IoT	The Internet of Things has changed the perceptions of patients, and they are now more conscious of their rights. However, increasing Internet usage does not alter the need to strengthen connections with patients (Davis, Bagozzi, and Warshaw 1989). Hence, more patients believe IoT, the faster Technology 4.0 will be introduced.
	Innovative clinical services	Continued advances in medical services are needed in the adoption of H4.0 technologies that will increase the productivity, competence, awareness, and quality of products and services (Zhou, Liu, and Zhou 2015).

(*Continued*)

Table 2.1 (Continued)   Health 4.0 Enablers

Sl. no.	Enabler	Description
	Patient feedback	This data enables healthcare administrators make wise decisions to constantly develop their healthcare processes and better respond to patient needs (Qin, Liu, and Grosvenor 2016).
	Sufficient maintenance and support systems	Smart maintenance systems are required for H4.0 implementation to avoid any disruption and breakdown (Lee, Kao, and Yang 2014).
	Compatibility in hardware and healthcare software	Production and IT equipment for healthcare procurement from various providers over time leads to compatibility of software (Schoenherr, Narayanan, and Narasimhan 2015).
	Well defined strategic goals	The coherence of the corporate priorities promotes the right time for companies to implement Health 4.0. Users can often have doubts, and their current status can be avoided. So, health managers can intelligently express their vision for workers before introducing Health 4.0 so that digital culture is well incorporated in the company (Koch et al. 2014).
	Healthcare organization culture	The implementation of H4.0 needs a shift in culture as companies are now turned into smart factories. The roles and responsibilities of organisations would change because of automation and decentralisation. (Bröring et al. 2017).
	Employee engagement and involvement	To understand its technology, the introduction of Health 4.0 involves advanced expertise and skills, and staff must be trained to understand and address this definition. On the one hand, the company is forced to build

(Continued)

Table 2.1 (Continued)   Health 4.0 Enablers

Sl. no.	Enabler	Description
		these capabilities and, on the other hand, the workers' embrace of the new technology is another obstacle. If workers are motivated, active, and trusted before Health 4.0 is introduced, that would certainly benefit organisations (Mueller, Chen, and Riedel 2017).
	Clarity of medical, legal, and IP regulations	New advances in H4.0 technology in the medical industry, such as trademarks, copyrights, and licences, etc., need to be treated with caution (Christians and Liepin 2017).

2.3 Research Methodology

2.3.1 ISM Methodology

ISM is a well-known technique in which the relationships are developed into a structured model (Warfield 1974). It helps to comprehend complex issues appropriately. This methodology is widely used in the research areas (Jharkharia and Shankar 2005, Prasanna Venkatesan and Sanket 2018, Jain and Quershi 2022, S. Jain et al. 2022, Jain et al. 2022, Aggarwal et al. 2022, Mittal et al. 2021). Lean implementation in healthcare (Ajmera and Jain 2019a), diabetic patients QOL (Ajmera and Jain 2019b). Medical tourism (Jain and Ajmera 2018). FMS (Raj, Attri, and Jain 2012, Jain and Raj 2014, 2015a,b, 2016, Jain and Soni 2019, Jain and Raj 2021). Biodiesel (Avinash, Sasikumar, and Murugesan 2018), Hotel services (Sarmah and Rahman 2018), online purchasing (Xiao 2018), waste recycling (Chauhan, Singh, and Jharkharia 2018), mobile phone industry (Maheshwari, Seth, and Gupta 2018), warehouse selection (Jha et al. 2018), automobile industry (Kumar, Singh, and Kumar 2017), medical device development (Rane and Kirkire 2017), TQM (Veltmeyer and Mohamed 2017), footwear industry (Purohit et al. 2016), healthcare waste management (Thakur and Anbanandam 2016), Telecom sector (Bhadani, Shankar, and Rao 2016), hospital inventory management (Kumar and Kumar 2015), and education management (Mahajan et al. 2014).

Different steps involved in the ISM approach are depicted in Figure 2.1.

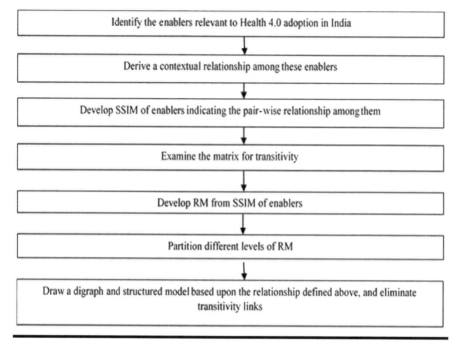

Figure 2.1   Flow Diagram of ISM.

2.3.2 DEMATEL Methodology

DEMATEL methodology were applied in different sectors as Jain and Ajmera (2020a) used DEMATEL for the evaluation of "FMS variables." Jain and Ajmera (2020b) applied for "Lean variables of the healthcare industry," "software upgradation" (Majumdar, Kapur, and Khatri 2019), "project management in construction" (Mavi and Standing 2018), "supply chain management" (Kaur et al. 2018), "supplier selection" (Liu, Deng, and Chan 2018), "barriers to manufacturing" (Potdar, Routroy, and Behera 2017), "agile manufacturing" (Vinodh, Balagi, and Patil 2016), "solar energy" (Luthra et al. 2016), "automotive parts remanufacturing" (Xia, Govindan, and Zhu 2015), "knowledge management adoption" (Patil and Kant 2014), and "business process management" (Bai and Sarkis 2013).

Different steps of the DEMATEL methodology are depicted in Figure 2.2 (Tzeng, Chiang, and Li 2007, Jain and Ajmera 2020a, Jain and Qureshi 2022).

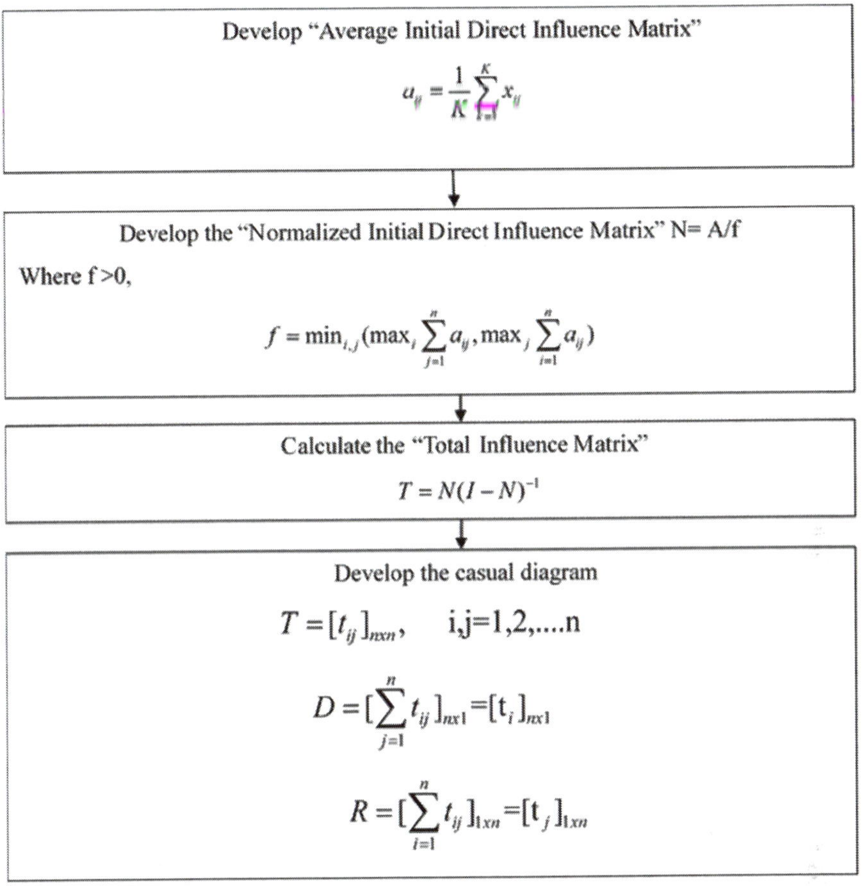

Develop "Average Initial Direct Influence Matrix"

$$a_{ij} = \frac{1}{K} \sum_{i=1}^{K} x_{ij}$$

Develop the "Normalized Initial Direct Influence Matrix" N= A/f

Where f >0,

$$f = \min_{i,j} (\max_i \sum_{j=1}^{n} a_{ij}, \max_j \sum_{i=1}^{n} a_{ij})$$

Calculate the "Total Influence Matrix"

$$T = N(I - N)^{-1}$$

Develop the casual diagram

$$T = [t_{ij}]_{n \times n}, \quad i,j=1,2,....n$$

$$D = [\sum_{j=1}^{n} t_{ij}]_{n \times 1} = [t_i]_{n \times 1}$$

$$R = [\sum_{i=1}^{n} t_{ij}]_{1 \times n} = [t_j]_{1 \times n}$$

Figure 2.2   Flow Diagram of DEMATEL.

2.4 Modeling the Enablers of the Indian Healthcare Industry by ISM Methodology

The steps are given below (Jain and Raj 2016):

1. Establish a contextual relationship:

Seventeen enablers of Health 4.0 relevant to the Indian healthcare industry were determined, and a contextual specific interaction was selected, which means that one enabler affects another variable. Symbolic representation showing this relationship direction (i and j) is presented in Table 2.2 (Jain and Ajmera 2018).

Table 2.2 Contextual Relationship

Symbol	Illustration
V	Enabler i influences or reaches to enabler j
A	Enabler j reaches to enabler i
X	Both enabler s i and j reach to each other
O	No relationship between enablers i and j

2. Development of SSIM matrix:

SSIM **"structural self-interaction"** is developed for 17 enablers and is described in Table 2.2. SSIM is depicted in Table 2.3.

3. Development of RM:

SSIM is converted into an initial RM **"reachability matrix"** in the binary form. This reachability matrix, called initial RM, is given in Table 2.4; transitivity is introduced to develop the final RM, which is depicted in Table 2.5 in which transitivity is designated as 1^*.

4. Partitioning the RM:

For this step, the reachability and antecedent set of each factor are needed; they are derived from the final RM (Jain and Raj 2016). After the development of RM, the structural model, called digraph, is established. Partitioning is then done for the set and subset of all the factors. Partitioning of the RM is shown in Table 2.6.

5. Development of digraph and model:

Indirect links are removed to achieve a final digraph. The digraph and model are depicted in Figures 2.3 and 2.4, respectively.

2.5 MICMAC Analysis of the Enablers

MICMAC analysis is carried out to estimate the drive and dependence power of enablers in four clusters, as discussed in Table 2.7 (Ajmera and Jain 2019c, Mandal and Deshmukh 1994).

We also carried out a MICMAC study in the current research with the aim of finding and evaluating Health 4.0 enablers in the Indian healthcare market.

Table 2.3 SSIM

Sl. no.	2	3	4	5	6	7	8	9	10	11	12	13	14	15	16	17
1	O	O	A	A	A	O	O	X	O	O	O	O	O	O	O	O
2		O	A	A	X	O	O	O	V	O	A	A	V	V	V	O
3			X	A	V	O	A	O	O	O	V	V	V	V	V	V
4				A	V	V	A	V	V	V	V	V	V	V	V	V
5					V	V	V	O	V	O	V	O	V	V	V	V
6						A	O	O	O	O	O	O	V	V	O	O
7							O	O	O	V	A	X	V	O	V	O
8								O	O	O	O	O	V	O	O	O
9									O	V	O	O	O	O	O	O
10										X	A	O	V	O	O	O
11											A	O	X	V	O	O
12												V	O	O	O	O
13													V	O	O	O
14														V	O	O
15															V	V
16																X

Table 2.4 Initial Reachability Matrix

Sl. no.	1	2	3	4	5	6	7	8	9	10	11	12	13	14	15	16	17
1	1	0	0	0	0	0	0	0	1	0	0	0	0	0	0	0	0
2	0	1	0	0	0	1	0	0	0	1	0	0	0	1	1	1	0
3	0	0	1	1	0	1	0	0	0	0	0	1	1	1	1	1	1
4	1	1	1	1	0	1	1	0	1	1	1	1	1	1	1	1	1
5	1	1	1	1	1	1	1	1	0	1	0	1	0	1	1	1	1
6	1	1	0	0	0	1	0	0	0	0	0	0	0	1	1	0	0
7	0	0	0	0	0	1	1	0	0	0	1	0	1	1	0	1	0
8	0	0	1	1	0	0	0	1	0	0	0	0	0	1	0	0	0
9	1	0	0	0	0	0	0	0	1	0	1	0	0	0	0	0	0
10	0	0	0	0	0	0	0	0	0	1	1	0	0	1	0	0	0
11	0	0	0	0	0	0	0	0	0	1	1	0	0	1	1	0	0
12	0	1	0	0	0	0	1	0	0	1	1	1	1	0	0	0	0
13	0	1	0	0	0	0	1	0	0	0	0	0	1	1	0	0	0
14	0	0	0	0	0	0	0	0	0	0	1	0	0	1	1	0	0
15	0	0	0	0	0	0	0	0	0	0	0	0	0	0	1	1	1
16	0	0	0	0	0	0	0	0	0	0	0	0	0	0	0	1	1
17	0	0	0	0	0	0	0	0	0	0	0	0	0	0	0	1	1

Table 2.5 Final Reachability Matrix

Sl. no.	1	2	3	4	5	6	7	8	9	10	11	12	13	14	15	16	17
1	1	0	0	0	0	0	0	0	1	0	1*	0	0	0	0	0	0
2	0	1	0	0	0	1	0	0	1*	1	1*	0	0	1	1	1	1*
3	0	1*	1	1	0	1	1*	0	1*	1*	1*	1	1	1	1	1	1
4	1	1	1	1	0	1	1	0	1	1	1	1	1	1	1	1	1
5	1	1	1	1	1	1	1	1	1*	1	1*	1	1*	1	1	1	1
6	1	1	0	0	0	1	0	0	1*	1*	0	0	0	1	1	1*	1*
7	0	1*	0	0	0	1	1	0	1*	1*	1	0	1	1	1*	1	0
8	1*	0	1	1	0	1*	1*	1	0	1*	1*	1*	1*	1	1*	1*	1*
9	1	0	0	0	0	0	0	0	1	1	1	0	0	1*	1*	0	0
10	0	0	0	0	0	0	0	0	0	1	1	0	0	1	1*	0	0
11	0	0	0	0	0	0	0	0	0	1	1	0	0	1	1	1*	1*
12	0	1	0	0	0	1*	1	0	0	1	1*	1	1	1*	1*	1*	0
13	0	1	0	0	0	0	1	0	1*	1*	1	0	1	1	1	1*	0
14	0	0	0	0	0	0	0	0	0	0	0	0	0	1	1	1*	1*
15	0	0	0	0	0	0	0	0	0	0	0	0	0	0	1	1	1
16	0	0	0	0	0	0	0	0	0	0	0	0	0	0	0	1	1
17	0	0	0	0	0	0	0	0	0	0	0	0	0	0	0	1	1

Table 2.6 Iterations

Sl. no.	Reachability set	Antecedent set	Intersection set	Level
16	16,17	2,3,4,5,6,7,8,11,12,13,14,15,16,17	16,17	I
17	16,17	2,3,4,5,6,8,11,14,15,16,17	16,17	I
15	15	2,3,4,5,6,7,8,9,10,11,12,13,14,15,	15	II
10	10,11,14	2,3,4,5,6,7,8,9,10,11,12,13,14	10,11,14	III
11	10,11,14	1,2,3,4,5,7,8,9,10,11,12,13,14	10,11,14	III
14	10,11,14	2,3,4,5,6,7,8,9,10,11,12,13,14	10,11,14	III
1	1,9	1,4,5,6,8,9	1,9	IV
9	1,9	1,2,3,4,5,6,7,9,13	1,9	IV
2	2,6	2,3,4,5,6,7,12,13	2,6	V
6	2,6	2,3,4,5,6,7,8,13	2,6	V
7	7,13	3,4,5,7,8,12,13	7,13	VI
13	7,13	3,4,5,7,8,12,13	7,13	VI
12	12	3,4,5,8,12	12	VII
3	3,4	3,4,5,8	3,4	VIII
4	3,4	3,4,5,8	3,4	VIII
8	8	5,8	8	IX
5	5	5	5	X

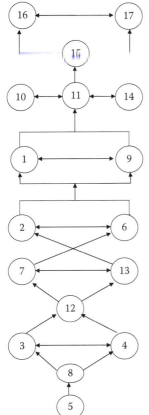

Figure 2.3   Digraph.

Different enablers are mapped in line with their driving and dependency. Table 2.8 demonstrates the stability and driving force of enablers. Figure 2.5 then displays the dependency and drive power diagram.

The enablers are grouped into four groups, i.e., autonomous, dependent, independent, and linked.

a. Group 1 "Autonomous": Enablers are positioned in the first quadrant and have both weak and weak driving power. Enabler 1 lies in this quadrant in the current work.

b. Group 2 "Dependent": Enablers are heavily dependent, but they are small. They are situated in the the second quadrant and inspired by different enablers. This quadrant is represented by the research items 9,10,11,14,15,16, and 17.

c. Group 3 "Linkage": Such enablers are both efficient driving and dependent. They are unpredictable and necessary since any behaviour they take directly

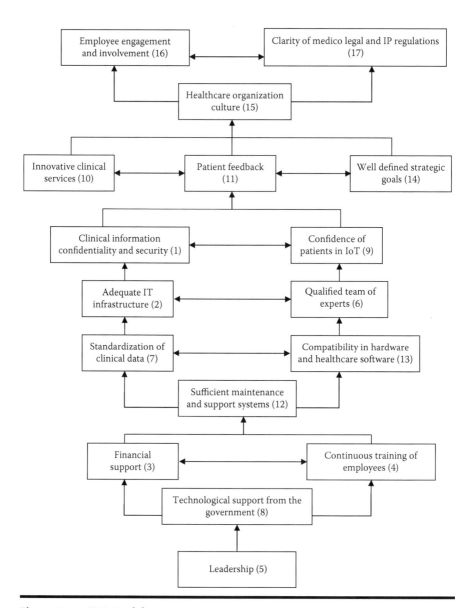

Figure 2.4 ISM Model.

impacts others and even responds to them. In this quadrant, there are no promoters in the present work.

d. Group 4 "Independent": These enablers are in the fourth quadrant of strong control but have weak strength of dependency. Enabler 2,3,4,5,6,7,8,12, and 13 are included.

Table 2.7 Cluster of MICMAC Analysis

Cluster no.	Cluster name	Properties
1	Autonomous Enabler	Poor driving and poor power dependency
2	Dependent Enabler	Heavy dependency, but poor driving strength
3	Linkage Enabler	Heavily dependent as well as powerful driving force
4	Independent Enabler	Strong driving and low power of dependency

2.6 DEMATEL Analysis of the Enablers

The direct and indirect effects of 17 enablers of H4.0 in healthcare are depicted in the Tables 2.9–2.11, and Table 2.11 indicates the ranking of enablers as 5>4>8>3>12>7>13>2>6>9>1>11>10>14>17>15>16.

The enablers are categorized into "cause and effect groups" by the "cause and effect diagram." The cause-and-effect diagram of H4.0 enablers is shown in Figure 2.6.

According to the figure, "Enabler 5 (leadership), 4 (continuous training of employees), 8 (technological support from the government), 3 (financial support), 12 (sufficient maintenance and support systems), 7 (standardization of clinical data), 13 (compatibility in hardware and healthcare software), 2 (adequate IT infrastructure), 6 (qualified team of experts) are the net causes while enabler 9 (confidence of patients in IoT), 1 (clinical information confidentiality and security), 11 (patient feedback), 10 (innovative clinical services), 14 (well-defined strategic goals), 17 (clarity of medico-legal and IP regulations),15 (healthcare organization culture), and 16 (employee engagement and involvement) are net effects. The enablers in the cause group are more important because they have a considerable effect on the entire system. So these enablers should be handled more carefully.

2.7 Discussion and Conclusion

"Leadership" was the most critical factor in successful implementation of H4.0 in Indian healthcare because this enabler has a very powerful guiding force in the current initiative. H4.0, the development and management of adequate infrastructural systems in the organisations, requires substantial initial investments. In addition, increased funding is needed to train personnel and maintain support services. All these important decisions are taken under the leadership of top

Table 2.8 Conical Matrix

Enablers	16	17	15	10	11	14	9	1	2	6	7	13	12	3	4	8	5	Sum
16	1	1	0	0	0	0	0	0	0	0	0	0	0	0	0	0	0	2
17	1	1	0	0	0	0	0	0	0	0	0	0	0	0	0	0	0	2
15	1	1	1	0	0	0	0	0	0	0	0	0	0	0	0	0	0	3
10	0	0	1	1	1	1	0	0	0	0	0	0	0	0	0	0	0	4
11	1	1	1	1	1	1	0	0	0	0	0	0	0	0	0	0	0	6
14	1	1	1	1	1	1	0	0	0	0	0	0	0	0	0	0	0	6
9	0	0	1	1	1	1	1	1	0	0	0	0	0	0	0	0	0	6
1	0	0	0	0	1	0	1	1	0	0	0	0	0	0	0	0	0	3
2	1	1	1	1	1	1	1	0	1	0	0	1	0	0	0	0	0	9
6	1	1	1	1	0	1	1	0	0	1	1	1	0	0	0	0	0	9
7	1	0	1	1	1	1	1	0	1	1	1	0	1	0	0	0	0	10
13	1	0	1	1	1	1	1	0	1	1	1	1	0	0	0	0	0	10
12	1	0	1	1	1	1	0	0	1	1	0	0	1	1	0	0	0	9
3	1	1	1	1	1	1	1	1	1	1	1	1	0	1	1	0	0	14
4	1	1	1	1	1	1	1	1	1	1	1	1	1	1	1	0	0	15
8	1	1	1	1	1	1	0	1	1	1	1	1	1	0	1	1	0	14
5	1	1	1	1	1	1	1	1	1	1	1	1	1	1	1	1	1	17
Sum	14	11	14	13	13	13	9	6	8	8	7	7	5	4	4	2	1	

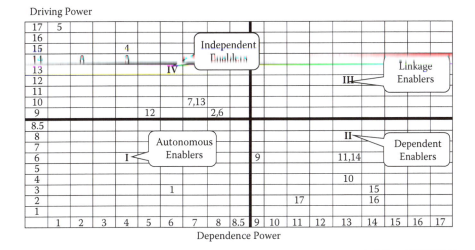

Figure 2.5   MICMAC Analysis.

management. If leaders are supportive and efficient, H4.0 implementation will be successful. It is necessary for leaders to consider and understand the value of H4.0 technology first so that H4.0 can be introduced in their organisations with high priority. "Technological support from the government" is the most significant element in the successful introduction of H4.0 technology. The government will also support the introduction of the Health 4.0 technology in the area of healthcare through the availability of Internet services at a lower cost. Uninterrupted Internet connectivity is important for Health 4.0 applications since the whole infrastructure is impaired by the poor signal power. The continuous training of workers is another significant aspect. Health 4.0 technologies require trained personnel since staff must use virtual artificial devices to manage and interpret clinical data. The medical industries must therefore stress the need to provide specialised training to ensure the use of H4.0 technologies. The workers often need to retrain so that they are completely informed of and run Health 4.0 apps.

The results of the ISM methodology is verified with the results of MICMAC and DEMATEL methodologies. Sufficient maintenance and support systems are another important enabler. During a period leading to software compatibility problems due to the lack of manufacturing and IT facilities in the resource organisations from different manufacturers, users faced difficulty using IT technologies and seeking an exact solution. Schoenherr research also suggests that hardware and software compatibility issues would improve the adoption of Industry 4.0 should it be treated correctly (Schoenherr, Narayanan, and Narasimhan 2015). With available information solutions, the complex data of health care is highly difficult to handle

Table 2.9 Normalized Initial Direct Influence Matrix N

	1	2	3	4	5	6	7	8	9	10	11	12	13	14	15	16	17
1	**0**	0.0000	0.0000	0.0000	0.0000	0.0000	0.0000	0.0000	0.0656	0.0000	0.0492	0.0000	0.0000	0.0000	0.0000	0.0000	0.0000
2	0.0000	**0**	0.0000	0.0000	0.0000	0.0656	0.0000	0.0000	0.0492	0.0656	0.0492	0.0000	0.0000	0.0656	0.0656	0.0656	0.0492
3	0.0000	0.0492	**0**	0.0656	0.0000	0.0656	0.0492	0.0000	0.0492	0.0492	0.0492	0.0656	0.0656	0.0656	0.0656	0.0656	0.0656
4	0.0656	0.0656	0.0656	**0**	0.0000	0.0656	0.0656	0.0000	0.0656	0.0656	0.0656	0.0656	0.0656	0.0656	0.0656	0.0656	0.0656
5	0.0656	0.0656	0.0656	0.0656	**0**	0.0656	0.0656	0.0656	0.0492	0.0656	0.0492	0.0656	0.0492	0.0656	0.0656	0.0656	0.0656
6	0.0656	0.0656	0.0000	0.0000	0.0000	**0**	0.0000	0.0000	0.0492	0.0492	0.0000	0.0000	0.0000	0.0656	0.0656	0.0492	0.0492
7	0.0000	0.0492	0.0000	0.0000	0.0000	0.0656	**0**	0.0000	0.0492	0.0492	0.0656	0.0000	0.0656	0.0656	0.0492	0.0656	0.0492
8	0.0492	0.0000	0.0656	0.0656	0.0000	0.0492	0.0492	**0**	0.0492	0.0492	0.0492	0.0492	0.0492	0.0656	0.0492	0.0492	0.0000
9	0.0656	0.0000	0.0000	0.0000	0.0000	0.0000	0.0000	0.0000	**0**	0.0492	0.0656	0.0000	0.0000	0.0492	0.0492	0.0000	0.0000
10	0.0000	0.0000	0.0000	0.0000	0.0000	0.0000	0.0000	0.0000	0.0000	**0**	0.0656	0.0000	0.0000	0.0656	0.0492	0.0000	0.0000
11	0.0000	0.0000	0.0000	0.0000	0.0000	0.0000	0.0000	0.0000	0.0000	0.0656	**0**	0.0000	0.0000	0.0656	0.0656	0.0492	0.0492
12	0.0000	0.0656	0.0000	0.0000	0.0000	0.0492	0.0656	0.0000	0.0000	0.0656	0.0656	**0**	0.0656	0.0492	0.0492	0.0492	0.0000
13	0.0000	0.0656	0.0000	0.0000	0.0000	0.0000	0.0656	0.0000	0.0492	0.0492	0.0492	0.0000	**0**	0.0656	0.0492	0.0492	0.0000
14	0.0000	0.0000	0.0000	0.0000	0.0000	0.0000	0.0000	0.0000	0.0000	0.0492	0.0656	0.0000	0.0000	**0**	0.0656	0.0000	0.0492
15	0.0000	0.0000	0.0000	0.0000	0.0000	0.0000	0.0000	0.0000	0.0000	0.0000	0.0000	0.0000	0.0000	0.0000	**0**	0.0000	0.0656
16	0.0000	0.0000	0.0000	0.0000	0.0000	0.0000	0.0000	0.0000	0.0000	0.0000	0.0000	0.0000	0.0000	0.0000	0.0000	**0**	0.0656
17	0.0000	0.0000	0.0000	0.0000	0.0000	0.0000	0.0000	0.0000	0.0000	0.0000	0.0000	0.0000	0.0000	0.0000	0.0000	0.0656	**0**

Table 2.10 Total Relationship Matrix T

	1	2	3	4	5	6	7	8	9	10	11	12	13	14	15	16	17	SUM
1	0.0043	0.0000	0.0000	0.0000	0.0000	0.0000	0.0000	0.0000	0.0659	0.0072	0.0547	0.0000	0.0000	0.0073	0.0077	0.0038	0.0038	0.1546
2	0.0078	0.0043	0.0000	0.0000	0.0000	0.0659	0.0000	0.0000	0.0531	0.0799	0.0639	0.0000	0.0000	0.0822	0.0863	0.0866	0.0772	0.6012
3	0.0143	0.0721	0.0043	0.0659	0.0000	0.0829	0.0635	0.0000	0.0693	0.0886	0.0880	0.0702	0.0789	0.1081	0.1114	0.1141	0.1022	1.1339
4	0.0774	0.0884	0.0659	0.0043	0.0000	0.0851	0.0789	0.0000	0.0905	0.1089	0.1115	0.0702	0.0800	0.1143	0.1174	0.1184	0.1053	1.3165
5	0.0852	0.0946	0.0748	0.0748	0.0000	0.0941	0.0873	0.0656	0.0805	0.1183	0.1055	0.0786	0.0731	0.1251	0.1276	0.1299	0.1161	1.5311
6	0.0696	0.0659	0.0000	0.0000	0.0000	0.0043	0.0000	0.0000	0.0572	0.0617	0.0196	0.0000	0.0000	0.0783	0.0824	0.0683	0.0623	0.5747
7	0.0087	0.0585	0.0000	0.0000	0.0000	0.0729	0.0043	0.0000	0.0597	0.0732	0.0872	0.0000	0.0659	0.0922	0.0796	0.0923	0.0746	0.7210
8	0.0597	0.0239	0.0702	0.0702	0.0000	0.0675	0.0654	0.0000	0.0230	0.0844	0.0866	0.0584	0.0665	0.1046	0.0916	0.0947	0.0845	1.0511
9	0.0659	0.0000	0.0000	0.0000	0.0000	0.0000	0.0000	0.0000	0.0043	0.0573	0.0767	0.0000	0.0000	0.0582	0.0611	0.0114	0.0114	0.3461
10	0.0000	0.0000	0.0000	0.0000	0.0000	0.0000	0.0000	0.0000	0.0000	0.0081	0.0707	0.0000	0.0000	0.0707	0.0589	0.0116	0.0116	0.2316
11	0.0000	0.0000	0.0000	0.0000	0.0000	0.0000	0.0000	0.0000	0.0000	0.0697	0.0092	0.0000	0.0000	0.0707	0.0742	0.0620	0.0620	0.3479
12	0.0016	0.0745	0.0000	0.0702	0.0000	0.0129	0.0702	0.0000	0.0113	0.0881	0.0889	0.0000	0.0702	0.0763	0.0775	0.0774	0.0726	0.6715
13	0.0077	0.0729	0.0000	0.0000	0.0000	0.0585	0.0659	0.0000	0.0596	0.0725	0.0723	0.0000	0.0043	0.0912	0.0785	0.0762	0.0746	0.6842
14	0.0000	0.0000	0.0000	0.0000	0.0000	0.0000	0.0000	0.0000	0.0000	0.0541	0.0697	0.0000	0.0000	0.0081	0.0733	0.0619	0.0619	0.3290
15	0.0000	0.0000	0.0000	0.0000	0.0000	0.0000	0.0000	0.0000	0.0000	0.0000	0.0000	0.0000	0.0000	0.0000	0.0000	0.0702	0.0702	0.1404
16	0.0000	0.0000	0.0000	0.0000	0.0000	0.0000	0.0000	0.0000	0.0000	0.0000	0.0000	0.0000	0.0000	0.0000	0.0000	0.0043	0.0659	0.0702
17	0.0000	0.0000	0.0000	0.0000	0.0000	0.0000	0.0000	0.0000	0.0000	0.0000	0.0000	0.0000	0.0000	0.0000	0.0000	0.0659	0.0043	0.0702
SUM	0.4022	0.5550	0.2151	0.2151	0.0000	0.5442	0.4355	0.0656	0.5743	0.9720	1.0045	0.2773	0.4388	1.0875	1.1275	1.1491	0.9114	

Table 2.11   The Direct and Indirect Influences

Sl. no.	Variable	Di	Ri	Horizontal axis Di+Ri	Vertical axis Di-Ri
1	Clinical information confidentiality and security	0.1546	0.4022	0.5567	−0.2476
2	Adequate IT infrastructure	0.6012	0.5550	1.1562	0.0463
3	Financial support	1.1339	0.2151	1.3491	0.9188
4	Continuous training of employees	1.3165	0.2151	1.5316	1.1014
5	Leadership	1.5311	0.0000	1.5311	1.5311
6	Qualified team of experts	0.5747	0.5442	1.1189	0.0305
7	Standardization of clinical data	0.7210	0.4355	1.1565	0.2855
8	Technological support from the government	1.0511	0.0656	1.1167	0.9855
9	Confidence of patients in IoT	0.3461	0.5743	0.9205	−0.2282
10	Innovative clinical services	0.2316	0.9720	1.2036	−0.7404
11	Patient feedback	0.3479	1.0045	1.3525	−0.6566
12	Sufficient maintenance and support systems	0.6715	0.2773	0.9489	0.3942
13	Compatibility in hardware and healthcare software	0.6842	0.4388	1.1231	0.2454
14	Well defined strategic goals	0.3290	1.0875	1.4165	−0.7585
15	Healthcare organization culture	0.1404	1.1275	1.2678	−0.9871
16	Employee engagement and involvement	0.0702	1.1491	1.2192	−1.0789
17	Clarity of medico legal and IP regulations	0.0702	0.9114	0.9816	−0.8413

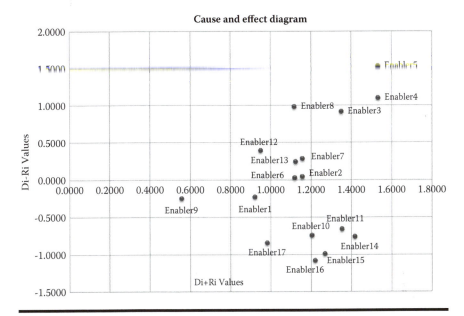

Figure 2.6   The Cause-and-Effect Diagram of H4.0 Enablers.

(Raghupathi and Raghupathi 2014). Therefore, sufficient steps toward the standardization of clinical data can prove beneficial for H4.0 implementation. An immense amount of sensitive information, open to all parties, is available online. This subject should also be treated with considerable caution.

2.8 Implications of Research

H4.0 is a remarkable phenomenon that will reshape the market by amalgamating the new technology with minimal capital consumption to reach optimum clinical performance. For health managers, the new research gives many ramifications. First, 17 significant enablers have been recognised in the Indian health sector relating to H4.0 technologies. Health managers can fully comprehend the leadership and reliability power of these enablers in advance, identify the enablers with strong driving force, and rely more on them to effectively adopt and implement H4.0 technology in their organisations. Second, the ISM approach will help to understand the relationships among these enablers. Third, the Health 4.0 model illustrates how various enablers impacting H4.0 adoption in the organizations affect each other. The Health 4.0 model will act as a boon for the healthcare industry since it will guide the healthcare managers who are trying to implement Industry 4.0 technologies in their organizations.

2.9 Limitations and Future Prospects of Research

Related forms of experiments in other countries can also be carried out in the future to examine the presence of other enablers. Some 17 enablers have been addressed in this report, but more enablers affecting H4.0 in the Indian healthcare industry can be found. The Fuzzy ISM model can also be created. The ISM model should be quantified and tested using statistical modelling and confirmatory factor analysis.

References

Aggarwal, Gaurav, Vineet Jain, Puneeta Ajmera, and Jose Arturo Garza-Reyes. 2022. Modeling and analysing the barriers to the acceptance of energy-efficient appliances using an ISM-DEMATEL approach. *Journal of Modelling in Management*, ahead-of-print. doi:10.1108/jm2-02-2022-0064

Ajmera, Puneeta, and Vineet Jain. 2019a. "A fuzzy interpretive structural modeling approach for evaluating the factors affecting lean implementation in Indian healthcare industry." *International Journal of Lean Six Sigma* vol. 11 (2):376–397. doi: 10.1108/IJLSS-02-2018-0016

Ajmera, Puneeta, and Vineet Jain. 2019b. "Modeling the factors affecting the quality of life in diabetic patients in India using total interpretive structural modeling." *Benchmarking: An International Journal* vol. 26 (3):951–970. doi: 10.1108/BIJ-07-2018-0180

Ajmera, Puneeta, and Vineet Jain. 2019c. "Modelling the barriers of Health 4.0–the fourth healthcare industrial revolution in India by TISM." *Operations Management Research* vol. 12 (3):129–145. doi: 10.1007/s12063-019-00143-x

Avinash, A, P Sasikumar, and A Murugesan. 2018. "Understanding the interaction among the barriers of biodiesel production from waste cooking oil in India-an interpretive structural modeling approach." *Renewable Energy* vol. 127:678–684.

Bagheri, Behrad, Shanhu Yang, Hung-An Kao, and Jay Lee. 2015. "Cyber-physical systems architecture for self-aware machines in industry 4.0 environment." *IFAC-PapersOnLine* vol. 48 (3):1622–1627.

Bahrin, Mohd Aiman Kamarul, Mohd Fauzi Othman, NH Nor Azli, and Muhamad Farihin Talib. 2016. "Industry 4.0: A review on industrial automation and robotic." *Jurnal Teknologi* vol. 78 (6–13):137–143.

Bai, Chunguang, and Joseph Sarkis. 2013. "A grey-based DEMATEL model for evaluating business process management critical success factors." *International Journal of Production Economics* vol. 146 (1):281–292.

Bates, David W, Suchi Saria, Lucila Ohno-Machado, Anand Shah, and Gabriel Escobar. 2014. "Big data in health care: Using analytics to identify and manage high-risk and high-cost patients." *Health Affairs* vol. 33 (7):1123–1131.

Bhadani, Abhay Kumar, Ravi Shankar, and D Vijay Rao. 2016. "Modeling the barriers of service adoption in rural Indian telecom using integrated ISM-ANP." *Journal of Modelling in Management* vol. 11 (1):2–25.

Bonczek, Robert H, Clyde W Holsapple, and Andrew B Whinston. 2014. *Foundations of decision support systems*. New York: Academic Press.

Bröring, Arne, Stefan Schmid, Corina-Kim Schindhelm, Abdelmajid Khelil, Sebastian Kabisch, Denis Kramer, Danh Le Phuoc, Jelena Mitic, Darko Anicic, and Ernest Teniente López. 2017. "Enabling IoT ecosystems through platform interoperability." *IEEE Software* vol. 34 (1):54–61.

Chauhan, Ankur, Amol Singh, and Sanjay Jharkharia. 2018. "An interpretive structural modeling (ISM) and decision-making trail and evaluation laboratory (DEMATEL) method approach for the analysis of barriers of waste recycling in India." *Journal of the Air & Waste Management Association* vol. 68 (2):100–110.

Chawla, Nitesh V, and Darcy A Davis. 2013. "Bringing big data to personalized healthcare: A patient-centered framework." *Journal of General Internal Medicine* vol. 28 (3):660–665.

Chen, Injazz J. 2001. "Planning for ERP systems: Analysis and future trend." *Business Process Management Journal* vol. 7 (5):374–386.

Christians, Andreas, and Michael Liepin. 2017. "The consequences of digitalization for German Civil Law from the National Legislator's point of view." *Zeitschrift fuer Geistiges Eigentum/Intellectual Property Journal* vol. 9 (3):331–339.

Davis, Fred D, Richard P Bagozzi, and Paul R Warshaw. 1989. "User acceptance of computer technology: A comparison of two theoretical models." *Management Science* vol. 35 (8):982–1003.

Gilchrist, Alasdair. 2016. *Industry 4.0: The industrial internet of things*. New York: Springer.

Harrison, Robert, Daniel Vera, and Bilal Ahmad. 2016. "Engineering methods and tools for cyber–physical automation systems." *Proceedings of the IEEE* vol. 104 (5):973–985.

Hecklau, Fabian, Mila Galeitzke, Sebastian Flachs, and Holger Kohl. 2016. "Holistic approach for human resource management in Industry 4.0." *Procedia CIRP* vol. 54:1–6.

Hung, M. 2016. Special report–IoT's challenges and opportunities in 2017.

Jain, Swati, Puneeta Ajmera, and Vineet Jain 2022. Modelling and analysis of the classroom communication barriers using ISM: an Indian teacher's perspective. *International Journal of Knowledge and Learning* vol. 15 (3):253–273.

Jain, Vineet, and Puneeta Ajmera. 2018. "Modelling the factors affecting Indian Medical Tourism Sector using Interpretive Structural Modeling." *Benchmarking: An International Journal* vol. 25 (5):1461–1479.

Jain, Vineet, and Puneeta Ajmera. 2020a. "DEMATEL method for evaluating FMS variables in the Indian manufacturing industry." *International Journal of Process Management and Benchmarking* vol. 11 (6):822–838. doi: 10.1504/IJPMB.2020.10039303

Jain, Vineet, and Puneeta Ajmera. 2020b. "Fuzzy TISM and DEMATEL approach to analyze Lean variables in Indian Healthcare Industry." *International Journal of Process Management and Benchmarking* vol. 12 (2):233–275. doi: 10.1504/IJPMB.2020.10039306

Jain, Vineet, Sandeep Phoghat, Puneeta Ajmera, and Anil Sirvi. 2022. Modeling the barriers of Indian healthcare supply chain management using ISM. *International Journal of Supply and Operations Management* vol. 9 (3):321–337.

Jain, Vineet, and Hanif Qureshi. 2022. "Modelling the factors affecting Quality of Life among Indian police officers: a novel ISM and DEMATEL approach." *Safety and Health at Work*, in press. doi: 10.1016/j.shaw.2022.07.004

Jain, Vineet, and Tilak Raj. 2014. "Modelling and analysis of FMS productivity variables by ISM, SEM and GTMA approach." *Frontiers of Mechanical Engineering* vol. 9 (3):218–232. doi: 10.1007/s11465-014-0309-7

Jain, Vineet, and Tilak Raj. 2015a. "A hybrid approach using ISM and modified TOPSIS for the evaluation of flexibility in FMS." *International Journal of Industrial and Systems Engineering* vol. 19 (3):389–406.

Jain, Vineet, and Tilak Raj. 2015b. "Modeling and analysis of FMS flexibility factors by TISM and fuzzy MICMAC." *International Journal of System Assurance Engineering and Management* vol. 6 (3):350–371. doi: 10.1007/s13198-015-0368-0

Jain, Vineet, and Tilak Raj. 2016. "Modeling and analysis of FMS performance variables by ISM, SEM and GTMA approach." *International Journal of Production Economics* vol. 171 (1):84–96. doi: 10.1016/j.ijpe.2015.10.024

Jain, Vineet, and Tilak Raj. 2021. "Study of issues related to constraints in FMS by ISM, fuzzy ISM and TISM." *International Journal of Industrial and Systems Engineering* vol. 37 (2):197–221.

Jain, Vineet, and Vimlesh Kumar Soni. 2019. "Modeling and analysis of FMS performance variables by fuzzy TISM." *Journal of Modelling in Management* vol. 14 (1):2–30. doi: 10.1108/JM2-03-2018-0036

Jee, Kyoungyoung, and Gang-Hoon Kim. 2013. "Potentiality of big data in the medical sector: focus on how to reshape the healthcare system." *Healthcare Informatics Research* vol. 19 (2):79–85.

Jha, Manoj Kumar, Rakesh D Raut, Bhaskar B Gardas, and Vaijayanti Raut. 2018. "A sustainable warehouse selection: An interpretive structural modelling approach." *International Journal of Procurement Management* vol. 11 (2):201–232.

Jharkharia, Sanjay, and Ravi Shankar. 2005. "IT-enablement of supply chains: Understanding the barriers." *Journal of Enterprise Information Management* vol. 18 (1):11–27.

Kagermann, Henning. 2015. "Change through digitization—Value creation in the age of Industry 4.0." In: Albach, H., Meffert, H., Pinkwart, A., and Reichwald, R. (eds) *Management of permanent change*, 23–45. Wiesbaden: Springer. doi: 10.1007/978-3-658-05014-6_2

Kamble, Sachin S, Angappa Gunasekaran, and Rohit Sharma. 2018. "Analysis of the driving and dependence power of barriers to adopt industry 4.0 in Indian manufacturing industry." *Computers in Industry* vol. 101:107–119.

Kamigaki, Tamotsu. 2017. "Object-oriented RFID with IoT: A design concept of information systems in manufacturing." *Electronics* vol. 6 (1):14.

Kaur, Jasneet, Ramneet Sidhu, Anjali Awasthi, Satyaveer Chauhan, and Suresh Goyal. 2018. "A DEMATEL based approach for investigating barriers in green supply chain management in Canadian manufacturing firms." *International Journal of Production Research* vol. 56 (1–2):312–332.

Koch, Volkmar, Simon Kuge, Reinhard Geissbauer, and Stefan Schrauf. 2014. "Industry 4.0: Opportunities and challenges of the industrial internet." *Strategy & PwC*. Available at: http://www.strategyand.pwc.com/reports/industry-4-0 (2017, March 10).

Kumar, Dinesh, and Dinesh Kumar. 2015. "Modelling hospital inventory management using interpretive structural modelling approach." *International Journal of Logistics Systems and Management* vol. 21 (3):319–334.

Kumar, Pardeep, and Hoon-Jae Lee. 2011. "Security issues in healthcare applications using wireless medical sensor networks: A survey." *Sensors* vol. 12 (1):55–91.

Kumar, Pravin, Rajesh K Singh, and Rakesh Kumar. 2017. "An integrated framework of interpretive structural modeling and graph theory matrix approach to fix the agility index of an automobile manufacturing organization." *International Journal of System Alvenneer Engineering and Management* vol. 0 (1):342-352.

Lasi, Heiner, Peter Fettke, Hans-Georg Kemper, Thomas Feld, and Michael Hoffmann. 2014. "Industry 4.0." *Business & Information Systems Engineering* vol. 6 (4):239–242.

Lee, Jay, Hung-An Kao, and Shanhu Yang. 2014. "Service innovation and smart analytics for industry 4.0 and big data environment." *Procedia Cirp* vol. 16:3–8.

Liu, Tianyu, Yong Deng, and Felix Chan. 2018. "Evidential supplier selection based on DEMATEL and game theory." *International Journal of Fuzzy Systems* vol. 20 (4):1321–1333.

Lorincz, Konrad, David J Malan, Thaddeus RF Fulford-Jones, Alan Nawoj, Antony Clavel, Victor Shnayder, Geoffrey Mainland, Matt Welsh, and Steve Moulton. 2004. "Sensor networks for emergency response: Challenges and opportunities." *IEEE pervasive Computing* vol. 3 (4):16–23.

Luthra, Sunil, Kannan Govindan, Ravinder K Kharb, and Sachin Kumar Mangla. 2016. "Evaluating the enablers in solar power developments in the current scenario using fuzzy DEMATEL: An Indian perspective." *Renewable and Sustainable Energy Reviews* vol. 63:379–397.

Mahajan, Ritika, Rajat Agrawal, Vinay Sharma, and Vinay Nangia. 2014. "Factors affecting quality of management education in India: An interpretive structural modelling approach." *International Journal of Educational Management* vol. 28 (4):379–399.

Maheshwari, Prateek, Nitin Seth, and Anoop Kumar Gupta. 2018. "An interpretive structural modeling approach to advertisement effectiveness in the Indian mobile phone industry." *Journal of Modelling in Management* vol. 13 (1):190–210.

Majumdar, Rana, PK Kapur, and Sunil Kumar Khatri. 2019. "Assessing software upgradation attributes and optimal release planning using DEMATEL and MAUT." *International Journal of Industrial and Systems Engineering* vol. 31 (1):70–94.

Mandal, Anukul, and SG Deshmukh. 1994. "Vendor selection using interpretive structural modelling (ISM)." *International Journal of Operations & Production Management* vol. 14 (6):52–59.

Mavi, Reza Kiani, and Craig Standing. 2018. "Critical success factors of sustainable project management in construction: A fuzzy DEMATEL-ANP approach." *Journal of Cleaner Production* vol. 194:751–765.

Mittal, Palka, Ajmera Puneeta, Jain Vineet, and Aggarwal Gaurav. 2021. Modeling and analysis of barriers in controlling TB: developing countries' perspective. *International Journal of Health Governance* vol. 26 (4): 362–383. doi: 10.1108/ijhg-06-2021-0060.

Mueller, Egon, Xiao-Li Chen, and Ralph Riedel. 2017. "Challenges and requirements for the application of industry 4.0: A special insight with the usage of cyber-physical system." *Chinese Journal of Mechanical Engineering* vol. 30 (5):1050.

Patil, Sachin K, and Ravi Kant. 2014. "Predicting the success of knowledge management adoption in supply chain using fuzzy DEMATEL and FMCDM approach." *International Journal of Business Performance and Supply Chain Modelling* vol. 6 (1):75–93.

Potdar, Pavan Kumar, Srikanta Routroy, and Astajyoti Behera. 2017. "Analyzing the agile manufacturing barriers using fuzzy DEMATEL." *Benchmarking: An International Journal* vol. 24 (7):1912–1936.

Prasanna Venkatesan, Shanmugam, and Joshi Sanket. 2018. "An integrated interpretive structural modeling and a graph-theoretic approach for measuring the supply chain complexity in the Indian automotive industry." *Journal of Manufacturing Technology Management* vol. 29 (3):478–514.

Purohit, Jayant K, ML Mittal, Sameer Mittal, and Milind Kumar Sharma. 2016. "Interpretive structural modeling-based framework for mass customisation enablers: An Indian footwear case." *Production Planning & Control* vol. 27 (9):774–786.

Qin, Jian, Ying Liu, and Roger Grosvenor. 2016. "A categorical framework of manufacturing for industry 4.0 and beyond." *Procedia Cirp* vol. 52:173–178.

Raghupathi, Wullianallur, and Viju Raghupathi. 2014. "Big data analytics in healthcare: Promise and potential." *Health information science and systems* vol. 2 (1):3.

Raj, T., R. Attri, and V. Jain. 2012. "Modelling the factors affecting flexibility in FMS." *International Journal of Industrial and Systems Engineering* vol. 11 (4):350–374.

Rane, Santosh B, and Milind Shrikant Kirkire. 2017. "Interpretive structural modelling of risk sources in medical device development process." *International Journal of System Assurance Engineering and Management* vol. 8 (1):451–464.

Rüßmann, Michael, Markus Lorenz, Philipp Gerbert, Manuela Waldner, Jan Justus, Pascal Engel, and Michael Harnisch. 2015. "Industry 4.0: The future of productivity and growth in manufacturing industries." *Boston Consulting Group* vol. 9.

Sarmah, Bijoylaxmi, and Zillur Rahman. 2018. "Customer co-creation in hotel service innovation: An interpretive structural modeling and MICMAC analysis approach." *Benchmarking: An International Journal* vol. 25 (1):297–318.

Schoenherr, Tobias, Sriram Narayanan, and Ram Narasimhan. 2015. "Trust formation in outsourcing relationships: A social exchange theoretic perspective." *International Journal of Production Economics* vol. 169:401–412.

Thakur, Vikas, and Ramesh Anbanandam. 2016. "Healthcare waste management: An interpretive structural modeling approach." *International Journal of Health Care Quality Assurance* vol. 29 (5):559–581.

Thuemmler, Christoph, and Chunxue Bai. 2017. *Health 4.0: How virtualization and big data are revolutionizing healthcare*. New York: Springer.

Tzeng, Gwo-Hshiung, Cheng-Hsin Chiang, and Chung-Wei Li. 2007. "Evaluating intertwined effects in e-learning programs: A novel hybrid MCDM model based on factor analysis and DEMATEL." *Expert systems with Applications* vol. 32 (4):1028–1044.

Veltmeyer, Johan, and Sherif Mohamed. 2017. "Investigation into the hierarchical nature of TQM variables using structural modelling." *International Journal of Quality & Reliability Management* vol. 34 (4):462–477.

Vinodh, S, TS Sai Balagi, and Adithya Patil. 2016. "A hybrid MCDM approach for agile concept selection using fuzzy DEMATEL, fuzzy ANP and fuzzy TOPSIS." *The International Journal of Advanced Manufacturing Technology* vol. 83 (9–12):1979–1987.

Warfield, John N. 1974. "Developing subsystem matrices in structural modeling." *IEEE Transactions on Systems, Man, and Cybernetics* vol. 4 (1):81–87.

Wei, Wei-Qi, and Joshua C Denny. 2015. "Extracting research-quality phenotypes from electronic health records to support precision medicine." *Genome Medicine* vol. 7 (1):41.

Willcocks, Leslie P, and Richard Sykes. 2000. "Enterprise resource planning: The role of the CIO and it function in ERP." *Communications of the ACM* vol. 43 (4):32–38.

Xia, Xiqiang, Kannan Govindan, and Qinghua Zhu. 2015. "Analyzing internal barriers for automotive parts remanufacturers in China using grey-DEMATEL approach." *Journal of Cleaner Production* vol. 87:811–825.

Xiao, Lin. 2018. "Analyzing consumer online group buying motivations: An interpretive structural modeling approach." *Telematics and Informatics* vol. 35 (4):629–642.

Zhou, Keliang, Taigang Liu, and Lifeng Zhou. 2015. Industry 4.0: Towards future industrial opportunities and challenges. Paper read at Fuzzy Systems and Knowledge Discovery (FSKD), 2015 12th International Conference on, at Zhangjiajie, China.

Chapter 3

Machine Learning Algorithms for Health Data Security: A Systematic Review

Naif Al Mudawi, Abdulwahab Alazeb,
Mohammed S. Alshehri, and Sultan Almakdi
Najran University

Contents

3.1 Introduction 54
3.2 Value of Fuels and Lignocellulose as Raw Material 55
3.3 Research Question 56
    3.3.1 Search and Selection Strategy 56
    3.3.2 Selection Criteria 57
    3.3.3 Thermochemical Routes for Biomass Conversion to Fuels 58
    3.3.4 Observation 58
3.4 Findings 60
    3.4.1 Systematic Search Results 60
3.5 Motivation and Algorithms 60
    3.5.1 Health Data Security Using ML and DL Strategy 60
    3.5.2 Health Data Security Using Traditional Approach 65
    3.5.3 Mathematical Interpretation of the ML Models 70
    3.5.4 Support Vector Machine (SVM) 70

DOI: 10.1201/9781003145189-3

3.5.5 Radial Basis Function (RBF) Kernel SVM.................................. 71
3.5.6 Decision Tree (DT) 72
3.5.7 Naïve Bayes Algorithm.. 72
3.5.8 Complexity Analysis of the ML Models.................................... 73
3.6 Conclusion and Future Work.. 74
References 75
Appendix 3.A.. 77

3.1 Introduction

The healthcare sector is being modernized from an integrated paper system to an electronic health record system by revolutionizing modern computational technology. With the advancement of information and communication technology, healthcare data has become increasingly digital and distributed [1]. Big data has profoundly transformed the procedure businesses handle, analyze, and use data in any organization—the encouraging areas where big data may make a difference in healthcare. Big healthcare data holds a lot of promise in improving patient outcomes, forecasting epidemic outbreaks, generating valuable insights, avoiding preventable diseases, cutting healthcare expenditures, and enhancing the overall quality of life. Turning into data security, privacy is a matter of great concern. More crucially, privacy refers to the confidentiality of individually identifiable healthcare information [2]. In contrast, patients are more likely to disclose their confidential information to healthcare practitioners, so maintaining a solid relationship between healthcare professionals and keeping trust in healthcare industries is significant.

Having the numerous benefits of electronic health records (EHR), individuals' digital health data is currently in grave danger. Because attackers routinely target e-health data, the data is incredibly vulnerable. Internal and external attacks such as hacking, unauthenticated internal sharing, and inappropriate disposal of unwanted yet sensitive material were revealed in a long-term review of data breaches. Email and network servers, on the other hand, are the most prevalent sites where private health data is accessible. Simply put, many intruders are targeting the healthcare industry. In addition, cyberattacks are universal, but in 2021, they have been relatively high, especially in the healthcare sector. According to the United States Federal Bureau of Investigation (FBI), records of more than 40 million patients have been compromised, and in sum, a record 40,099,751 people have been invaded by vulnerability reported to the federal authorities so far this year [3]. Traditional security methods make it difficult to detect previously unknown security threats. This, in turn, brings us to a big question: Are we ready to prevent unauthorized access to the EHR data in the healthcare industry? Moreover, we need a system that can automatically enable health data security and tighten security protocols in the healthcare sector.

Machine-learning (ML) techniques are essential in many cyber security applications [4]. Machine-learning and deep-learning models are currently being used to detect and respond to attacks in almost all aspects of cyber security. On the defensive side, machine-learning models help develop more robust and automated ways to boost performance and early detection of attacks, lowering the impact and damage. This study is a systematic review to illustrate the analysis and interpretation of the latest approach based on machine learning to solve the issues related to healthcare data security. This report also discusses the advantages and disadvantages of all modern techniques to healthcare data security. In addition, a better security model has been presented based on background research of all conceivable solutions to the problem. It will help readers comprehend machine-learning models and their application in the healthcare field. Each section and subsection will highlight distinct parts of the research. We included research questions, a search and selection approach for papers relating to our problem, and inclusion and exclusion criteria in the research methods section, which helped us conduct the review effectively. The section on results and discussions displays the systematic search results and observations that led to identifying prevalent strategies for preventing cyberattacks and their limits and comparison. We also conducted an algorithm complexity analysis. Finally, we finished the review paper. This review will act as a baseline and play an important part in future researchers' efforts to secure healthcare data and improve their performance.

3.2 Value of Fuels and Lignocellulose as Raw Material

A practical approach is being used to comprehend the research problem of this study, which assists the author in recognizing numerous thoughts and clarifications while also comprehending the research problem and quality. As a result, the strategy was created using the findings of the initial literary analysis and important and supplemental research questions. As illustrated in Figure 3.1, the initial stage one, 'primary research,' consists of three sections: planning, configuration, and reporting.

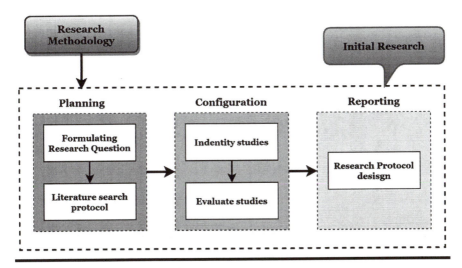

Figure 3.1 Preliminary Search Strategy.

3.3 Research Question

To assure security for healthcare data, an increasing number of unique solutions are based on numerous machine-learning (ML) and deep-learning (DL) frameworks. However, our analysis focuses on whether the DL models developed from this vast number of research investigations are feasible for increasing healthcare data security. To better grasp the fundamental issue, we've devised a study question: **"How effective are many researchers' current suggested artificial intelligence and machine-learning methods for ensuring the security of healthcare data?"**

3.3.1 Search and Selection Strategy

As illustrated in Figures 3.2 and 3.3, we explored several electronic databases from December 2017 to 2020. We identified relevant published papers using Google Scholar, PubMed, and IEEE since they are well-established and provide a wide selection of peer-reviewed, up-to-date publications, information, and reports. Scholarly publications from numerous areas, such as pure science, technology or engineering, medicine, and so on, are available on Google Scholar. PubMed, a part of the National Library of Medicine in the United States, provides multi-disciplinary research in machine learning, artificial intelligence, biotechnology, biochemistry, and many more. IEEE is an extensive digital archive of scientific and technological information. Following "A structured method to documenting a search strategy for publishing," a systematic literature search strategy was devised in [5]. We employed four search terms (deep learning, machine learning, data protection, and healthcare data security) and Boolean operators like "and"

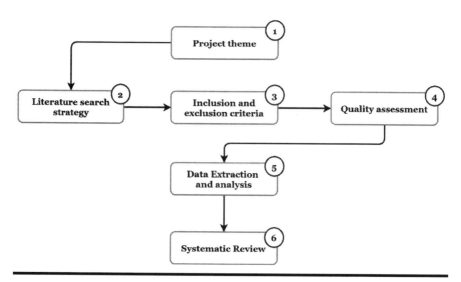

Figure 3.2 Overall Research Methodology.

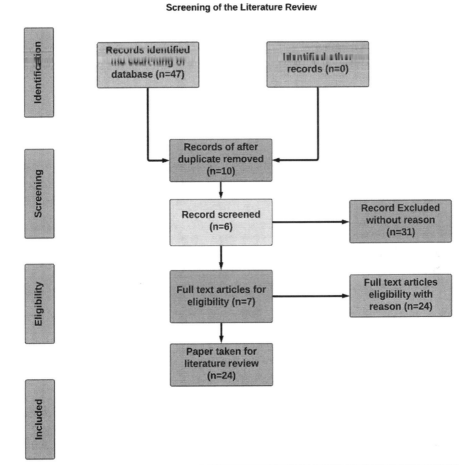

Screening of the Literature Review

Figure 3.3 Paper Selection and Screening Procedures.

between the search keywords during the search process. The keywords are chosen in response to the research topic. After the initial selection, each manuscript is verified against the quality assessment tool to qualify for the review.

3.3.2 Selection Criteria

We have set our selection criteria for accepting a research article based on the following key criteria and retrieved only articles meeting these conditions.

a. **Inclusion Criteria**
   - Select any type of journal article or conference paper that discusses DL and ML-based methods for protecting the data in the healthcare sector.
   - Reviewed and published 2017–2020.

b. **Exclusion Criteria**
  - Early works or preprint.
  - Any published journal article or conference papers that do not discuss any new methods based on AI/ML/DL healthcare data security.
  - Editorials, review papers, and research letter.

3.3.3 Thermochemical Routes for Biomass Conversion to Fuels

We have also divided this section into several subsections based on the literature. We have presented the observation in Section 3.3.1 and findings in Section 3.3.2. Figure 3.4 shows the overall structural overview of cyberattack identification in the healthcare sector.

3.3.4 Observation

Many diverse approaches were discovered while analyzing further research studies on machine-learning approaches for healthcare data security. The most widely used traditional machine-learning algorithms are decision tree, random forest, KNN, support vector machine (SVM), and Naive Bayes. Through the combination of network and biometric aspects with an ML method, a real-time EHMS (enhanced healthcare monitoring system) with the implementation of fuzzy-based analytical network process (ANP) and multi-criteria decision making was presented (MCDM). These are used to assess the precision of machine-learning algorithms in proposing an effective data security strategy for digital healthcare. There have also

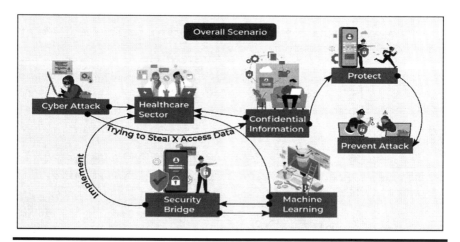

Figure 3.4 Overall Cyberattack Identification with Machine-Learning Algorithms.

been several deep-learning algorithms developed to safeguard healthcare data. Deep-learning approaches have unique ways, such as using five neurons in the hidden layer to maintain anonymity and the learning-based deep-Q-network (LDQN) methodology. The LDQN approach is thought to have the lowest error rate, which leads to an increase in malware detection rate. Some options, such as integrating cloud storage with the machine-learning model, appeared to be effective as well. Furthermore, a clustering approach known as the Gaussian mixture model algorithm has been applied in data privacy. Figure 3.5 presents machine learning mechanism to identify different types of attacks in the healthcare sector.

The outcomes of the methodologies have not been compared to secure healthcare data in any of these research investigations, which is the fundamental focus of this systematic review. In this research, deep learning, machine learning, and learning combined with cloud storage are all used. Even so, because no state-of-the-art technology has been applied, concluding the most efficient technique for healthcare data protection utilizing the machine is difficult. All of the ideas are implemented, but they are not compared to other current approaches to determine the best or most effective answer to the healthcare data-security challenge. At the same time, it's unclear whether the machine-learning and deep-learning models'

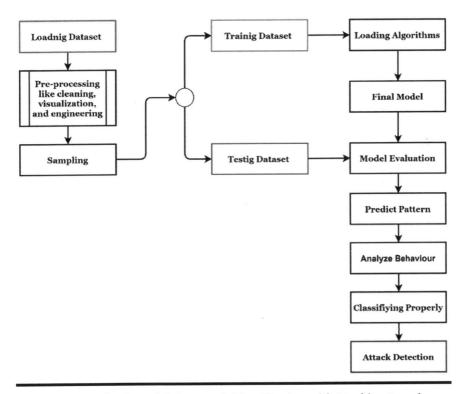

Figure 3.5   Mechanism of Cyberattack Identification with Machine Learning.

expected outputs and outcomes are applicable in real life. The research authors merely trained and evaluated their models in a lab setting, with no real-world deployment. As a result, it's unclear how these models will fare with the real-world data. As a result, more study into the real-world use of machine-learning and deep-learning models to protect healthcare data is needed, and more research into the privacy of healthcare data utilizing machine learning is needed, too.

3.4 Findings

This section is divided into several subsections and, each of them will address the following parameters of the study. In Section 3.4.1, we have presented systematic search results. In Section 3.5, we have presented motivation & algorithms. In Section 3.5.3, we have presented the mathematical interpretation of the ML models, and finally, in Section 3.5.8, we have introduced the computational complexity of the ML models.

3.4.1 Systematic Search Results

In the initial primary research, 47 titles were retrieved and collected for the title review, comprising 10 titles from Google Scholar, 11 titles from PubMed, 13 from Science Direct, and 13 titles from the IEEE. At the subsequent phase, the rest of the titles were inspected for replication and availability, and a total of 10 titles were deleted for duplication and one article for availability. The papers were then checked according to exclusion criteria. During the abstract review, several articles were found not to propose new DL models so, after excluding these 31 articles, a total of 24 papers were included for full-text review. After that, the study has applied the quality assessment (Appendix A) tool to qualify the papers according to the threshold values. This study defines the threshold value around 70. After successfully applying the quality assessment tools, the reseach found 18 qualified papers. So, finally, we have included 18 documents for the full review. Figure 3.6 shows the year by the publication of the selected manuscripts. This figure clearly indicates that the study adopted the highest number of manuscripts only in 2018.

3.5 Motivation and Algorithms

3.5.1 Health Data Security Using ML and DL Strategy

Newaz et al. (2019) [6] proposed HealthGuard, which uses Artificial Neural Network, Decision Tree, Random Forest, k-Nearest Neighbor, to analyze the performance against three malicious threats for eight types of intelligent medical

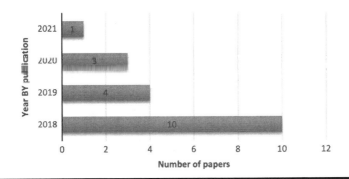

Figure 3.6 Number of Papers Adopted for Review According to the Publication Year.

devices in 12 benign events turning to the four ML-based detection techniques. This modern ML-based security framework provides a precision of 91% when distinguishing the vital signs of devices connected and patients' body functions in the innovative healthcare system (SHS).

When using different ML approaches for proposing a real-time EHMS (enhanced healthcare monitoring system) testbed, which identifies the patient's biometrics and gathers network flow metrics, Hady et al. (2020) [7] incorporate network and biometric features that improve functioning by 7% to 25% for intrusion detection. The information gathered is sent to a remote server for further treatment and diagnostic considerations. The proposed system's validity demonstrates that it is simple to detect intrusions (Figures 3.7 and 3.8).

Begli et al. (2019) [8] were motivated to build an enormous pipeline that assures the remote healthcare system's security. The concept contains a structure in terms of distant healthcare scheme that secures data and protects it from typical network threats such as denial of service (DoS) and user-to-root (U2R) assaults. The suggested intrusion-detection system (IDS) employs the support vector machine (SVM). The efficiency of the proposed method is then demonstrated using the IDS layered architecture's assessment parameters. The proposed approach has the strength of making a multi-agent-based healthcare network with individual conditions, as well as providing healthcare services and allocating intrusion-detection systems to a single category of representatives to store caliver and computational expenditure of a particular network. The authors intend to test the system using actual medical data and evaluate the results using additional machine-learning approaches.

Boddy et al. (2017) [9] addressed the lack of security architecture monitoring potential active threats inside the network once a hostile person has gained access through a backdoor. The authors presented a method that uses advanced data analytics and visualization approaches to detect unexpected data activity. The technology uses machine learning to learn data trends and profile user behavior. The system is a cyber-security machine-learning system that learns from security

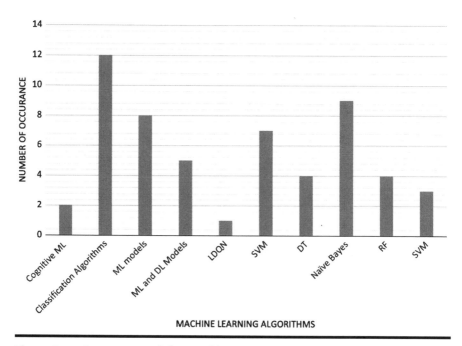

Figure 3.7 Occurrence of the Machine-Learning Algorithms on Cyber Security in Healthcare Sector.

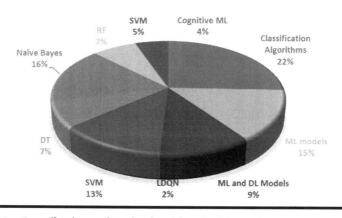

Figure 3.8 Contributions of Each Algorithm in this Study.

analysts and increases accuracy. The proposed solution faces a barrier in processing datasets provided by healthcare infrastructure using big data analytics. The system's strength is that it contributes to the healthcare infrastructure's defense-in-depth strategy by autonomously assessing the network's unique design. The dataset presented in this paper comprises a snapshot of data on three crucial hospital servers, which is a drawback of the proposed work. The authors hope to include datasets collected over a more extended period in the future.

Kaur et al. (2018) [10] provide a revolutionary approach for handling big data in the medical business that uses machine learning and advanced security methods to introduce big data and its applicability in healthcare. Their approach consists of four interconnected modules. For the case of unbalanced data, the first module always incorporates to measure their patterns. In terms of the heterogeneous data, the second layer is their further consideration. To protect patients' confidential information, activity-monitoring components also integrated in the security and privacy layer. Automtic diagnosis, medication, epidemic breakout predictions, data analytics, and visualization are all submodules of the machine-learning-based application in this proposal. Machine-learning approaches such as Naive Bayes, support vector machines, decision trees, evolutionary algorithms, and others are proposed for the submodules in this study. Finally, it is advocated that machine-learning techniques include soft computing techniques to achieve superior outcomes in terms of performance and accuracy. To enhance the idea generating phase and receive understanding from data, the predictive layers are constructed using sophisticated data methodologies. Healthcare information services and applications are encapsulated under this layer. Following that, machine learning, SQL queries, and medical imaging analytics are offered for presenting the generated data.

Uddin et al. (2020) [11] presented a strategy for storing health data that considers the preferences of patients. Even with streamed data, this will aid in making quick storage decisions in real time. The model is used to map health data into repositories. Applying a machine-learning consolidated technique followed by medical information, the mapping between each repository's health data features and attributes is learned. In the repositories, there is a model created for health data. A machine-learning-based classifier mediated by clinical rules is used to understand how to design between each repository's health data features and characteristics. Second, these features are used to create a dataset, with each instance representing the needs for saving a specific portion of data. Following that, the features are established by combining expert ratings. To establish the target of every parameter in the collection, statistical correlation and clinical heuristic principles are applied. In a real-world scenario, experts may give storage repositories to an example that isn't described by any rules. As a result, data requirements for storage repositories can be generalized using a machine-learning classifier executed on the testing dataset.

Mohanta et al. (2019) [12] offered an artificial intelligence-combining approach such as smart wearable devices with powerfull lightweight sensors that assist monitor, gather, and diagnose disease based on symptoms extracted from sensory data; and robot nurses to monitor patients' health status. The innovative healthcare concept entails remotely regulating, accessing, and manipulating various components of the hospital application. The primary controller is in charge of all modules. Because medical data is enormous, it is kept on a cloud platform for efficient management and storage. The acquired data is subsequently sent to the appropriate departments via the cloud for future investigation and generating observation. Each department has sensors and actuators in place for data collection and transmission. With the use of AI models, pathologists and doctors assess and identify abnormalities in various forms, such as scan documents, X-ray reports, and smears.

To safeguard the medical image, Marwan et al. (2018) [13] employed image segmentation. Several image-segmentation techniques are being addressed during the project, including support vector machine (SVM) and fuzzy C-means (FCM), which have not been implemented to improve cloud service data security. To complete the task, the pixel level color of the input image was extracted first, and these pixels were then used as input to the SVM algorithm for classification. To improve the efficacy of the linear classification, the fuzzy C-means (FCM) algorithm was used to train the SVM algorithm. The suggested research focused on extracting the pixel-level color of the input photos, and it is claimed that this can improve data security. This research has yielded significant benefits, which might be emphasized as a strength. One of the most evident advantages is machine learning in cloud-computing services. Despite the beneficial impact, several shortcomings can be rectified, such as the authors' use of the pixel texture as an additional parameter, which would have increased security. Furthermore, a large dataset is required for healthcare research to train machine learning algorithms, which was not observed in this study.

Sreeji et al. (2020) [14] presented a client-server architecture. The system is comprised of two phases: training and prediction. The training phase retrieves the classifiers from the server, fits them with weights from the client, and returns the importance to the server. The trained data is then transmitted to the server. As a result, the system generates a reliable prediction model. Using the created prediction model, hospitals can foresee the likelihood of cardiac disease. The various hospitals upload the text files containing the patient's information. Most present systems rely on anonymization techniques to secure patient information. A central server in the system trains the hospitals' data servers. Hospitals want to forecast heart illness using a trained algorithm, but they'll need data from other hospitals to do so. As a result, the dataset from each institution is obtained in this manner, preserving the anonymity of the data. The prediction method in this study had a superior accuracy of 98% for five neurons in the buried layer. This demonstrates that the prediction system is more accurate. They present a new distributed deep-learning architecture for hospitals' secure and private prediction models. Anonymization techniques are already used to protect the confidentiality and security of healthcare data. The suggested approach makes no use of anonymization methods.

Shakeel et al. (2018) [15] investigate the safe health data transaction and access procedure related to the Internet of Things (IoT) utilizing the learning-based deep-Q-network (LDQN) technique. At the beginning, the IoT device was reviewed applying a robust neural network, which examines every aspect to verify the device and eliminate unwanted access and assaults. Each request traffic feature is retrieved from the database request to assess malware activity and additional safety matters following the authentication procedure. The extracted features are analyzed using the feature-state technique and related operations, which aids in determining the secured data. In addition, to measure the efficacy of the IoT system, a deep convolution neural network is used to examine the features. The LDQN approach achieves a poor rate (0.12), which improves malware identification rates (98.79%). Uddin et al. (2020) [16] were also motivated to combine an artificial health data storage suggestion model. In this study, a training dataset with the label for each instance of the dataset is required—a deep learning strategy for testing the correctness of our synthetic datasets. The simulated dataset is loaded into a deep learning network, achieving approximately 89% accuracy.

MacDermott et al. (2019) [17] used machine-learning technology to determine the possible way to predict and recognize flaws and assaults. Feature identification can increase classifier learning adaptibility, reduce computing complexity, and help design better machine-learning models. Experiments were carried out utilizing Weka and a network-assault dataset. Their subsequent concentration was on top of a gain ratio attribute evaluation, where they realized that matter of enhancing the average merit to have more forecasting features. The examination of information gain attributes is comparable to the variant. This experiment measures the knowledge received about the class to determine the worth of an attribute.

Chowdhury et al. (2018) [18] used four fundamental classifiers in the WEKA to test the system's accuracy, including support vector machine (SVM), Naive Bayes, decision tree, and random forest. Step-by-step procedures were followed during the experimentation. To eliminate the Windows API call functionality, they adopted a virtual environment. They next use a DCFS measure to filter the collected features and select the most relevant API requests. The virus and non-malware samples were then converted to WEKA format. Finally, we used the WEKA platform to train the classifiers and then used the test dataset to evaluate their performance. Each classifier is validated using k-fold cross-validation in this study. They look into the differences in parameters and how they affect the algorithm's performance.

3.5.2 Health Data Security Using Traditional Approach

Seh et al. (2021) [19] researched recognizing healthcare data breaches that lead to privilege misuse demonstrates the importance of dynamic security measures for monitoring anomalous patient behaviour. To detect varying user access in EHS (electronic healthcare records), an ML-based security framework is developed, using a fuzzy-based analytical network process (ANP) and multi-criteria decision-making (MCDM) to evaluate the precision of ML approaches in proposing proactive data security for digital healthcare.

Cheng et al. (2020) [20] have addressed the fact that, while encryption is an amazing technique to preserve privacy, it is ineffective when discussing and evaluating medical cases. To effectively handle privacy difficulties, this article suggested a federated learning-verification model, which is a combination of blockchain technology. Furthermore, an FL-EM-GMM algorithm has been provided to train the model without data exchange to preserve patients' privacy. Finally, an experiment on the federated job of datasets from two organizations demonstrates that the system can overcome privacy difficulties. The results show that the system has improved usability, data security, and efficacy compared to the model developed using the traditional machine-learning algorithm.

Godi et al. (2020) [21] created a foundation for an e-health care monitoring system (EHMS). It is an application model that incorporates several machine-learning techniques. The EHMS uses a few Internet of Things (IoT) health wearable devices that collect real-time data from the human body. The primary function of EHMS is to collect real-time patient information through a wearable sensor device linked to a distant server. Wireless sensor networks, routing antennas, and base stations connect these wearable sensor devices. At regular intervals, the collected data will be routed to the admin server. These restricted devices and IoT applications are mainly dealing with additional obstacles. EHMS is an Internet of Things program that can manage online monitoring and periodic check-ups for a variety of chronic conditions. More importantly, the EHMS program can quickly identify the patient's criticality and abnormality state.

A conceptual architecture has been proposed by Zheng et al. (2018) [22], exchanging health data using blockchain technology. In addition, to give control over data quality, a machine-learning techniques has been developed. The main objective of this solution is to allow users to securely share their health data in a general data protection regulation (GDPR). Apart from the research community, it is also allow the commercial information consumers to obtain standard quality health information.

AlZubi et al. (2021) [23] were inspired to develop a cognitive machine-learning model to communicate healthcare data safely. Machine-learning models like cognitive algorithm can measure the pattern of cyberattack, and having this data to make observations can aid healthcare workforces. Their solution is related to a patient-centered design that secures data on a known device, such as end-user mobile phones. It gives the end user regulate over data transmitting. In comparison to other current models, their proposed model has a 96.5% attack prediction ratio, a 98.2% accuracy ratio, a 97.8% efficiency ratio, a 21.3% latency, and an 18.9% communication cost.

Yirui et al. (2020) [24] examined attack detection approaches that make use of the power of deep-learning techniques. Before discussing many successful deep-learning-based solutions, the authors first review the fundamental difficulties of network security and attack detection. They concentrate on attack detection approaches based on deep learning classification, such as autoencoders, generative adversarial networks, recurrent neural networks, and convolutional neural networks. They then give some benchmark datasets with descriptions and compare the performance of different representing approaches to demonstrate the current state of attack detection systems based on deep learning architecture. Finally, they review the paper and explore potential methods for improving attack detection performance using deep retaining structures.

Rocio et al. (2018) [25] were persuaded to experiment with the machine learning algorithm for the case of intrusion detection in SCADA applying an accurate data set from a gas pipeline. This paper contributes in two ways: 1) The accuracy, precision, recall, and F 1 score of the support vector machine (SVM) and random forest (RF) for intrusion detection are examined. 2) The accuracy, precision, recall, and F 1 score of the support vector machine (SVM) and random forest (RF) for intrusion detection are examined. Binary and categorical classifications are the two types of classifications. Their results show that RF can efficiently measure intrusions in each situation, with an F1 score of > 99%.

Eirini et al. (2021) [26] use the Jacobian-based saliency map attack to study how adversarial learning might target supervised models by creating adversarial samples and assessing classification behavior. The project also looks into how such occurrences can improve the robustness of supervised models with adversarial training. The experiments given here were created using data from a real-world power grid. The classification performance of two frequently used classifiers, random forest and J48, fell by 6 and 11 percentage points, respectively, when adversarial samples were included. Their performance enhanced after adversarial training, suggesting their resistance to such attacks.

Iqbal et al. (2020) [27] describe an intrusion detection tree ("IntruDTree"). This model not only predicts unknown test samples accurately but also reduces the model's complexity by reducing feature dimensions. Finally, they put IntruDTree model to the test by running tests on cybersecurity datasets and computing precision, recall, f-score, accuracy, and ROC values. To assess the usefulness of the resulting security model, we compare the findings of the IntruDTree model to those of many common traditional machine-learning approaches, including the Naive Bayes classifier, logistic regression, support vector machines, and k-nearest neighbor (Table 3.1).

A generative adversarial network (GAN) has been developed to deal with the scenario. It merely needs to learn the normal status distribution and identify abnormal status by comparing it to the learned distribution to demonstrate its high generating ability. On the other hand, existing GAN-based models are inadequate for processing data with discrete values, leading to a considerable loss in detection performance. To deal with the discrete features, Hongyu et al. (2019) [28] offer an efficient GAN-based model with a custom-designed loss function. Experiments show that their approach outperforms state-of-the-art techniques on discrete datasets while significantly decreasing overhead.

In this paper, Jia et al. (2020) [29] investigate the art of steganography with GANs in terms of data-hiding tactics such as cover modification, cover selection, and cover synthesis. The properties of the three GAN-based steganography strategies, as well as their evaluation criteria, are reviewed. Finally, several current GAN-based image steganography difficulties are summarized and analyzed. Topics for future research have also been predicted.

Table 3.1 Summarizing the Key Information from the Recent Literature

Model used	Objective	Publication	Novelty	Accuracy
SVM, Naïve Bayes, DT, RF	Applying machine-learning algorithms to detect malware	2018	Integrating a refinement algorithm for increasing detection accuracy	
Cognitive machine-learning attack detection model	Using computational strategies to measure the pattern of the cyber attack	2021	The authors have addressed the state-of-the-art techniques for preventing cyberattacks	**96.5%**
Machine-learning models	Using conventional procedures for detecting faults and attacks in terms of data security	2019	Their experiment measures the knowledge received about the class to determine the worth of an attribute.	–
Machine learning and deep learning	Recommends an appropriate storage repository based on the sensitivity of the health data, the quality of performance, and the patient's security and privacy preferences.	2020	Automaticall notifying health repositories for a specific data module, the system employs supervised learning.	–
LDQN	IoT-based secure health data transaction	2018	The feature explain and related operations are used to assess the quality value.	**98.79%**

SVM, FCM	Applying image segmentation approach to have the medical image secured.	2018	The proposed research concentrated on extracting the pixel-level colour of the input images, and it is claimed that the data security can be enhanced in that way.	—
Naïve Bayes, SVM, DT	Advanced security mechanisms to handle the big data in the medical industry	2018	Big data technologies are used to create predictive layers to improve decision-making and gain insight from data.	—
SVM	Securing the healthcare data from denial of service (DoS) and user-to-root (U2R) attacks.	2019	There is a multi-agent-based healthcare system with distinct regulations and security safeguards to deal with any threats.	—
ANN, DT, RF, SVM	Applying the computational strategies for preventing cyber attacks	2019	Analyze the performance against three malicious threats for eight intelligent medical devices in 12 benign events turning to the four ML-based detection techniques.	**91%**

3.5.3 Mathematical Interpretation of the ML Models

Based on the above information stated in the Section 3.5.2, it can be observed that the artificial neural network (ANN), support vector machine (SVM), decision tree (DT), and random forest (RF) algorithms frequently appeared for the case of preventing healthcare data security. In addition, to using the other conventional methods, these algorithms have satisfactory performance for the possibility of healthcare data prevention from cyberattacks. The following mathematical interpretations are explained to understand the technical mechanisms of these algorithms because researchers will be able to utilize them and perform effectively for working in this field.

3.5.4 Support Vector Machine (SVM)

Support vectors are the data points that make up the difference between the classes at the end of the different classes of datasets. The support vector machine algorithm can be used for both classification and regression problems. However, SVMs are quite popular for relatively complex types of small or medium classification datasets. In this algorithm, the data points are separated by a hyperplain, in which case the kernel determines what the hyperplain will look like. We can illustrate that any hyperplane can be written as shown in Equation 3.1 (Figure 3.9):

$$\vec{w} \cdot \vec{x} + b = 0 \tag{3.1}$$

Here, w is the (not necessarily normalized). The "margin" is the area or region bordered by these two hyperplanes, and the maximum margin hyperplane is the hyperplane that lies halfway between them. With a normalized or standardized dataset, the following equations can characterize these hyperplanes.

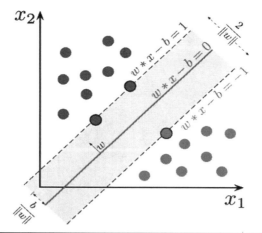

Figure 3.9 Hyperplanes with a Maximum Margin and SVM Margins for Samples of Two Classes Trained.

$$\text{Plus} - \text{plane} = \vec{w} \cdot \vec{x} + b = 0$$

$$\text{Minus} - \text{plane} = \vec{w} \cdot \vec{x} - b = 0$$

So, we can write the width or the margin of the two hyperplanes for data classification as the following equation:

$$width = \frac{\vec{W}}{abs(\vec{W})} \tag{3.2}$$

3.5.5 Radial Basis Function (RBF) Kernel SVM

The linear and nonlinear data efficiency of the support vector machine (SVM) has been demonstrated. With this approach, the radial base function was introduced to categorize nonlinear data. When it comes to placing information into the function space, the kernel function is crucial. In many circumstances, if we plot more than one variable in a standard scatter plot, we won't be able to distinguish between two or more data classes. The kernel of a support vector machine is a method for converting lower-dimensional input into higher-dimensional space and distinguishing between categories. There are three types of support vector machine kernels: linear kernel, polynomial kernel, and radial-basis function kernel. The radial-basis function is a nonlinear function as well. The support vector machine's most common function is this one. Any input can be mapped to an infinite-dimensional space with this kernel.

$$K(x_1, x_2) = \exp\left(-\frac{|x_1 - x_2|^2}{2\sigma^2}\right) \tag{3.3}$$

The radial-basis function (RBF) kernel is another name for a Gaussian function. A feature map (Φ) separates the input space in Figure 3.3. By applying equation (3.1), we get:

$$f(X) = \sum_i^N \alpha_i y_i k(X_i, X) + b \tag{3.4}$$

We get a new function by applying equation (3.3) in (3.4), where N represents the trained data.

$$f(X) = \sum_i^N \alpha_i y_i \exp\left(-\frac{|x_1 - x_2|^2}{2\sigma^2}\right) + b \tag{3.5}$$

3.5.6 Decision Tree (DT)

Both classification and regression problems can be solved with the classification and regression tree or CART algorithm. The decision tree looks a lot like a tree branch. The decision trio starts from the 'root node' just as the tree starts from the root. From the root node, the branches of this tree spread through different decision conditions; such nodes are called decision nodes. These nodes are called leaf nodes after making final decision. For a training set that comprises p positive and n negative, an applied math modeling [30] addressed feature selection within the tree to address this issue.

$$H\left(\frac{p}{n+p}, \frac{n}{n+p}\right) = -\frac{p}{n+p}\log_2\frac{p}{n+p} - \frac{n}{n+p}\log_2\frac{n}{n+p} \qquad (3.6)$$

The training set E is separated into prefixes of E1, E2 ... Ek by selecting K in the attribute with the unique value. After the attempt in the attribute (branches I = 1, 2 ... k), the expected entropy (EH) will remain, including:

$$EH(A) = \sum_{i=1}^{K} \frac{p_i + n_i}{p+n} H\left(\frac{p_i}{n_i + p_i}, \frac{n_i}{n_i + p_i}\right) \qquad (3.7)$$

For this trait, the information gain (I) or decrease in entropy is:

$$A(I) = H\left(\frac{p}{n+p}, \frac{n}{n+p}\right) - EH(A) \qquad (3.8)$$

3.5.7 Naïve Bayes Algorithm

Suppose you have a data point. $\vec{x} = \{x_1, ..., x_n\}$ of n n features, Naive Bayes forecasts the class C_k for $\vec{x}$. According to the probability metrics.

$$p(C_k|\vec{x}) = p(C_k|x_1, ..., x_n) \text{ For } k = 1, ..., K \qquad (3.9)$$

Using Bayes' Theorem, this can be delineated as

$$p(C_k|\vec{x}) = \frac{p(\vec{x}|C_k)p(C_k)}{p(\vec{x})} = \frac{p(x_1, ..., x_n|C_k)p(C_k)}{p(x_1, ..., x_n)} \qquad (3.10)$$

Applying the chain rule, the factor, $p(x_1, ..., x_n|C_k)$ in the numerator can be again illustrated as

$$p(x_1, \ldots, x_n | C_k) = p(x_1 | x_2, \ldots x_n, C_k) p(x_2 | x_3, \ldots, x_n, C_k) \ldots$$
$$p(x_{n-1} | x_n, C_k) p(x_n | C_k)$$

The "naive" conditional independence assumption is used at this point. This can be expressed as follows, using the previous decomposition:

$$p(x_i | x_{i+1}, \ldots, x_n | C_k) = p(x_i | C_k) \Rightarrow p(x_1, \ldots, x_n | C_k) = \prod_{i=1}^{n} p(x_i | C_k)$$
$$p(C_k | x_1, \ldots, x_n) \propto p(C_k, x_1, \ldots, x_n)$$
$$\propto p(C_k) p(x_1, \ldots, x_n | C_k) \tag{3.11}$$
$$\propto p(C_k) p(x_1 | C_k) p(x_2 | C_k) \ldots p(x_n | C_k)$$
$$\propto p(C_k) \prod_{i=1}^{n} p(x_i | C_k)$$

3.5.8 Complexity Analysis of the ML Models

Machine-learning computational complexity is a quantitative examination of the possibilities for effective computer learning. It is based on recently applied machine-learning models based on computational complexity theory and focuses on successful and general learning methods. The bounds of the algorithms for dense data are shown in Table 3.2. The following approximations are obtained by labeling n as the number of training samples, p as the total amount of features, n "trees" as the number of characteristics (for methods based on various trees), n sv as

Table 3.2 Measure the Computational Complexity of Machine-Learning Algorithms

Algorithm	Classification/ Regression	Training	Prediction
Decision Tree	C+R	$O(n^2 p)$	$O(p)$
Random Forest	C+R	$O(n^2 p n_{trees})$	$O(p n_{trees})$
GradientBoosting (n_{trees})	C+R	$O(n p n_{trees})$	$O(p n_{trees})$
SVM (Kernel)	C+R	$O(n^2 p + n^3)$	$O(n_{sv} p)$
k-Nearest Neighbours	C+R	–	$O(np)$
Neural Network	C+R	?	$O(p n_{l_1} + n_{l_1} n_{l_2} + \ldots)$
Naive Bayes	C	$O(np)$	$O(p)$

the number of support vectors, and n (l I as the number of neurons at layer I in the neural network.

Decision tree-based models: Clearly, ensemble techniques multiply the complexity of the original model by the number of "voters" in the model and replace the size of each bag with the training size. A split must be discovered before a maximum depth of d is achieved while training a decision tree. The method for determining this split is to look for the various thresholds (there are up to n of them) for each variable (there are p of them), as well as the information gained (evaluation in $O(n)$). The use of $\sqrt{}$ p predictors for each (weak) classifier is suggested in the Breiman implementation and classification.

Support vector machine: The classical techniques require evaluating the kernel matrix K, whose general term is $K(x_i, x_j)$, where K is the defined kernel. It is assumed that K can be evaluated with an $O(p)$ complexity is valid for standard kernels (Gaussian, polynomials, sigmoid). This statement may be untrue in the case of other kernels. The restricted quadratic algorithm is then "morally identical" to inverting a square matrix of dimension n with a complexity of $O(n^3)$.

3.6 Conclusion and Future Work

Healthcare data security is considerably significant nowadays, and researchers are currently applying several techniques to ensure unauthorized access. The objective of this research is achieved. This research identified the most frequently automated artificial intelligence-enabled models used to ensure data security. We have compared most of the well-known models here and have identified the efficiency of the various models by describing some of the unique processing techniques, which are extremely important in the field of big data security analytics. These findings will help us, and future researchers pursue any of the frameworks and improve these models. Even though the cyber-attack is being increased exponentially and healthcare sectors are vulnerable, early detection and preventing healthcare data from intruders using computational technology like machine learning can be an effective approach in terms of enhancing the organization's security. As several machine-learning algorithms and traditional methods are figured out in this study using healthcare research, it is crucial to know their mathematical interpretation from which model analysis can be possible. In addition, the computational complexity of the frequently applied algorithms is delineated in this study. This will be a benchmark for the research community to select an ideal model for data security. Finally, this research will be extended by implementing an attack-detection model that will tighten healthcare security and keep the healthcare data secure.

References

[1] Obenshain, M. 2004. Application of data mining techniques to healthcare data. *Infection Control & Hospital Epidemiology.* 25:690–695.

[2] Barrows, R. C. Jr. and P. D. Clayton 1996. Privacy, confidentiality, and electronic medical records. *Journal of the American Medical Informatics Association.* 3:139–148.

[3] Jercich, K. 2021. The biggest healthcare data breaches of 2021. Available: https://www.healthcareitnews.com/news/biggest-healthcare-data-breaches-2021

[4] Salloum, S. A., Alshurideh, M., Elnagar, A. and K. Shaalan. 2020. Machine learning and deep learning techniques for cybersecurity: A review. in *AICV.* 4:50–57.

[5] Kable, A. K., Pich, J. and S. E. Maslin-Prothero. 2012. A structured approach to documenting a search strategy for publication: A 12 step guideline for authors. *Nurse Education Today.* 32:878–886.

[6] Newaz, A. I., Sikder, A. K., Rahman, M. A. and A. S. Uluagac. 2019. Healthguard: A machine learning-based security framework for smart healthcare systems. in *2019 Sixth International Conference on Social Networks Analysis, Management and Security (SNAMS).* 5:389–396.

[7] Hady, A. A., Ghubaish, A., Salman, T., Unal, D. and R. Jain. 2020. Intrusion detection system for healthcare systems using medical and network data: A comparison study. *IEEE Access.* 8:106576–106584.

[8] K. Shaukat, S. Luo, V. Varadharajan, I. A. Hameed, and M. Xu, "A survey on machine learning techniques for cyber security in the last decade," *IEEE Access.* 8:222310–222354.

[9] Boddy, A., Hurst, W., Mackay, M. and A. E. Rhalibi. 2017. A study into data analysis and visualisation to increase the cyber-resilience of healthcare infrastructures. in *Proceedings of the 1st International Conference on Internet of Things and Machine Learning.* 34:1–7.

[10] Kaur, P., Sharma, M. and M. Mittal. 2018. "Big data and machine learning based secure healthcare framework," *Procedia Computer Science.* 132:1049–1059.

[11] Uddin, M. A., Stranieri, A., Gondal, I. and V. Balasubramanian. 2020. Dynamically Recommending Repositories for Health Data: A Machine Learning Model. in *ACSW.* 24:125–210.

[12] Mohanta, B., Das, P. and S. Patnaik. 2019. Healthcare 5.0: A paradigm shift in digital healthcare system using artificial intelligence, IOT and 5G communication. in *2019 International Conference on Applied Machine Learning (ICAML).* 7:191–196.

[13] Marwan, M., Kartit, A. and H. Ouahmane. 2018. Security enhancement in healthcare cloud using machine learning. *Procedia Computer Science.* 127:388–397.

[14] Sreeji, S., Shiji, S., Vysagh, M. and T. A. Amma. 2020. Security and Privacy Preserving Deep Learning Framework that Protect Healthcare Data Breaches. *International Journal of Research in Engineering, Science and Management.* 3:148–152.

[15] Shakeel, P. M., Baskar, S., Dhulipala, V. S., Mishra S. and M. M. Jaber. 2018. Maintaining security and privacy in health care system using learning based deep-Q-networks. *Journal of medical systems.* 42:1–10.

[16] Uddin, M. A., Stranieri, A., Gondal, I. and V. Balasubramanian. 2020. Rapid health data repository allocation using predictive machine learning. *Health Informatics Journal.* 26:3009–3036.

[17] MacDermott, Á., Kendrick, P., Idowu, I., Ashall, M. and Q. Shi. 2019. Securing things in the healthcare internet of things. in *2019 Global IoT Summit (GIoTS).* 3:1–6.

[18] Chowdhury, M., Jahan, S., Islam, R. and J. Gao. 2018. Malware detection for healthcare data security. in *International Conference on Security and Privacy in Communication Systems.* 4:407–416.

[19] Seh, A. H., Al-Amri, J. F., Subahi, A. F., Agrawal, A., Kumar, R. and R. A. Khan. 2021. Machine Learning Based Framework for Maintaining Privacy of Healthcare Data. *Intell. Autom. Soft Comput.* 29: 697–712.

[20] Cheng, W. Ou, W. Yin. et al. 2020. A privacy-protection model for patients. *Security and Communication Networks.* 6:56–83.

[21] Godi, B., Viswanadham, S. A., Muttipati, S., Samantray, O. P. and S. R. Gadiraju. 2020. E-healthcare monitoring system using IoT with machine learning approaches. in *2020 International Conference on Computer Science, Engineering and Applications (ICCSEA).* 5:1–5.

[22] Zheng, X., Mukkamala, R. R., Vatrapu, R and J. Ordieres-Mere. 2018. Blockchain-based personal health data sharing system using cloud storage. in *2018 IEEE 20th International Conference on e-Health Networking, Applications and Services (Healthcom).* 1–6.

[23] AlZubi, A. A., Al-Maitah, M. and A. Alarifi. 2021. Cyber-attack detection in healthcare using cyber-physical system and machine learning techniques. *Soft Computing.* 25:12319–12332.

[24] Kumar, A. Glisson, W. and H. Cho. 2020. Network attack detection using an unsupervised machine learning algorithm. Hawaii International conference on system sciences, 2020.

[25] Perez, R. L., Adamsky, F., Soua, R. and T. Engel. 2018. Machine learning for reliable network attack detection in SCADA systems. in *2018 17th IEEE International Conference On Trust, Security And Privacy In Computing And Communications/12th IEEE International Conference On Big Data Science And Engineering (TrustCom/BigDataSE).* 633–638.

[26] Anthi, E., Williams, L., Rhode, M., Burnap, P. and A. Wedgbury. 2021. Adversarial attacks on machine learning cybersecurity defences in industrial control systems. *Journal of Information Security and Applications.* 58:102717.

[27] Sarker, I. H., Abushark, Y. B., Alsolami, F. and A. I. Khan. 2020. Intrudtree: A machine learning based cyber security intrusion detection model. *Symmetry.* 12:754.

[28] Chen H. and L. Jiang. 2019. Efficient GAN-based method for cyber-intrusion detection. *ArXiv preprint arXiv:1904.02426.* 8.

[29] Liu, J., Ke, Y., Zhang, Z. et al. 2020. Recent advances of image steganography with generative adversarial networks. *IEEE Access.* 8:60575–60597, 2020.

[30] De Mántaras, R. L. 1991. A distance-based attribute selection measure for decision tree induction. *Machine Learning.* 6:81–92.

Appendix 3.A

Table: Study Quality Assessment Tools Retrieved from NIH (https://www.nhlbi. nih.gov/health-Topics/study-Quality-Assessment-Tools)

No	Question	Yes	No	Other	Score
	Threshold Score Level >=?				
	Paper Name:				
1	Is the review based on a focused research question that is adequately formulated and described?				
2	Were eligibility criteria for included and excluded studies predefined and specified?				
3	Did the literature search strategy use a comprehensive systematic approach?				
4	Were titles, abstracts, and full-text articles dually and independently reviewed for inclusion and exclusion to minimize bias?				
5	Was the quality of each included study rated independently by two or more reviewers using a standard method to appraise its internal validity?				
6	Were the included studies listed along with essential characteristics and results of Machine Learning Algorithms for Health Data Security?				
7	Did the study include unique features of Machine Learning Algorithms for Health Data Security?				

(Continued)

	Threshold Score Level >=?				
	Paper Name:				
No	*Question*	*Yes*	*No*	*Other*	*Score*
8	Was the study easily implementable in the real-life problem?				
9	Were the primary data collected and stored in the study?				
10	How consistent is the information obtained from the study compared to the other study?				
Quality Rating	**Good**	**Fair**	**Poor**	**Total score**	
Rater 1 initials					
Rater 2 initials					

Chapter 4

Fog Computing in IoT-Based Healthcare Systems

Azadeh Zamanifar and Ali Yamini

Science and Research Branch of Azad University

Contents

4.1 Introduction 80
4.2 Concepts in Fog Computing 80
4.3 Healthcare Systems 81
4.4 Properties of Fog-Based Computing 82
    4.4.1 Privacy 82
    4.4.2 Energy Efficiency 82
    4.4.3 Bandwidth 82
    4.4.4 Scalability 82
    4.4.5 Dependability 83
4.5 Fog Computing in IoT-Based Healthcare 83
    4.5.1 Computation Center 83
    4.5.2 Latency and Throughput 84
    4.5.3 Reliability 85
    4.5.4 Security 85
    4.5.5 Automatic Fog Computing 86
    4.5.6 Energy Effectiveness 87
4.6 Conclusion 87
References 87

DOI: 10.1201/9781003145189-4

4.1 Introduction

The industry (Hu et al. 2015) invented the fog computing term as a metaphor for architecture's main idea and invented behind it: fog is a place between the cloud (data centers) and the ground, where the user's devices reside. The synonymous term used often is edge calculations and describes tasks as opposed to the cloud at the edge of the network. The term "edge" can refer to different classes of architecture. In an industrial environment, the edge often refers to a manufacturing plant's nodes that reside with the user, for example, as part of a machine controller or network gateway (Bonomi et al. 2012). ETSI terms (Hu et al. 2015) consider Internet service providers' views and consider edge as the operator network boundary, like in an LTE base station. Our understanding of fog covers both views.

Cloud-based systems allow data from different sites and devices to be collected, and output is again sent to the desired device, causing the response delay in response and requiring high bandwidth for large data. Data security and user privacy are also a major concern. These are the reasons why individuals are hesitant to use the cloud. Fog computing has been proposed to fix these problems. To address these issues, researchers have proposed other comparable computing paradigms to fog computing, such as edge computing, mist computing, the cloud of things, and cloudlets (Pareek et al. 2021).

4.2 Concepts in Fog Computing

The main feature of fog calculation is its topology, which means that geographically distributed nodes perform computations and provide storage and network services. Computational resources may be integrated with general network functions in access points, routers, and network gateways. There may also be specific computational fog nodes, such as mobile edge computing servers in the base stations (LTE) and the access points described by ETSI (Hu et al. 2015). Other devices can be proprietary, such as home automation centers. Various specific fog actions depend on the application and specific scope. In general, tasks include collection, aggregation, analysis, and temporary storage.

Fog computing can be performed in a computational fog node or commonly inside multiple nodes, improving scalability and creating redundancy and elasticity. If additional computing power is needed, more fog nodes are added (Awaisi et al. 2020). The usage of mechanisms such as virtualization and sandboxing helps to run these programs. For this reason, fog computing share many of the principles of cloud computing. The centrality of fog computing is the concept of the computing loading level, which is being used by cloudlets in research and can also be found in the mobile fog (Fernando et al. 2013). Similarly, collective computing concentrates on the use of distributed and provided computing power by mobile devices. Fog computation is one possible solution to overcome the gap between sensors and analysis in health informatics. Fog computation is a style of architecture in distributed systems where the specific program logic is not only in the cloud or close to user systems but also in the infrastructure components between them. Fog computation provides new possibilities for solving healthcare challenges, such as relaxed patient mobility and increasing uninterrupted patient control. In general, a large number of publications related to the principles of fog computing refer to applications in healthcare. However, in most cases, discussion about locations where performing computation tasks is necessary has not occurred.

4.3 Healthcare Systems

Health systems in most countries face tremendous challenges due to increased population and increasing chronic diseases. Many countries also face a growing shortage of nursing staff. Simultaneously, there is a demand for reducing costs while maintaining high-quality patient care (Catarinucci et al. 2015). As a result, the healthcare industry offers a model of information-based healthcare delivery (Nigam and Bhatia 2016). Part of this delivery model provides access to patients via remote control, leading to increased accessibility, quality, efficiency, and continuity of healthcare for patients and reducing the overall cost of healthcare (Mandellos et al. 2009).

Today, with manual measurement of biometric parameters and data transmission between systems, including pen and paper, much time is wasted. Remote monitoring frees time for administrators. Other enhancements are similar to automated monitoring that can replace manual monitoring. Bertini and colleagues (Bertini et al. 2016) compare the benefits of remote monitoring with those reported within the hospital, including positive effects on survival, which is another context for improving hospital processes. Many processes are manually planned, instead of using resources more efficiently, so they run sequentially. Besides, sensors facilitate accessing accurate information about the current status and position of pieces of equipment, caregivers, and patients. Sensors also provide a more accurate patient picture because they can continuously record data and provide insight into increasing biometric parameters' diversity (Jain et al. 2021). Remote monitoring will revolutionize diagnosis and treatment. Topol (Toole 2013) calls this human digitalization. When this new patient image is compatible with analytic techniques, new insights will change early diagnosis, diagnosis, drug, and treatment. A prerequisite for this change is that the data should not be treated in isolated silos but combined with other resources and visible in the text.

Another process is rooted in reaction therapy. Only after an accident do patients undergo treatment at the hospital and take more preventative care (MacIntosh et al. 2016). Moreover, increasing the possibility of monitoring patients at home will give them greater freedom than at the hospital. Generally, this means that borders between hospitals, homes, and other care places become increasingly blurry. It is essential to note that healthcare frequently happens everywhere.

4.4 Properties of Fog-Based Computing

Compared to the system to fog architecture, placing processing near the machine can reduce the latency time because the physical distance is less, and the possible response time in a data center can be omitted. In this comparison, only a latency device can be reduced because the intensive computational tasks that take a long time for sensor devices limited to resources can transfer fog computing nodes and predict the latency time (Deng et al. 2015).

4.4.1 Privacy

In comparison to the system for fog architecture, fog computing can reduce data diffusion; for example, by analyzing the sensitive data at the local gate instead of the data center outside the user's control, it can improve user data privacy (Vaquero and Rodero-Merino 2014).

4.4.2 Energy Efficiency

Several methods for fog computing can improve the energy efficiency in sensor devices. First, the gateways can act as a communication proxy so that the machines can increase their sleep period. During sleep mode, the gate will respond to any request or update, and then the sensor is processed by awakening the device. Second, heavy energy consumer computations and other services can be removed from battery nodes (Deng et al. 2015).

4.4.3 Bandwidth

Compared to the device to fog architecture, fog computing can reduce the volume of data sent to data centers. This reduction can happen in a few ways: raw data can be used, analyzed, preprocessed, and compressed, so only a small amount of data needs to be sent (Cao et al. 2015, Xu et al. 2016). Local nodes can also respond to system requests based on stored local data, so it is unnecessary to communicate with data centers at all (Gia et al. 2015).

4.4.4 Scalability

Fog computing can improve the scalability of the system. Local computation can reduce the load from concentrated resources and expand as needed.

Vaquero and Rodero-Merino (Vaquero and Rodero-Merino 2014) refer to scalability as using "mini-clouds."

4.4.5 Dependability

Fog computation can increase the reliability of the system in two ways. By allowing multiple nodes in the network, the same function can be used as redundancy. Moreover, it can perform closer computations to sensor nodes that are less dependent on network connection availability to more concentrated sources (Yannuzzi et al. 2014).

4.5 Fog Computing in IoT-Based Healthcare

Fog computations also activate new applications: by adding a higher level of independence and intelligence on edge, fog computing creates delay and response time and energy saving for wearable and low-cost devices. At the same time, it performs complicated tasks such as crash detection (Cao et al. 2015). The next generation of healthcare devices without using simple algorithms and with limited accuracy replace expensive and complicated machines. Fog computing enables these devices and eventually leads to the "Internet of health issues." Fog computing is not cloud computing. It is an extension of it. Meanwhile, health systems in many countries struggle with significant challenges due to population growth and increased disease. Many countries face a growing shortage of nursing personnel. As a result, the healthcare industry offers an information-based healthcare model (Nigam and Bhatia 2016). Part of this delivery model allows remote control of patients, leading to increased availability, quality, effectiveness, and continuity of healthcare for patients and reduces healthcare costs (Mandellos et al. 2009). Fog computation in new applications causes latency and response time and cost savings for wearable and low-cost sensors. In the next generation, healthcare systems replace expensive and complex machines by adding a higher level of independence and intelligence at the edge.

4.5.1 Computation Center

In the previous section, data from BAN to fog is performed at several network levels. This indicates that computational tasks' distribution should not be easily centralized at a node's hierarchical level. Placing the computational tasks in the infrastructure is not trivial. The different roles and computational resources of the available machines require careful consideration of the transaction and the completion of possible choices (Deng et al. 2015). Even if it is considered for some operations, a high-consumer environment through cloud computing is preferred to the other with fewer capabilities. Limitations such as privacy may limit the number of available alternatives. For example, prevention of information leakage from the hospital site.

It is also observed that despite the general acceptance of fog computers in each location between the cloud and an IV-A device, health features establishing scenarios impact decisions related to the fog concept significantly. In health informatics, when comparing the responsibilities of fog in hospitals, or other locations where health activities are available, fewer resources are available (i.e., hospital physicians and older homes). Many examples of this effect are significant.

When considering different levels that can be done through the device to the cloud, the execution of local processing (i.e., inside a center) may be of higher importance to discussing reliability (i.e., VI-C). This local process does not discredit the collaboration between servers connected to the local node. They can overlap together, but if the connection to the outer side is declined, it presents additional guarantees and may be necessary for vital systems. Privacy and regulations that occur with a particular scenario, especially in health informatics, may create more stringent restrictions, and the need to perform assigned tasks is in specific restrictions.

4.5.2 Latency and Throughput

Previous works show that the calculation of the loading rate offered by fog computing in the vicinity of limited devices can reduce the latency time to 2.88 times (Gordon et al. 2012), compared to the amount of cloud loading. The available local resources and resources used in the cloud strongly influence the result. These resources depend solely on the number of servers used (i.e., access to the network infrastructure is almost negligible) with the mobile network's wide coverage networks 4.4 and increasing data send rate. However, increasing the number of nodes and highly specialized sensors will increase the scalability concerns. The latency-sensitive programs may require improved mechanisms to control the latency between the sensors and the cloud (Deng et al. 2015).

Theoretically, (Xu et al. 2016) using dedicated servers at the edge of the network (i.e., cloudlets), there is an improvement, but it ignores the extensive usage of IoT devices and their specific feature. Also, this is a visual point that local executing of computation tasks should improve latency, throughput, and even energy consumption (Tang et al. 2015). However, throughput and latency may be improved by fog computing by reducing the amount of data transmitted between the source and the destination, destroying the network core and the overall system (Aazam and Huh 2014). This load reduction may also reduce the probability of transmission errors and can be achieved by performing computing operations such as elimination, feature extraction, or prediction (Gomes et al. 2017).

Practical applications related to face recognition and speech recognition require a large amount of data, and it is shown that local computing can reduce latency (Hossain and Muhammad 2015). However, improving resource-limited devices' performance depends on whether devices are capable of bridging networks. Fog computations need to use the diversity of resources limiting resources and their capabilities in the entire hierarchy of network infrastructure to scale and present more rapid response time.

4.5.3 Reliability

Reliability of health programs, particularly for the use case class, is critical to vital monitoring and critical control. Every point of simple breakdown needs to be carefully reviewed. According to cloud-based solutions, data centers' availability is generally high, but the power outage is still problematic, even with redundancy (Gunawi et al. 2016).

The network path to data centers may break down. Finally, each connected to the central data center in different deployment scenarios can top working, although some are more exposed. Ambulances can pass through areas without cell phone coverage, or patients may interrupt their connection with wi-fi. This question arises concerning what degree of cloud services can be used for critical cases. In describing many use cases, it seems that these aspects have not been adequately addressed.

Local computation can be used to completely replace essential tasks performed in data centers or for the use of local processing in case of limitations in the cloud (Byers and Wetterwald 2015), for instance, feature extraction for analyzing the patient's ECG data in real time (Gia et al. 2015), (López et al. 2010). If caregivers depend on the performance to monitor patients' well-being, the analysis should not be interrupted. When the task finishes in a close gateway, it can also be done when the data center or its connection is disconnected. For the use case class of data collection, what is essential is that the data may eventually reach some database; the fog nodes may also buffer data locally to be transferred at a time when they can be further transferred (Mutlag et al. 2019).

As in the cloud, fog computing nodes may also be subject to failure. However, the consequences and nature of failure are different from cloud computing. The failure in the cloud or network can affect the entire hospital. In contrast, when the resources of a lower network hierarchy are lost, the consequences of a separate region, such as hospital wing or discrete parts and handling such partial events, are more manageable considering re-equipment or replacement. It can also lead to local redundancies at the local level (Al-Khafajiy et al. 2018).

4.5.4 Security

Davis et al. (Davies et al. 2016) argue that privacy concerns due to the "excessive focus" of IoT systems are an important barrier to their growth. Even if data are protected within the cloud and data centers, a suitable solution to protect data is to prevent them from being sent in the first location and processing them to the primary source (Vaquero and Rodero-Merino 2014). In the vicinity of fog devices, which can be located in lower infrastructure, they may provide the required trust and apply the necessary privacy mechanisms that threaten cloud computing in critical scenarios—for example, the program for the analysis of speech patients with Parkinson's disease (Monteiro et al. 2016).

Instead of sending audio recordings to a data center, analysis occurs locally, and only the result is sent. Although privacy is still a problem in decentralized solutions such as fog computing, trust and authentication must be used, especially when considering multiple vendors and fully wireless devices. The separation between the node and access points, or gateways, enables disobedient or compromised fog nodes to prevent local benefits (Yi et al. 2015), (Stojmenovic and Wen 2014). Implementors must implement reliable models and software and physical security mechanisms to protect networks and nodes and primarily achieve a decentralized network between mobile nodes, fog nodes, and sensors. The other way to calculate the computation work in an invalid fog computing node is the real computation (Gennaro et al. 2010), considering that computational tasks can be effectively mapped to the existing operation in these conditions.

The fog node can also contribute to security operations. Since they often have more computational power than sensor-limiting devices, they may help carry out cryptographic operations (Hummen et al. 2014). Symmetric encryption supported by many embedded sensor nodes protects the link between the sensor device and the BAN gateway. BAN may secure the patient's data before transmitting it to the network using concepts explained in (Hummen et al. 2014). The fog may also host other security functions such as intrusion detection (Shi et al. 2015) or direct information control that may leave the location (Davies et al. 2016).

Sweeping everything and technological innovations may also create a new era for human and computer interaction and its relevance to users' security and nodes. These systems require identification mechanisms that do not jeopardize machines' operation and their mobility between different networks.

4.5.5 Automatic Fog Computing

Fog computing, in comparison to ground computing, provides flexibility. To reduce further complexity along with this ability, dynamic managed behaviors on the IoT and fog computing patterns (Yi et al. 2015), (Vaquero and Rodero-Merino 2014) using available resources and coordination of actions expected to improve overall performance. Specific conditions of the scenario are fundamental to the possibility of independent and efficient management in fog computing and aligning the Internet with IoT to gain full advantage of its potential (Cerf and Senges 2016). Using big data, especially as a possibility for knowledge of context management (Salman et al. 2015), is very important considering the nodes and their different infrastructure roles. However, these considerations must control the heterogeneity of devices and vendors without introducing additional and unbearable costs.

Several parameters to improve fog computing management must be scaled by releasing the IoT devices and their specific applications. This requires nodes to decide if they need previous corrections without compromising their purpose in the system while participating in decision-making. The node's autonomy or self-awareness enhances such a process by standard protocols (Orwat et al. 2008). These standardized mechanisms are essential to ensure the interoperability between the devices (Cerf and Senges 2016), and "crossing the gap" of IoT (Davies et al. 2016).

4.5.6 Energy Effectiveness

The primary energy consumers are in sensor-computation networks and data transmission, in addition to the real measurement method's energy. Fog computing justifies the energy efficiency by the expensive calculation of the sensor machines. Huetal et al. (Hu et al. 2016) show how the cloud properties of colorizing clouds can significantly improve mobile devices' energy consumption. These results are for mobile apps. For BANs, the transmission cost may be different since it decreases the energy from less processing by increasing the cost of transmission. For the first time, the fog computing nodes are rich in energy, so they are suitable. However, if the fog nodes like mobile are moving in the mobile-deployment scenario, there is a compromise between mobile energy consumption and the sensor device; such compromises may require independent reasoning inside the device to determine which strategy is more efficient.

4.6 Conclusion

In this chapter, we review fog computing concept. Then, we review IoT-based healthcare systems. Next, we present fog computing features that provides more efficient healthcare systems. We also discuss the challenges that still exist in this area.

References

Aazam, M. and E.-N. Huh (2014). Fog computing and smart gateway based communication for cloud of things. 2014 International Conference on Future Internet of Things and Cloud, IEEE.

Al-Khafajiy, M., L. Webster, T. Baker and A. Waraich (2018). Towards fog driven IoT healthcare: challenges and framework of fog computing in healthcare. Proceedings of the 2nd International Conference on Future Networks and Distributed Systems.

Awaisi, K. S., S. Hussain, M. Ahmed, A. A. Khan and G. Ahmed (2020). "Leveraging IoT and Fog Computing in Healthcare Systems." *IEEE Internet of Things Magazine* 3(2): 52–56.

Bertini, M., L. Marcantoni, T. Toselli and R. Ferrari (2016). "Remote monitoring of implantable devices: Should we continue to ignore it?" *International Journal of Cardiology* 202: 368–377.

Bonomi, F., R. Milito, J. Zhu and S. Addepalli (2012). Fog computing and its role in the internet of things. Proceedings of the First Edition of the MCC Workshop on Mobile Cloud Computing.

Byers, C. C. and P. Wetterwald (2015). "Fog computing distributing data and intelligence for resiliency and scale necessary for IoT: The internet of things (ubiquity symposium)." *Ubiquity* **2015**(November): 1–12.

Cao, Y., S. Chen, P. Hou and D. Brown (2015). FAST: A fog computing assisted distributed analytics system to monitor fall for stroke mitigation. 2015 IEEE International Conference on Networking, Architecture and Storage (NAS), IEEE.

Catarinucci, L., D. De Donno, L. Mainetti, L. Palano, L. Patrono, M. L. Stefanizzi and L. Tarricone (2015). "An IoT-aware architecture for smart healthcare systems." *IEEE Internet of Things Journal* **2**(6): 515–526.

Cerf, V. and M. Senges (2016). "Taking the internet to the next physical level." *IEEE Annals of the History of Computing* **49**(02): 80–86.

Davies, N., N. Taft, M. Satyanarayanan, S. Clinch and B. Amos (2016). Privacy mediators: Helping iot cross the chasm. Proceedings of the 17th International Workshop on Mobile Computing Systems and Applications.

Deng, R., R. Lu, C. Lai and T. H. Luan (2015). Towards power consumption-delay tradeoff by workload allocation in cloud-fog computing. 2015 IEEE International Conference on Communications (ICC), IEEE.

Fernando, N., S. W. Loke and W. Rahayu (2013). "Mobile cloud computing: A survey." *Future Generation Computer Systems* **29**(1): 84–106.

Gennaro, R., C. Gentry and B. Parno (2010). Non-interactive verifiable computing: Outsourcing computation to untrusted workers. Annual Cryptology Conference, Springer.

Gia, T. N., M. Jiang, A.-M. Rahmani, T. Westerlund, P. Liljeberg and H. Tenhunen (2015). Fog computing in healthcare internet of things: A case study on ecg feature extraction. 2015 IEEE International Conference on Computer and Information Technology; Ubiquitous Computing and Communications; Dependable, Autonomic and Secure Computing; Pervasive Intelligence and Computing, IEEE.

Gomes, A. S., B. Sousa, D. Palma, V. Fonseca, Z. Zhao, E. Monteiro, T. Braun, P. Simoes and L. Cordeiro (2017). "Edge caching with mobility prediction in virtualized LTE mobile networks." *Future Generation Computer Systems* **70**: 148–162.

Gordon, M. S., D. A. Jamshidi, S. Mahlke, Z. M. Mao and X. Chen (2012). {COMET}: Code Offload by Migrating Execution Transparently. 10th {USENIX} Symposium on Operating Systems Design and Implementation ({OSDI} 12).

Gunawi, H. S., M. Hao, R. O. Suminto, A. Laksono, A. D. Satria, J. Adityatama and K. J. Eliazar (2016). Why does the cloud stop computing? lessons from hundreds of service outages. Proceedings of the Seventh ACM Symposium on Cloud Computing.

Hossain, M. S. and G. Muhammad (2015). "Cloud-assisted speech and face recognition framework for health monitoring." *Mobile Networks and Applications* **20**(3): 391–399.

Hu, W., Y. Gao, K. Ha, J. Wang, B. Amos, Z. Chen, P. Pillai and M. Satyanarayanan (2016). Quantifying the impact of edge computing on mobile applications. Proceedings of the 7th ACM SIGOPS Asia-Pacific Workshop on Systems.

Hu, Y. C., M. Patel, D. Sabella, N. Sprecher and V. Young (2015). "Mobile edge computing—A key technology towards 5G." *ETSI White Paper* **11**(11): 1–16.

Hummen, R., H. Shafagh, S. Raza, T. Voig and K. Wehrle (2014). Delegation-based Authentication and Authorization for the IP-based Internet of Things. 2014 Eleventh Annual IEEE International Conference on Sensing, Communication, and Networking (SECON), IEEE.

Jain, R., M. Gupta, A. Nayyar and N. Sharma (2021). Adoption of fog computing in healthcare 4.0. *Fog computing for healthcare 4.0 environments*, Springer: 3–36.

López, G., V. Custodio and J. I. Moreno (2010). "LOBIN: E-textile and wireless-sensor-network-based platform for healthcare monitoring in future hospital environments." *IEEE Transactions on Information Technology in Biomedicine* **14**(6): 1446–1458.

MacIntosh, E., N. Rajakulendran, Z. Khayat and A. Wise (2016). "Transforming health: Shifting from reactive to proactive and predictive care." *MaRS White Paper* **14**(6).

Mandellos, G. J., D. K. Lymberopoulos, G. V. Koutelakis, M. N. Koukias and T. C. Panagiotakopoulos (2009). *Requirements and solutions for advanced telemedicine applications*, INTECH Open Access Publisher.

Monteiro, A., H. Dubey, L. Mahler, Q. Yang and K. Mankodiya (2016). Fit: A fog computing device for speech tele-treatments. 2016 IEEE International Conference on Smart Computing (SMARTCOMP), IEEE.

Mutlag, A. A., M. K. Abd Ghani, N. a. Arunkumar, M. A. Mohammed and O. Mohd (2019). "Enabling technologies for fog computing in healthcare IoT systems." *Future Generation Computer Systems* **90**: 62–78.

Nigam, V. K. and S. Bhatia (2016). "Impact of cloud computing on health care." *International Research Journal of Engineering and Technology* **3**(5): 2804–2810.

Orwat, C., A. Graefe and T. Faulwasser (2008). "Towards pervasive computing in health care–A literature review." *BMC Medical Informatics and Decision Making* **8**(1): 1–18.

Pareek, K., P. K. Tiwari and V. Bhatnagar (2021). Fog computing in healthcare: A review. IOP Conference Series: Materials Science and Engineering, IOP Publishing.

Salman, O., I. Elhajj, A. Kayssi and A. Chehab (2015). Edge computing enabling the Internet of Things. 2015 IEEE 2nd World Forum on Internet of Things (WF-IoT), IEEE.

Shi, Y., S. Abhilash and K. Hwang (2015). Cloudlet mesh for securing mobile clouds from intrusions and network attacks. 2015 3rd IEEE International Conference on Mobile Cloud Computing, Services, and Engineering, IEEE.

Stojmenovic, I. and S. Wen (2014). The fog computing paradigm: Scenarios and security issues. 2014 Federated Conference on Computer Science and Information Systems, IEEE.

Tang, B., Z. Chen, G. Hefferman, T. Wei, H. He and Q. Yang (2015). A hierarchical distributed fog computing architecture for big data analysis in smart cities. *Proceedings of the ASE Big Data & SocialInformatics* **2015**: 1–6.

Toole, B. (2013). *The creative destruction of medicine: How the digital revolution will create better health care*: E. Topol, New York: Basic Books, 2012, 303 pp. ISBN-13: 9780465025503, Taylor & Francis.

Vaquero, L. M. and L. Rodero-Merino (2014). "Finding your way in the fog: Towards a comprehensive definition of fog computing." *ACM SIGCOMM Computer Communication Review* **44**(5): 27–32.

Xu, K., Y. Li and F. Ren (2016). An energy-efficient compressive sensing framework incorporating online dictionary learning for long-term wireless health monitoring. 2016 IEEE International Conference on Acoustics, Speech and Signal Processing (ICASSP), IEEE.

Xu, Y., V. Mahendran and S. Radhakrishnan (2016). Towards SDN-based fog computing: MQTT broker virtualization for effective and reliable delivery. 2016 8th International Conference on Communication Systems and Networks (COMSNETS), IEEE.

Yannuzzi, M., R. Milito, R. Serral-Gracià, D. Montero and M. Nemirovsky (2014). Key ingredients in an IoT recipe: Fog computing, cloud computing, and more fog computing. 2014 IEEE 19th International Workshop on Computer Aided Modeling and Design of Communication Links and Networks (CAMAD), IEEE.

Yi, S., Z. Hao, Z. Qin and Q. Li (2015). Fog computing: Platform and applications. 2015 Third IEEE Workshop on Hot Topics in Web Systems and Technologies (HotWeb), IEEE.

Yi, S., Z. Qin and Q. Li (2015). Security and privacy issues of fog computing: A survey. International Conference on Wireless Algorithms, Systems, and Applications, Springer.

Chapter 5

Medical Imaging and Healthcare Applications Using 5G

Enjie Liu[1], Youbing Zhao[2], and Abimbola Efunogbon[1]

[1]*University of Bedfordshire, UK*
[2]*University of Bedfordshire, UK and Communication University of Zhejiang, China*

Contents

5.1 Introductions: Background and Constraints of Traditional Healthcare
Applications 92
5.2 Opportunities Provided by Cloud Computing and 5G 93
5.3 Medical Imaging with Cloud and 5G 93
    5.3.1 Medical Image Storage 94
    5.3.2 Medical-Image Processing.. 95
    5.3.3 Machine-Learning and AI 95
    5.3.4 Visualization and Virtual Reality (VR)/Augmented
    Reality (AR).. 96
5.4 The Impacts of 5G on Cloud Computing 96
5.5 5G in Healthcare 97
    5.5.1 5G in Healthcare Applications with High Processing
    Requirements.. 97
    5.5.2 Benefit of 5G to Healthcare Applications 98
    5.5.3 An Example Application 98
5.6 Introduction to 5G Technology 101

DOI: 10.1201/9781003145189-5

5.7 Software Defined Network in 5G 101
5.8 5G Architecture 103
    5.8.1 Logical Structure of 5G 103
    5.8.2 Slicing and Integrating with Broadband 105
5.9 Edge Computing 106
5.10 Conclusion 107
References 108

5.1 Introductions: Background and Constraints of Traditional Healthcare Applications

As an enabling technology for sharing data and computing power, the cloud has brought significant changes to many industries, including the medical and healthcare sector. With 5G on the horizon, ultra-fast and low-latency data transmission on the cloud and via the Internet will enable more medical and health applications, which formerly may have been constrained by data size and transmission latency.

The integration of the 5G technology and cloud computing generate even more opportunities for medical and healthcare applications, free them from a variety of physical and nonphysical constraints, including:

■ Storage constraint

Medical and healthcare data are commonly high-dimensional, heterogeneous, longitudinal and serve a large population. A large volume is required to store, query, share and archive these data, with medical-imaging studies a typical example. Limited storage will be a serious constraint for most practical medical institutions in the digital era.

■ Location and sharing constraint

Traditionally medical data are owned by different medical institutions. Therefore, sharing these data among different locations and different entities is difficult.

■ Computing power constraint

Nowadays, medical and healthcare applications heavily involve data mining, machine learning, and artificial intelligence, which are all computationally demanding. For example, the mining of EHRs and the analysis of medical images demand more and more computing power. Standalone computers can hardly satisfy these computational demands.

■ Expertise constraint

Traditionally, the diagnosis and analysis of medical data are also limited by the expertise of individual physicians who might provide a different diagnosis on the same data

5.2 Opportunities Provided by Cloud Computing and 5G

■ Cloud storage

With cloud storage, massive medical and healthcare data, including medical images and EHRs can be stored on the cloud, which is not only more scalable but also more cost-effective.

■ Data sharing

Cloud computing provides data sharing via the Internet, making the sharing of healthcare data much more convenient. Furthermore, data sharing can promote the use of wearable devices, remote monitoring devices, various IoT devices, remote visualization, and remote diagnosis, empowering physicians as well as patients to store, acquire, share, and utilize medical data in a much larger extent.

■ Computing resource sharing

Cloud computing can share powerful computing resources among different entities, making deep mining and processing of the medical data possible.

■ Expertise sharing and empowering

Cloud computing not only provides sharing of expertise via remote diagnosis, but also gathers and shares intelligence via machine-learning algorithms, exposing best expertise and knowledge to a wide range of institutions.

5.3 Medical Imaging with Cloud and 5G

Medical services such as medical imaging can be significantly enhanced and transformed by cloud technologies [Kagadis 2013, Daher 2018]. Collaboration among clinical services and hospitals can be promoted by sharing medical data and images. Patient empowerment may be achieved by enabling patients to have access to their health data via cloud services. Experts with different medical backgrounds can meet in remote diagnosis and remote surgery through the cloud and 5G.

Medical imaging, as a major medical data type, due to its nature of data-intensive, storage-intensive, and computation intensive, is very appropriate as an example to introduce the importance of cloud computing and 5G technology in the medical and healthcare sector. In the following subsections, the role of cloud computing will be introduced, with medical imaging as the example.

5.3.1 Medical Image Storage

The discovery of X-ray technology by Roentgen revolutionized medicine and healthcare. The application of the X-ray in the biomedical field makes it possible to examine the interior of a live body with little harmful impacts, creating the new branch of nuclear medicine; it led healthcare into the era of medical imaging. The invention of a variety of technologies, including X-ray, ultrasonography, CT, MRI, PET, etc. profoundly enhanced the capability of medical imaging. Most of medical images acquired today by tomography devices such as CT, MRI, and PET are essentially 3D images presented with 2D slices.

The invention of digital computers heralded the era of digital images. Before the wide application of digital images, the most common media for preserving medical images are still films, which are difficult to store, carry, share, and digitalize. The advent of CT and MRI posed an extra burden by producing a large number of images in one study. Early digital storage might be tape-based, which is slow for reading and requires a large number of tapes for image archiving. The storage challenge of medical imaging is that it requires increasingly large data volumes to be preserved long term.

The digital revolution and standardization of PACS and DICOM brought medical imaging into the digital-networking era. Compared to traditional films, digital transmission, sharing, storage, and processing of medical images are much more convenient.

Compared to the common X-ray study, the storage requirements for CT and MRI medical images are more demanding since many slices are acquired in one study. Moreover, with the rapid renovation of medical-imaging techniques and devices, the space as well the time resolution of medical images has been significantly improved, leading to the considerably increased size of medical images and the demand for storage surges. In addition, multi-modal tomography study and processing is a common practice today [Tawfik et al. 2021], which means more storage is needed for medical images from the same patient.

Cloud computing is a solution of distributed computing and data interchange over the Internet. It provides a more economic and robust means for storage and sharing of medical images, satisfying the massive data storage that medical images need. It also provides services to query and access those data conveniently.

Cloud computing also makes sharing of medical images among different entities such as hospitals, physicians, and even patients possible. With reuse of medical images boosted, unnecessary imaging studies can be avoided, leading to extensive saving of time and money as well as reduction of radiation dose for patients.

To wrap up, cloud-based PACS-compatible medical-imaging solutions are more cost-effective, more convenient for storing data, and more accessible to physicians and patients. 5G-based fast data acquisition will further improve the efficiency and user experience of cloud-based storage.

5.3.2 *Medical-Image Processing*

Medical-image processing and analysis requires intensive computing power. Cloud computing provides shared computing power over the Internet, available any-where, even suitable for portable devices, home caring, and smart ambulance, achieving fast processing of large medical-image datasets.

The benefits of cloud-enabled medical image processing include:

- Cloud-based image storage: Seamless integration with cloud storage for storing massive medical-image datasets
- Cloud-based image retrieval: Medical images can be accessed, queried, re-trieved via the cloud, which encourages sharing and remote diagnosis
- Cloud-based image diagnosis: Easier access to multi-modal images, which might be important for medical image reconstruction and fusion
- Cloud-based image processing: Sharing of high-end computing power, lowering the cost of medical-image processing
- Cloud-based image analysis: Suitable for mining and deep learning of massive medical data; suitable for distributed and parallel processing algorithms
- Cloud-based intelligence: Easier access to shared data models, mature AI, and machine-learning algorithms

5.3.3 *Machine-Learning and AI*

Medical-image analysis, including segmentation, registration, classification, re-construction, and visualization, is heavily dependent on machine-learning and AI algorithms. Intelligent medical-image processing and analysis is the future as it replaces human expertise with machine intelligence. The wide application of AI, together with cloud computing and 5G, may significantly change the future of medicine and healthcare [Alexander 2019].

AI algorithms are typically data and computing intensive. In recent years, the popular topic in AI is deep learning, whose application on medical-imaging processing has been studied by many researchers [Singh 2020]. Since most medical-image data are essentially 3D, the widely used deep-learning models for medical-image segmentation, registration, and classification are 3D deep-learning models, which are more data and computing intensive. Deep learning needs to leverage massive datasets to infer a convincing model, which makes them very suitable for cloud-storage platforms. Moreover, deep learning requires high-end GPU computing powers, which make them suitable for GPU clouds. With decreased storage and computational costs via the cloud available, it has become more accessible to analyze 3D medical images using 3D deep-learning with the cloud. In addition, with the help of the cloud, integrated data mining of imaging data, EHR data, and even data from wearable devices is made possible, which might produce better mining results and new insights.

5.3.4 Visualization and Virtual Reality (VR)/Augmented Reality (AR)

The result of medical-image analysis needs to be presented by medical-image visualization. Medical-image analysis and visualization inherently are analysis and visualization of human or other biological tissues and structures. Medical imaging represents 3D spatial structures by a series of 2D images; radiologists traditionally reconstruct the 3D anatomies in their mind. However, with the advancement of VR and AR technologies, as well as the revolutionary advances in graphics capabilities, realistic 3D scenes can be rendered in real time, which boost 3D medical applications.

Cloud computing and 5G play critical roles in medical VR/AR applications since fast access to data and fast processing of the data can utilize the cloud and 5G technologies. On the one hand, the reconstruction and visualization time can be reduced or even achieved in real time. On the other hand, the data can be transmitted to the end user much more quickly, which makes interactive or even real-time visualization possible. With the empowerment of the cloud and 5G, the technology trend will move more medical-image visualization capabilities to the remote ends, even to portable devices, freeing them from location and computing constraints.

5.4 The Impacts of 5G on Cloud Computing

5G, when coupled with cloud computing, is capable of transforming the cloud, propelling the operational efficiency of the cloud and accommodating more interactive applications [Moyers 2020]. Some of the major impacts of 5G on cloud computing are listed below:

■ Promoting cloud efficiency, accessibility, scalability, and usability

Faster data transfer with 5G network increases the data efficiency and data size managed by the cloud. Faster accessing of medical and healthcare data from much larger databases could be achieved. Data access time will be significantly reduced, enhancing the usability of cloud-based applications.

■ Promoting use of mobile devices and IoT devices

Faster data transfer, low data latency, better scalability, and pervasive clouds promote the use of mobile devices and IoT devices. More medical mobile devices and sensors could be used in and out hospitals, enabling remote monitoring, remote diagnosis, and home care.

■ Promotes interactive cloud applications

Faster data transfer and low data latency reduce data-retrieval time and improve responsiveness and interactivity of applications. This may stimulate more interactive cloud-based applications. Remote and mobile medical and healthcare applications, including VR/AR applications, may benefit from this improvement.

■ Promoting data analytics on the cloud

Big-data-based data mining and deep learning requires access to large volumes of data and huge computing power. Faster data access and a more scalable data cloud support mining and learning based on larger datasets. Better responsiveness means the results of data analysis can be presented and interacted in a quicker way. Within the domain of medical and health data analytics, this responsiveness will promote remote and interactive data analytics applications backed by the cloud.

5.5 5G in Healthcare

5.5.1 5G in Healthcare Applications with High Processing Requirements

Healthcare applications often include remote diagnosis and intervention, long-term monitoring using sensors for chronic diseases, remote surgery, and homecare with robots. The driving technologies for these applications include, but not limited to: monitoring devices, robotics, virtual/augmented reality, AI technologies, and data analysis. Here we summarise a few applications that demand intensive computations, where the high data rate and low latency ensured by 5G may contribute significantly. In addition, the flexibility brought by 5G also enriches the possibilities and coverage of the services.

■ Robotics – Robots are widely used in healthcare, at home or in the hospital. In [Voigtländer 2017], the authors proposed an approach allowing off-loading of time critical, computational-exhaustive operations onto a cloud server. uRLLC slice is used for the communication between the robot and the cloud server.

■ Image processing plays an important role in remote surgery where intensive computations and highly availability of resources are essential for achieving the required spontaneous services. Authors in [Schmoll 2018] demoed a VR game with the capability to migrate game servers across the world with uninterrupt service.

■ Authors in [Healy 2017] provided AI-assisted detections to first responders of medical emergency services. The system is capable of detecting a patient's demeanour on the scene of an incident using an Intel RealSense camera system. The authors demonstrated the system in a lab setting with 5G mobile-edge node.

5.5.2 Benefit of 5G to Healthcare Applications

5G Trends [2020] summarizes the benefits that brought by 5G in various sectors, Table 5.1 lists benefits to the healthcare sector.

The indicative list in Table 5.2 is a compilation of key 5G features summarised by 5G PPP from a number of funded projects. The table lists a snapshot of the most important 5G features.

5.5.3 An Example Application

VIAPA [2019] presents a hybrid operating room equipped with advanced imaging systems, such as fixed C-arms (X-ray generator and intensifiers), CT scanners (computer tomography) and MR scanners (magnetic resonance). Below are some requirements:

Table 5.1 Benefit Examples Drawn from Verticals Sector – Healthcare (Contents Retrieved from [5G Trends 2020])

Benefit categories	Benefit examples drawn from verticals
Society critical	Enable fully and connected digitized emergency ambulance operations, ambulance teleguidance, ambulance routing; Save lives through, e.g., smart wearables; Life-saving applications, e.g., wireless operating room calling on remote experts; video application for health purposes.
Quality increase	Smart wearables for health monitoring, emergency localization, and secure access to patient records

Table 5.2 Demonstrated and Planned 5G Functionalities in Verticals (Adapted from [5G Trends 2020], Authors Filled with Their Own Contents)

5G features	Healthcare
Network slicing	Four types of network slices have been specified by 3GPP so far, namely eMBB, URLLC, mMTC, and Vehicle-to-Everything (V2X) services. up to 256 such slice types can be allocated in the current 3GPP Release 16 specification.
Mobile edge computing	High intensive computation demand for imaging process, AI, AR/VR, etc will be processed at the edge that close to the applications. It reduces the transmission time. In addition, edge node provides better computation and memory facilities.
Smart network management	Splitting of control plane and data plane ensures that the network resources can be better controlled at the control plane. In addition, intelligence can be applied to manage the network resources. With the smart management, the applications can be delivered based on Quality of Service (QoS) requirements. providing automated mechanisms that will allow the fast and easy deployment of network slices along with the necessary network and computing resources, their dynamic adaptation during the lifetime of a service, and their eventual release when these are no longer needed.
Location services & context awareness	Identifying exact location is one example for context awareness. This is essential for some healthcare applications, for example, ambulance services or response to call from home care. High-accuracy localization not only fulfils the demanding QoS of 5G and beyond 5G, but also enhances the intelligence of user applications.
5G NR capabilities	With the new radio technologies, the access method of the 5G terminals for healthcare will be enhanced.

(*Continued*)

Table 5.2 (Continued) Demonstrated and Planned 5G Functionalities in Verticals (Adapted from [5G Trends 2020], Authors Filled with Their Own Contents)

5G features	Healthcare
Softwarization	Softwarization enables flexible management of network resources. It de-couples the network functions from its hardware, removes impact for hardware changes to the applications, and shortens the time taken for deployment of an application. It eases the network resources and management.
Service chaining	The service chain concept composes and imposes the order in which service functions are invoked for a particular service. SDN and VNF support the dynamic creation and management of service function chaining. It enables to efficiently utilise the network resources, to meet requirement for healthcare application, where heavy computations are needed, such as in the imaging processing.
Guaranteed QoS	Quality of Service needs to be guaranteed for various application requirements, such as requirement for low latency, large data rate, or real time. Healthcare is no different froms other applications, and therefore, QoS requirements needs to be met.

■ Ultra-high resolution video: generated by endoscopes that produce up to 8K uncompressed (or compressed without quality loss) video. It supports high dynamic range (HDR) for larger colour gamut management (up to 10 bits per channel), as well as high frame rate (HFR), i.e., up to 120 frame per second. The graphics allow surgeons to distinguish small details like thin vessels and avoid any artefacts that could potentially induce surgeons to make wrong decisions.

■ 2D ultrasound images: 2D ultrasound requires data rate of 160 Mbit/s up to 500 Mbit/s. The data stream includes uncompressed images of 512 × 512 pixels with 32 bits per pixel at 20 fps (up to 60 fps in the fastest cases).

■ 3D ultrasound volumes: dedicated 3D probes requires higher data rates, i.e., above 1 gbit/s of raw data, and are expected to reach multi gigabit data rates in the future. That is 3D Cartesian volumes of 256 × 256 × 256 voxels, each encoded with 24 bits at 10 volumes per second.

■ CT/MR scans: images can range from a resolution of 1024 × 2024 to 3000 × 3000 pixels where higher resolutions are used for diagnosis purpose and lower ones are more suitable to fluoroscopy. The frame rate is typically at 5 to 30 frames per second. Higher rates are possible to monitor moving organs in real time.

Research and trials are undertaken to identify and measure the performance KPIs when 5G supports different applications. Clause 7.5 of 3GPP TS 22.261 [5G Service 2019] listed performance requirements for highly reliable machine-type communication, which is fundation of tele-diagnosis or tele-monitoring systems.

5.6 Introduction to 5G Technology

Having discussed healthcare applications empowered by 5G, we now move on to discuss the networking environment where the application, which, equipped with image-processing functions, will be deployed. Medical application is a generic term covering medical devices and applications involved in the delivery of care to patients [VIAPA 2019]. The applications will be used in a hospital, home, and on the run (e.g., ambulance).

5G mobile communication has been deployed since 2020. One of the features of 5G is its seamlessly merging with the cloud infrastructure and technology. The typical features of 5G are fast data transmission rates and ultra-low latency compared to the previous generations of the mobile communications. In some medical applications, such as remote surgery and ambulance services, real-time imaging processing is required. In remote surgery, a real and virtual combined environment, where human-machine interaction generates realistic experiences, robots obtain and handle information on behalf of humans. Mobility introduced by mobile communication added an extra benefit to such applications. And high bandwidth and low latency brought by 5G ensure that KPIs for such applications can be guaranteed.

In the next sessions, the architecture and features of 5G and their connections with medical and healthcare applications are introduced in detail.

5.7 Software Defined Network in 5G

The technology used for network slice deployment is network functional virtualization (NFV), supported by a software defined network (SDN). NFV consists of the network functions that form a slice or a service to be implemented as virtual network functions. Network function virtualization replaces network functions provided by dedicated hardware elements, such as routers, load balancers, and firewalls, with virtualized instances running as software on commercial off-the-shelf hardware. NFV transforms the way networks are built and services are delivered. With NFV, a wide array of network functions is simplified and efficiencies are maximized. As a result, introducing new revenue-generating services is faster and easier than ever before. NFV is a key enabler of the 5G infrastructure. NFV enables network slicing, a virtual network architecture that allows multiple virtual networks to be created atop a shared physical infrastructure. The virtual networks can then be customized to meet the Quality of Service (QoS) needs of applications, services, devices, customers, or operators. NFV enables the distributed cloud and helps to create flexible and programmable networks for the needs of future mobile communications. NFV applies to entire 5G networks, including core networks, radio access networks (RAN), and network management systems [NetVirtual 2017].

Different types of virtualization technologies based on full virtual machine (VM) implementations can be adopted in 5G. NFV softwarization also covers all the requirements of 5G networks and has already been used in coexistence with full VMs and container-based virtualization. These three technologies: full VMs, containers, and Unikernels, with different properties, may coexist in the same infrastructure and may be chosen opportunistically depending on the requirements of the scenarios and workloads.

The infrastructure of the 5G networks is based on SDN. It provides the communication between the applications and services in the cloud and the mobile terminal. Therefore, the network benefits from resource virtualization, and it can be managed dynamically and in real time. The concept of SDN-based connectivity between virtualized network functions (VNFs) enables multidimensional carrier-grade communication paths without utilizing of tunneling protocols. The main idea of introducing SDN is to separate the control plane from the data plane and enable external control of data through a logical software component called the controller. As a result, network hardware, such as switches and routers, behaves as simple forwarding devices without the ability to make routing decisions. Separating control plane and data plane can be achieved by a well-defined programming interface between the switches and the SDN controller.

With 5G being actively researched and worked on by the WGs and TSGs from different standardization bodies, it promises to provide more than just high-speed Internet. Release 16 in 2020 by 3GPP addresses the standardization of 5G [ETSI 2017]. For this reason, three types of network slices have been specified by 3GPP so far, they are: eMBB, URLLC, and mMTC services. Up to 256 such slice types can be allocated in the 3GPP release 16 specification [NFV 2017]. mMTC is introduced to support massive machine-type communication, where currently, pervasive human-centric applications dominate the market. Autonomously communicating devices will create mobile traffic that significantly differs in characters compared to the human-to-human traffic. The coexistence of human-centric and machine-type applications will impose diverse functional and KPI/performance requirements that 5G networks will have to support.

5G defined the following types of slices:

- eMBB (enhanced Mobile Broadband) slicing is for applications that demand high speed, such as augmented reality, high quality video, and real-time video services. To meet the high bandwidth requirement, caching can be deployed in the mobile cloud engine of a local data center to ensure high-speed services located in close proximity to users; therefore, bandwidth requirements are reduced from the backbone networks.
- URLLC (ultra reliable low latency communications) slicing is for applications that demand strict latency, such as self-driving, assisted driving, and remote management. RAN real-time and non-real-time processing function units must be deployed onsite to reduce latency.
- mMTC (massive machine-type communications) slicing is for applications that involve a small amount of network data interaction and a low frequency of signaling interaction. These services include: IoT applications, such as smart meters.

5.8 5G Architecture

5G standization is still in progress, and deployment is in its very early stage. So-called vertical application is at early stage of development. The healthcare application is regarded as one of the vertical applications that will potentially benefit from 5G technologies. The actual function and scenario are yet to be defined. However, medical-imaging processing, assisted by AI algorithms, will certainly be needed in healthcare applications.

5G system architecture, defined by ETSI [5GS 2020], supports data connectivity and services to deployments using techniques such as NFV and SDN. The architecture is designed with the key principles and concepts. Here are some of them [5GS 2020]:

- Separate the user plane and control plane functions, which allows the planes to independently scale and evolve, and ensures flexible deployment;
- Modularize the function design to enable flexible and efficient network slicing;
- Minimize dependencies between the access network (AN) and the core network (CN);
- Support a unified authentication framework

5.8.1 Logical Structure of 5G

Figure 5.1 illustrates 5G network functions from the viewpoint of the logical and physical network softwarization and programmability.

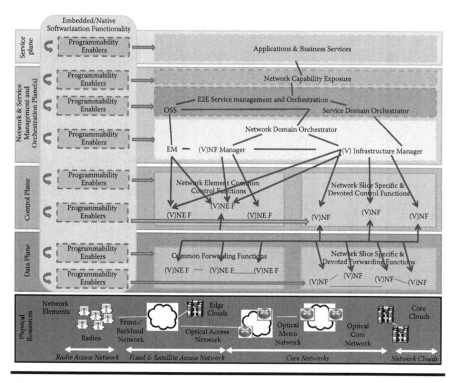

Figure 5.1 5G Logical and Physical Network Softwarisation and Programmability Viewpoint (Adapted from [5G PPP 2017]).

- The physical resources layer consists of the underlying hardware facilities. The multi-domain network operating system facilities include different adaptors and network abstractions. This system is responsible for allocation of (virtual) network resources and maintaining network state to ensure network reliability in a multi-domain environment.
- The data-plane layer comprises VNFs and physical network functions (PNFs); it carries and processes the user data traffic.
- The control-plane layer accommodates the two main controllers, software defined for mobile network coordination (SDM-X) and software defined for mobile network control (SDM-C), as well as other control applications. Following the SDN principles, SDM-X and SDM-C translate decisions of the control applications into commands to VNFs and PNFs. SDM-X, SDM-C, and other control applications can be executed as VNFs or PNFs by themselves.
- Management and orchestration (MANO) plane(s) manage(s) the virtual resources based on the QoS requirements of each application. MANO is also responsible for slice orchestration and re-claims the slices when they are no longer needed by the allocated services. ETSI NFV MANO functions include virtualized infrastructure manager (VIM), VNF manager, and the NFV

orchestrator (NFVO). An inter-slice broker handles cross-slice resource allocation and interacts with the service management function. The MANO layer also accommodates domain-specific application management functions, element managers (EM), and network management (NM) functions. Those functions would also implement ETSI NFV MANO interfaces to the VNF manager and the NFVO.

■ The service plane layer comprises business support systems (BSSs) and business-level policy and decision functions. It supports applications and services operated by the tenant. This includes the end-to-end orchestration system.

5.8.2 Slicing and Integrating with Broadband

Network slice applies at different part of the network, as shown in Figure 5.2, to handle diverse vertical requirements. In Figure 5.2, the slices are also mapped to the core network, transport network, and access network, respectively.

In addition to the slice type, each network slice is further categorized via a slice differentiator to widen the support for different vertical applications. These network slices are essentially logical networks operating on top of the same physical infrastructure. Network slices may operate in total isolation among themselves or they may share resources and network functions. A vertical service may require one or more network slices, which may be controlled or operated by more than one a mobile network operator and the vertical application provider.

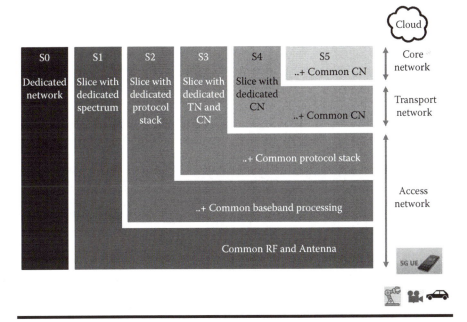

Figure 5.2 Different Types of Slicing (Adapted from [Slicing 2017]).

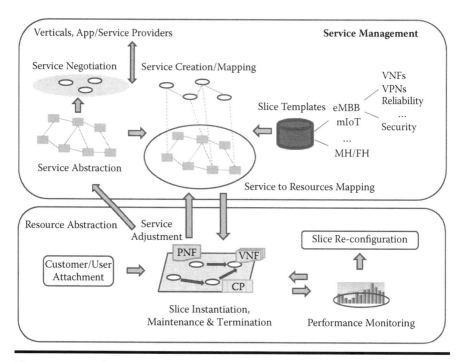

Figure 5.3 Service Management (Adapted from [ZSM 2020]).

From the end-to-end perspective, transport network slicing management needs to be integrated with broadband network services. Transport network slicing is a fundamental enabler for migrating the multi-service broadband network (MSBN) from "one architecture fits all" to the "network per service." The transport network slicing is clarified into three types: the network service as a service focusing on fixed networks, supporting 5G-related 3GPP-use cases, and slicing across fixed-mobile converged networks. As shown in Figure 5.3, service management and network slice control supported by MSBN require a continuous process of analyzing the service requirements and assuring the desired performance, even when the conditions of the network change or the requirements from the customer perspective evolve with time. Combining the network slice management with the service management as transport management domain provides capabilities such as service abstraction, service negotiation, service operations, service adjustment, and service template-to-vertical applications, application/service providers, and third parties for end-to-end service management.

5.9 Edge Computing

Edge computing brings content and computing resources closer to the users, reducing latency and load on the backhaul [ETSI MEC 2015]. In edge computing, a data centre is placed at the edge of the Internet, close to mobile devices, sensors, and end users. Increased networking capabilities of 5G potentially strengthened the connections between the edge devices and the data centres in cloud.

In the case of smart ambulance, the equipment act as edge computer within each car handles real-time processing, such as safely navigating intersections. However, some decisions require cloud-based information, navigation decisions, and route-planning; they will be originated and executed in the cloud. Carefully allocating computations to the edge and the cloud and efficiently communicating between the edge and the cloud are essential in achieving the best performance.

In the home-care application, smart apps and connected apps are used. The applications often require instant communication and connection with data analytic mechanisms for real-time decision making. When critical actions are being completed by these types of smart apps, latency needs to be as low as possible to minimize machine error. Edge computing brings processing closer to the user (or device), and hence, reduces delay caused by transmission.

Due to limitation on the computing resources of the terminal, even in the case of robotics embedded with powerful computation facilities, when intensive training is needed, a common practice is to offload the tasks to computing systems with sufficient computing resources, i.e., data centers in the cloud. However, the drawbacks of offloading are that it incurs high latency and network congestion in the IoT infrastructures. In this case, edge computing appears as an appealing solution.

5.10 Conclusion

As an enabling technology for sharing data and computing power, the cloud has brought significant changes to many industries, including the medical and healthcare sector. With 5G on the horizon, ultra-fast and low-latency data transmission on the cloud and via the Internet will enable more intelligent and interactive medical and health applications. This chapter presents a survey of 5G technologies and their related applications in medicine and healthcare in the background of cloud computing. 5G will transform traditional cloud computing to allow larger data volume to be accessed quicker and easier for medical and healthcare applications. Use of mobile devices and IoT devices will be encouraged by 5G technologies, and interactive applications will become more prevalent. Furthermore, medical analytics based on data mining and deep learning will also benefit from 5G-powered clouds. For future medicare services, 5G may not only mean faster data retrieval and larger data storage, but it might also revolutionize the whole Medicare industry by distributing more reliable Medicare services via 5G-powered clouds, decentralizing traditional roles of hospitals and physicians. Community-based and patient-oriented medical services might benefit from 5G-powered remote diagnosis and IoT sensors. More accurate analysis and diagnosis can be achieved with larger datasets and better computing power. To conclude,

5G-powered clouds will be one of the most important driving forces for transforming the Medicare industry in the coming years.

References

Alan Alexander, Megan McGill, Anna Tarasova, Cara Ferreira, Delphine Zurkiya, 'Scanning the Future of Medical Imaging', *Journal of the American College of Radiology*, 16(4), 2019, 501–507.

Empowering Vertical Industries through 5G Networks; Current Status and Future Trends, V1.0, 5G PPP Technology Board & 5G IA Verticals Task Force, August, 2020.

ETSI, 'Mobile Edge Computing a Key Technology towards 5G', ETSI White paper No. 11, September, 2015, available: http://www.etsi.org/images/files/ETSIWhitePapers/etsi_wp11_mec_a_key_technology_towards_5g.pdf

ETSI, Mobile Edge Computing; Market Acceleration; MEC Metrics Best Practice and Guidelines, ETSI GS MEC-IEG 006 V1.1.1, 2017-01.

ETSI TS 123 501 V16.6.0, 5G; System architecture for the 5G System (5GS), (3GPP TS 23.501 version 16.6.0 Release 16), 2020.

Gábor Fodor, Nandana Rajatheva, Wolfgang Zirwas, Lars Thiele, Martin Kurras, Kaifeng Guo, Antti Tölli, Jesper H. Sørensen, and Elisabeth de Carvalho, 'An Overview of Massive MIMO Technology Components in METIS', *IEEE Communications Magazine*, 55(6), 2017, 155–161.

George C. Kagadis, Christos Kloukinas, Kevin Moore, Jim Philbin, Panagiotis Papadimitroulas, Christos Alexakos, Paul G. Nagy, Dimitris Visvikis, William R. Hendee, 'Cloud Computing in Medical Imaging', *Medical Physics*, 40(7), 2013.

Healy, M., Walsh, P. 'Detecting Demeanor for Healthcare with Machine Learning', Proceedings of IEEE International Conference on Bioinformatics and Biomedicine (BIBM), 2017, Kansas City, USA.

IEEE 5G and beyond Technology Roadmap White paper, https://futurenetworks.ieee.org/roadmap

Martin Moyers, Impact of 5G on the Cloud Computing World, 2020, https://www.colocationamerica.com/blog/imapct-of-5g-on-cloud-computing

Nadim Michel Daher, 'Cloud Computing in Medical Imaging: Not a Matter of if, but When', 2018, https://www.openaccessgovernment.org/43155-2/43155/

Nahed Tawfik, Heba A. Elnemr, Mahmoud Fakhr, Moawad I. Dessouky, Fathi E. Abd El-Samie, 'Survey Study of Multimodality Medical Image Fusion Methods', *Multimedia Tools and Applications*, 80, 2021, 6369–6396.

Network Functions Virtualisation White Paper on NFV Priorities for 5G, http://portal.etsi.org/NFV/NFV_White_Paper_5G.pdf, February 21, 2017.

Prepared by GSA with contributions from Ericsson, Huawei and Nokia; 5G Network Slicing for Vertical Industries, September, 2017.

Schmoll, R., Pandi, S., Patrik, J., Braun, P. J., Fitzek, F. 'Demonstration of VR/AR off-loading to Mobile Edge Cloud for low latency 5G gaming application', Proceedings of 15th IEEE Annual Consumer Communications & Networking Conference (CCNC), January, 2018, Las Vegas, USA.

Satya P. Singh, Lipo Wang, Sukrit Gupta, Haveesh Goli, Parasuraman Padmanabhan, Balázs Gulyás, '3D Deep Learning on Medical Images: A Review', *Sensors*, 20(18), 2020, 5097.

3GPP TS 22.261 V18.0.0, Service requirements for the 5G system; Stage 1 (Release 18), 2019.

3GPP TS 22.263 V1.0.0, Services and System Aspects; Service requirements for Video, Imaging and Audio for Professional Applications (VIAPA); STAGE 1, (Release 17), 2019.

View on 5G Architecture (Version 2.0); 5G PPP Architecture Working Group, July, 2017.

Voigtländer, F., Ramadan, A., Eichinger, J., Lenz, C., Pensky, D., Knoll, A. '5G for Robotics: Ultra-Low Latency Control of Distributed Robotic Systems', Proceedings of 2017 International Symposium on Computer Science and Intelligent Controls, 2017, Budapest, Hungary.

Zero-touch network and Service Management (ZSM); Landscape, ETSI GR ZSM 004 V1.1.1, March, 2020.

Chapter 6

The Application of Cloud-Computing Technology to Improve Patients' Medical History Access to Clinicians for Quality of Care in the Fourth Industrial Revolution

Ngoako Solomon Marutha

Department of Information Science, University of South Africa, Pretoria, South Africa

Contents

6.1 Introduction and Background 112
6.2 Cloud-Computing Technology and Healthcare Services 113
6.3 Problem Statement 117
6.4 Purpose and Objective of the Study 118
6.5 Methodology 118

DOI: 10.1201/9781003145189-6

111

6.6 Discussion and Recommendations...119
  6.6.1 Proposed Framework...120
6.7 Concluding Remarks 122
References 122

6.1 Introduction and Background

Access and sharing of patients' health and medical history in and among the healthcare facilities is still a dream for another day in Africa and across the world. In the public healthcare facilities, the situation is far worse due to a resistance in the adoption and application of the latest technologies, such as cloud computing. "Technological advancements have brought about dramatic changes to the management and disposition of records since cloud computing emerged" (Shibambu & Marutha 2021). Cloud-computing technologies offer many innovations, including ease of access to, and sharing of, patients' information. "Cloud computing is widely used in various healthcare institutions, facilitating decision-making and communication on various levels" (Intellectsoft US 2021). In the current circumstances, healthcare facilities across the world are functioning in silos without sharing patients' healthcare and medical history; even though they have the same patients in service delivery. In African countries, the situation is far worse. The different facilities rendering healthcare services to the same citizens have no means of sharing their patients' information with each other when patients attend various healthcare facilities to receive different healthcare services. This lack of sharing applies to public healthcare facilities and private healthcare facilities. Healthcare service is not like a vehicle dealership where a vehicle may be serviced without perusing its prior service history because there are no implications in this situation. Instead, for the healthcare service to be rendered, without keeping abreast of the health and clinical history of the patient, a very serious health risk may be posed, one that may even result in death or critical implications for the patient. The absence of a patient's medical and health history is a very serious health-threatening risk.

A key problem in Africa, especially in the Sub-Saharan countries, is that records management is still operated manually in a paper-based format and medium. Although everything has advantages and disadvantages, manual records creation and management have not had much or significant advantages as compared to the electronically created and managed records in a digital form and medium. Some of the key advantages of electronic records management are that records may be accessed in a matter of seconds, and the same records may be accessed and used by an unlimited number of users at the same time. Maintenance of the electronic records storage and systems may be costly yet very simple, in comparison to manual paper-based records storage maintenance. The electronic records storage upgrade may also be simple and easy but involves a significant amount of money.

Imagine a situation in a country where records in different healthcare facilities are created and managed manually in a paper-based format. These facilities must share the health and medical history of each patient as the patient moves from facility to facility for consultation. If the sharing of patients' records is a priority for such facilities, it will mean they will need to employ the service of vehicles and drivers moving around different facilities with files. The time spent on such activities would be significant, and the turnaround time for clinicians to access patients' information would also be significant. This may be much more time consuming as compared to sharing patients' information on a network in a matter of seconds when electronic records are managed using the appropriate technological systems, such as cloud computing. This topic has resulted in this study to investigate a framework for the application of cloud-computing technology to improve patients' medical history access for clinicians to ensure quality of care in the fourth industrial revolution.

6.2 Cloud-Computing Technology and Healthcare Services

Cloud computing is a technology that makes records accessible to users for different business purposes on a network over the Internet by ensuring that the records stored are maintained, backed up, and remotely available to users at all times (Neelima & Padma 2014). This implies that users can access and store records remotely using the latest technology on gadgets such as smartphones, tablets, and laptops with compatible Internet applications. Shibambu and Marutha (2021) underscore that cloud computing is "storing data with a cloud service provider rather than on local systems such as an external hard drive, a compact disc and many more." Cloud computing may be used to serve as a central repository in which facilities store and share their records (Marutha 2016). To ensure proper control over the records stored on the cloud, organisations or governments will need to have a clear policy guideline that govern storage, security, and access to such records (Decman & Vintar 2013; Marutha 2016). Decman and Vintar (2013) further underscore that the organisation must be ready to spend to see a successful implementation of cloud-computing technology that comes with more advantages. They further elaborate that the policy for the management of cloud computing will need to be informed by legislation and international standards. Implementation has a high need for hardware and software that is standardised across the facilities involved in sharing to ensure interoperability and compatibility (Asogwa 2012:206; Decman & Vintar 2013:418). Cloud computing provides for a technological solution that is centralised in the preservation, management, archiving, access, and sharing of digital records (Decman & Vintar 2013). They further underscore that cloud computing connected to the latest technological solution may enable access to, and the sharing of, patients' information through smartphones, tablets, or laptops at any time and place where clinicians find themselves needing to render service to specific patients. This ability implies that with this nature of technology, healthcare providers may be able to move around helping patients at their homes or within hospital wards and clinics carrying only a smartphone or tablet. These devices can be enabled with applicable applications for creating and capturing recent patients' records and be used to access previous health and medical history records of patients.

In order to share patient records through cloud computing with ease, healthcare facilities will need to meet certain key requirements pertaining to the system operated in their facilities for patients' administration and record-keeping. For instance, healthcare facilities will have to agree to use common electronic records management systems for interoperability (Decman & Vintar 2013:415). In the event that facilities form a consortium for cloud-computing development or subscription, it may bring further benefits, such as cost effectiveness in terms of technology, a reduction or the elimination of record duplications across the facilities, and support service staff (Decman & Vintar 2013:415). In case the facilities belong to government, there should be a support structure made up of technical expert staff across the country to attend to problems and system challenges at a facility levels. The funding for hardware and software may also come from the national level of government to ensure successful implementations. Cloud-computing technology will "ensure that all healthcare institutions are able to access the medical records for each patient wherever and whenever they attend to patients' illnesses" (Marutha 2016).

Cognizant (2021) underscore that "cloud infrastructure powers provisioning and virtual workstations in the cloud, enable developers to deploy resources quickly and work remotely." Cloud computing is even more relevant and provides further advantages during the current COVID-19 pandemic, where most countries introduced a robust lockdown requiring people to stay indoors to curb the spread of the virus, enabling medical practitioners to operate remotely without the necessity of assistance from any other colleagues. Intellectsoft US (2021) add that "cloud computing is one of the leading trends in digital transformation for 2021." They further state that with the cloud-computing technology, supplying companies like "IBM, Dell and Iron Mountains" are also dominated, especially now with the rise of the coronavirus pandemic to enable healthcare facilities to operate virtually with ease and lower costs. Cloud-computing technology enables the building of an ecosystem that is self-sufficient and cost-effective (Intellectsoft US 2021). "Cloud computing creates shared hardware accessed through a network connection, applicable for various healthcare purposes" (Intellectsoft US 2021). Intellectsoft US (2021) further elaborates that

> ... *healthcare practitioners mostly apply cloud computing to communication, decision-making, and forecasting. The technology can create an entire IT infrastructure that unites hospitals, patients, insurance companies, and R&D centers inside a sole informative ecosystem.*

According to Intellectsoft US (2021), cloud computing may be implemented following two alternative models in the healthcare fraternity. The two models are the distribution model, which considers hardware and software; and the deployment model, which considers ownership of the cloud. The distribution model provides three technological things as a service, namely: software, infrastructure, and platform. Regarding "Software as a Service," the cloud service provider offers information-technology infrastructure and the healthcare facilities provide their own applications and operating system. Regarding "Infrastructure as a Service" the cloud service provider offers the information-technology infrastructure and operating system; then the healthcare facilities as the clients provide only the applications for the system to kick-start. In the case of "Platform as a Service" the cloud service provider supplies everything including information-technology infrastructure, the operating system, and the applications to make the system ready for use; the healthcare facility just starts with operation to use the system (Intellectsoft US 2021).

Furthermore, the development model is made up of four elements or options: private, community, public, and hybrid. The application of a private cloud involves one organisation operating on the platform with its own branches and divisions. Community cloud computing is suitable for a group of organisations with a common modus operandi, interest, objectives, and vision. This may be a form of consortia in the same subject area as healthcare service institutions in both private and public such as hospitals, clinics, pharmacies, and blood-test laboratories, to list only few. Public cloud computing may be applicable to only public institutions sharing the same interests as public hospitals, clinics, pharmacies, and blood-test laboratories, to name but a few. Hybrid cloud computing provides for a combination of different clouds for options in access. This system is like a combination of different clouds that can be centrally integrated for access by both public and private participating bodies or facilities (Intellectsoft US 2021).

Cloud computing brings about many benefits in the healthcare service sector. The empowerment of both healthcare providers, patients, and other stakeholders, with intellectual insight obtained from accurate and complete patient information, is a tremendous benefit. Cloud computing enables the healthcare providers to foresee the health risks and challenges beforehand through e-predictions for anticipated services. Multiple data-source technologies can provide meaning to a complex picture in the healthcare service to patients. Cloud-computing technology can handle big data effectively with clear data analysis. Cloud computing can reduce a significant number of medical errors by supporting clinicians with analytical information for accurate decision making and treatments. The software for cloud computing is also cost-effective as most things, including reports, are accessed automatically through analytic technology. Cloud-computing technology also brings opportunity for flexibility to the organisation since it is able to change with the passing of time as the organisation evolves to keep abreast of industry changes. The system also enables the organisations to be transparent enough, as required by most legislation in different countries, as transparency enables both clinicians and patients access to the information affecting them (Intellectsoft US 2021). In a way, this simplifies accountability too.

Nevertheless, like many other technologies, cloud computing also has its own barriers, but they are outweighed by many benefits (Shibambu & Marutha 2021). Intellectsoft US (2021) also add that there are challenges and issues pertaining to the implementation and adoption of cloud-computing technology for different organisations. Stratosphere Network (2021) and Shibambu and Marutha (2021) show that once the records are kept and managed on the cloud, cloud-service providers control the information from the organisation that created it and the entitled owners of such records; cloud systems may have some shortfalls in the provision of some of the functionalities required. This is the reason Shibambu and Marutha (2021) underscore that adopting or subscribing to cloud computing does not warrant the organisation to do away with their own local servers, hoping that all will be well with only the cloud server. Instead, local servers may still be maintained as a backup since cloud technology is still beyond the organisation's control. This will be used as a fall back in case cloud storage gives problems pertaining to information access in the future. Bandwidth also needs to be sufficient for the organisation to allow timely system response during retrieval and storage of records (Shibambu & Marutha 2021). According to Intellectsoft US (2021), other challenges include the unavailability of system specialists, limited functionalities, and security issues. There are very limited companies that deal with or may be able to satisfactorily supply cloud-computing services.

Intellectsoft US (2021) advise that even after applying cloud computing for the organisation, other technologies such as smart-connected services, artificial intelligence, and master data management technologies are still needed. Lavinski (2019) shows that cloud computing comes with some risks to the organisation, such as data confidentiality and security, network connectivity that may be very low, problems that are very technical, compliance to local or national legislation, vulnerability, and total Internet dependency. For instance, Intellectsoft US (2021) shows that in the healthcare sector, wireless networks may lead to cyberattack and the hacking of patients' important information that may also identify them, including personal or demographic information, treatments, diagnosis, banking details, and so forth. This is the reason there is still great concern pertaining to wireless systems and remote access to information in the healthcare industry. Security is one of the major challenges in the wireless network environment, healthcare fraternity not exclusive (Intellectsoft US 2021).

There is no problem that does not have a solution. Solutions can start with the regulation of access and use by introducing legislation and policies, coupled with different types of technical security measures. For instance, Ngoepe and Saurombe (2016) and Jackson and Shelly (2012) advise that records and information stored and preserved on the network platform require regulation by adhering to legislation and policies that impose mandates and obligations on people involved to discharge functions in a proper manner, as required by the organisation. Shibambu and Marutha (2021) underscore that legislation, policies, and procedures may help the organisations involved with a strategy and the strength to enforce common or uniform practice in their modus operandi.

In addition, cloud computing has more advantages than disadvantages, namely, to swiftly support healthcare facilities' missions for quality patient care, provide for a community of healthcare providers that are smart in rendering their services to clients, and ensure reliable intervention to challenges through the network established through the system (Intellectsoft US 2021). Stratosphere Network (2021) add that cloud computing is not difficult to implement because users are able to retrieve and access data at any time and whenever they may be finding themselves needing information to discharge their day-to-day responsibilities. They further attest that with cloud computing, the organisation does not need to acquire any hardware; instead, they may own a local server as a backup for their data on the cloud. It also offers measurable and controllable costs per user and is flexible for upgrade to higher or lower levels through enhancements (Stratosphere Network 2021).

Since cloud-computing technology relies on an international network, clients may be able to access their organisational information or records from any place outside the organisational premises across the world (Galloway 2013). With cloud computing, people can work virtually or remotely across the globe storing, accessing, and sharing the common information for discussion, decision making, and problem solving (Shibambu & Marutha 2021). This may be an ideal system for healthcare providers operating at different healthcare facilities assisting same patient or patients with common healthcare problems or even communicating challenges and solutions for communicable illness outbreak purposes. For instance, Intellectsoft US (2021) attest that cloud-computing technology also provides the advantage of communicating timely about communicable diseases across scattered communities in their sphere of influence. Shibambu and Marutha (2021) shows that "many cloud consumers are sharing a disc that has been partitioned by the cloud service provider with an intention to save costs."

Overall, the success in the implementation of cloud computing relies considerably on organisations and stakeholders that are unified and gives a dedicated time and effort to work on the system until it meets their common needs and is ready for implementation or rollout. To maximise benefit from the cloud-computing end product with ease, healthcare facilities will need to work on a common methodology and plan for development and implementation. The healthcare institutions will also need to deploy reputable and professional organisations with expertise, skills, and experience for the development of effective and efficient cloud-computing systems and technology (Intellectsoft US 2021).

6.3 Problem Statement

In different healthcare facilities across the world, clinicians and healthcare providers render different healthcare services to the same patients without any knowledge or information about treatments, diagnosis, or prescriptions rendered to these patients by their previous practitioners. The current practice is that each facility creates and keeps medical and health records that contain patients' health and medical history at their respective facilities without sharing the information. The purpose of keeping these records is to ensure that when the patient returns for further healthcare, healthcare practitioners will be able to refer back to previous records regarding treatments and illnesses. This access helps the practitioner understand the implication of the current treatment in terms of risks by considering the previous treatment. The problem is that each facility is only able to check a patient's medical history pertaining to treatments administered at their own facilities and not treatments administered at previous facilities, which may place the patient at risk. The main cause may be due to a lack of collaborative strategies and systems that enable all facilities to share information about a patient's medical history in the course of discharging their duties to the same patient. This kind of system may also help the healthcare fraternity to collaborate and provide a benchmark as some may have expertise that others do not. Again, the practitioners may also be able to communicate with each using the system enabled by cloud computing about the previous critical service rendered. This will guide the current doctor in terms of what to do and what to prescribe to patient.

6.4 Purpose and Objective of the Study

The purpose of the study was to investigate a framework for the application of the cloud-computing technology to improve patients' medical history access for clinicians to provide quality of care in the fourth industrial revolution. The objective of the study was:

- to propose a framework for the application of cloud-computing technology to improve patients' medical history access to clinicians for quality of care in the fourth industrial revolution.

6.5 Methodology

This qualitative study applied the literature to investigate a framework for the application of cloud-computing technology to improve patients' medical history access to clinicians for quality of care in the fourth industrial revolution. During the study, the literature was searched using the keywords from the title of the study using the Google search engine. The Google search engine then would take the researcher to the appropriates site hosting required articles. The keywords used include: *cloud computing, technology, patients' records, healthcare quality, medical history, clinicians, and fourth industrial revolution*. This enabled the researcher to limit the searches to specific subject areas. The Google search engine provided the results in summary and titles of articles, so the researcher was able to analyse each summary to determine its relevancy before opening any of the documents. Once the summary showed that the article may contain the information addressing issues in the study, it was opened and reviewed, and cited in the article discussion. The researcher went through all the summaries until reaching the saturation.

6.6 Discussion and Recommendations

In the healthcare facilities, a patient's medical and health history plays a very important role in enabling the quality of patient care for the healthcare service providers. The fact of the matter is that should the patient be treated without reference to their medical history, then the possibility exists that the incorrect treatment or prescription may be administered. This may affect the health and life of the patient negatively since some treatments may result in certain implications for the patients. In addition, certain medical prescriptions may also end up giving patients some side effects if unnecessarily repeated or coupled with previous prescriptions obtained from other healthcare facilities. It is irrelevant if treatment duplications and prescription repetitions were rendered at the same facility or different facilities. The only solution is for healthcare providers to know which treatments and prescriptions were given to patients, regardless of the place or facility they attended before being treated. Healthcare facilities need to work together as one, regardless of their scattered facilities. They need to work toward sharing patients' medical histories so as to avoid mistakes that may easily be avoidable; this will ensure quality patient care at all the times. This will eliminate a situation where patient records are not easily accessible from different facilities. Healthcare facilities need to come together and form a collaborative consortium in the interest of patient quality healthcare. This will enable them to adopt and use common electronic systems, which will help them keep and share patients' medical and healthcare history records. Treatment and prescription errors will be minimised, as well as duplicate recordkeeping. Malpractice litigation will also be minimised and record storage capacity reduced. Implementation of the solution will also depend on the scope coverage of the facilities. For instance, implementation could be national, thus covering facilities within a particular country; regional, thus covering facilities within certain countries; continental, thus covering countries across a particular continent, like Africa; or international, thus covering facilities across the entire world. Depending on the coverage, a project may be led by the leading or controlling entity or government body. For example: a country project may be led by the national department of health; a regional project could enlist the Southern African Development Community (SADC) countries to assist; a continental project may be led by a continental body like the African Unity (AU) for Africa; and, internationally, the World Health Organization (WHO) may take the lead.

6.6.1 Proposed Framework

The study therefore proposed a framework in Figure 6.1 for the application of cloud-computing technology to improve patients' medical history access to clinicians for quality of care in the fourth industrial revolution. The framework was developed based on the literature and discussion in the study to ensure that implementation of the findings was guided accordingly. The framework proposes the adoption of cloud computing to ensure proper storage, retrieval, sharing, and disposal of patient records during healthcare service delivery. Disposal may be discharged in a form of destruction or transferred to an archive's repository, depending on the value of the records that need to be disposed of. Only records with enduring value are suitable for transfer to an archive repository, while ephemeral records should be destroyed in any preferable way when they are deemed impractical for the service; destruction should be based on the set retention periods. Looking at item number 1 in Figure 6.1, healthcare facilities may need to collaborate to ensure effective sharing of patients' information about their medical and health history when rendering service to such patients. At the same time, this may create room or opportunity for facilities to benchmark with each other on matters, strategies, or decisions pertaining to patients' treatments. Item number 2 in the framework shows that collaborated facilities must ensure that the system is powered with appropriate security and safety measures to ensure confidentiality, integrity, and authenticity of the records stored and shared on the cloud. In other words, the system should have safety and security measures to protect the records when they are created, stored, and retrieved during a patient's consultation. The intention is to maintain the characteristics of the records, such as integrity and authenticity, and to ensure confidentiality for patients' personal information. In other words, the system must restrict access to unauthorised people. Item number 3 shows that the system must make records accessible and available. This implies that clinicians are not supposed to struggle when they need patients' records; it must be a matter of pressing the button or opening the application on a smart phone, laptop, or desktop computer. Records must be available and accessible at all times when healthcare providers need them to help patients. Item 4 clearly indicates there should be appropriate governance during the process of applying the system, creating storage, and when sharing patients' information. Governance may be implemented through the creation and implementation of legislation, policies, and procedures. This also controls human behaviour and ensures conformance to operational rules, standards, and procedures. Issues pertaining to safety, security, confidentiality, integrity, and the authenticity of records will need to be addressed in the governance documents and guidelines. Other matters will be the creation storage, preservation, access, and disposal of the records stored in the shared cloud, as well as collaboration strategies and interactions among different facilities and practitioners involved in the healthcare practice.

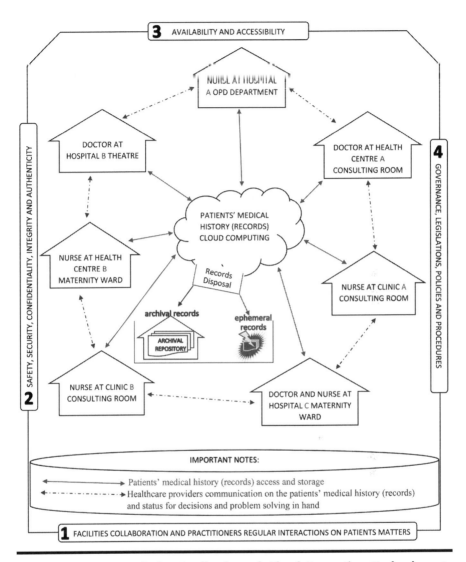

Figure 6.1 Framework for Application of Cloud-Computing Technology to Improve Patients' Medical History Access to Clinicians for Quality of Care in the Fourth Industrial Revolution.

It is hoped that the proposed framework for the application of cloud-computing technology to improve patients' medical history access to clinicians for quality of care in the fourth industrial revolution in Figure 6.1 will bring about a closing of gaps in accessing a patient's medical history when providing healthcare services to patients. This may ensure that practitioners have access to a patient's full medical and health history, whenever they render healthcare services to them.

6.7 Concluding Remarks

It is not a matter of overemphasising that it does not matter by whom and where the patients' records were created. If certain parts of a patient's medical and health history are not available, the record is still incomplete. Patients usually do not stay at one facility or healthcare provider, but rather visit different facilities and in-stitutions, especially if the illness takes long to be cured or resolved. Instead, the possibilities are that these patients may receive similar treatments and prescriptions from different practitioners at different facilities, whether it be private or public practices. The negative impact of this outcome is very severe because it affects the quality of the patient's care, life, and health. The problem encountered is a lack of cooperative collaboration and integrative technology to ensure that a patient's information is properly and effectively shared in the process of rendering healthcare services. It is high time that healthcare institution owners and practitioners realise that they need to focus on quality patient care and not business competition at the expense of patients' lives. This kind of business is supposed to be seen as a calling, not competition with counterparts.

References

Asogwa, B.E. (2012). The challenge of managing electronic records in developing countries: Implications for records managers in sub-Saharan Africa. *Records Management Journal,* 3(22): 198–211.

Cognizant. (2021). Cloud solution secure remote employee productivity. Available at: https://www.cognizant.com/case-studies/remote-employee-cloud-solution?cid=p831713456-0025&gclid=CjwKCAjwwqaGBhBKEiwAMk-FtBb8tGQ-9MxLjeXw4JOSDcmaDZ5JWT15QKlsOH7o_cimnMC1amcnPRoCC6wQAvD_BwE (accessed 16 June 2021).

Decman, M. and Vintar, M. (2013). A possible solution for digital preservation of e-government: A centralised repository within a cloud computing framework. *Aslib Proceedings: New Information Perspectives,* 4(65): 406–424.

Galloway, J.M. (2013). *A cloud architecture for reducing costs in local parallel and distributed virtualised cloud environments,* PhD Thesis, The University of Alabama: AL.

Intellectsoft US. (2021). *Cloud Computing in Healthcare as the Future of the Industry.* Available at: https://www.intellectsoft.net/blog/cloud-computing-in-healthcare/ (accessed 16 June 2021).

Jackson, M. and Shelly, M. (2012). *Electronic Information and the Law,* Thomson Reuters Professional Australia Limited, Sydney.

Lavinski, S. (2019). *10 Disadvantages & Risks of Cloud Computing,* available at: https://medium.com/faun/10-disadvantages-risks-of-cloud-computing-35111de75611 (accessed 19 June 2021).

Marutha, N.S. (2016). *A framework to embed medical records management into the healthcare service delivery in Limpopo Province of South Africa,* PhD thesis, University of South Africa: Pretoria.

Neelima, M.L. and Padma, M. (2014). A study on cloud storage, *IJCSMC,* 3(5): 966–971.

Ngoepe, M. and Saurombe, A. (2016). Provisions for managing and preserving records created in networked environments in the archival legislative frameworks of selected member states of the Southern African Development Community, *Archives and Manuscripts*, 44(1). 24–41.

Shibambu, A. and Marutha, N.S. (2021). A framework for management of digital records on the cloud in the public sector of South Africa. *Information Discovery and Delivery*. DOI: 10.1108/IDD-10-2020-0128

Stratosphere Network. (2021). *Advantages and Disadvantages of Cloud Computing*, available at: www.stratospherenetworks.com/advantages-and-disadvantages-of-cloud.html (accessed 19 June 2021).

Chapter 7

Diagnostic Imaging and Associated Services: Toward Interoperability and Cloud Computing

Cezar Miranda Paula de Souza and
Itamir de Morais Barroca Filho
Universidade Federal do Rio Grande do Norte – UFRN

Contents

7.1 Introduction 126
7.2 DICOM and DICOMWeb 128
    7.2.1 DICOMWeb Search Service (QIDO-RS – Query Based
        on ID for DICOM Objects) 134
    7.2.2 DICOMWeb Retrieve Service (WADO-RS – Web Access to
        DICOM Persistent Objects) 135
    7.2.3 DICOMWeb Storage Service (STOW-RS – STore
        Over the Web) 136
    7.2.4 DICOMWeb Worklist Service (UPS-RS – Unified Procedure
        Step) 138
    7.2.5 DICOMWeb Capabilities Service 138

DOI: 10.1201/9781003145189-7

7.3 Discussion 140
7.4 Conclusion and Future Work.. 143
References 144

7.1 Introduction

Evaluated at 15.9 billion in 2020, the global medical-imaging market is expected to expand at a compound annual growth rate (CAGR) of 5.2% from 2021 to 2028, according to GVG (2020). Market size is estimated at 20.1 billion US dollars in 2021, with key factors driving growth, including increasing demand for early-stage diagnostics of chronic disease and rising aging demographics. Key players in the market include GE Healthcare, Philips Healthcare, Siemens Healthcare, Canon Medical Systems Corporation, Fujifilm Holdings, Shimadzu Corporation, Toshiba Medical Systems Corporation, and Hitachi Medical Corporation, among others.

As these numbers suggest, it's a tens-of-billions global industry with key service providers and manufacturers across the globe, and that's not even accounting for the installed base of medical-imaging devices already in use.

In terms of numbers of imaging exams being performed, historically, X-ray is the most frequently used imaging technique with more than 100 million X-ray exams being performed per year globally, followed by MRI, PET, SPECT, CT, and nuclear medicine, according to IQ4I (2015).

In England alone, 44.9 million imaging tests were reported from March 2019 to March 2020, compared with 44.8 million in the previous period (2018–2019), an increase of 0.3%, according to NHS (2020). Plain radiography (X-ray) was most common with 23.2 million procedures, followed by diagnostic ultrasonography (ultrasound, 10.3 million), Computerized axial tomography (CT scan, 6.0 million), and magnetic resonance imaging (MRI, 3.8 million). July 2019 was the month with the most reported activity, 4.04 million tests, with the following months impacted by the COVID-19 pandemic (ongoing at the time of this writing) and the national lockdown.

While on that subject, Richards (2020) observes that although the need for radical investment and reform of diagnostic services was already recognized before the COVID-19 pandemic hit (major expansion of diagnostic capacity was already clearly identified as being needed), the pandemic has highlighted and further amplified the importance and the need for radical change in the provision of diagnostic services, while also providing an opportunity for change. Many beneficial improvements concerning diagnostic pathways, such as increased use of virtual consultations and community services have already been made, but must now be embedded.

According to NHS (2021), most medical services groups in operation in England today provide their own imaging services, using operating models that need investment in premises, IT, and equipment.

But that's not exclusive to England since it is the norm for medical services across the globe.

Providers are also competing for increasingly scarce medical and non-medical staff. The capability to share digital images remotely and in real time is fundamental to the creation of an imaging network, but, as of today's standards, the right solution will not be the same for every network: it will vary according to a range of different contextual factors, such as existing systems and contract end dates.

In that sense, there is much that needs to be done to deliver key benefits to patients and healthcare professionals, such as:

- sustained local services so patients can be scanned close to where they live but also have access to specialist opinion across a wider geographic area,
- faster turnaround times for reports,
- reduced risk of missed diagnosis,
- availability of images and other test results to the clinician at the point of treatment, reducing the need for multiple visits for treatment,
- greater service resilience where small or remote sites are struggling to recruit,
- improved IT interoperability, rapid transfer of images in emergencies,
- improved access to multidisciplinary training environments through "academy style" models,
- more flexible working opportunities, "home reporting" and flexible retirement options for professionals,
- access to better training and continuing professional development, being able to work across different sites and gain experience, for professionals,
- more opportunities for professionals to increase skill mix levels and both advanced practice and assistant practitioner roles.

With current standards in IT interoperability, cloud and edge computing could go a long way in addressing some if not all of those concerns, but there's a catch.

Like everything that permeates medicine (and especially with regard to information of private and personal nature, where medical confidentiality is seen as an ethical guarantee, something considered a fact), treatment, storage, transmission, access, and everything that involves digital-medical examination is strictly governed by rigid standards.

In this context, **digital imaging and communications in medicine (DICOM)**, established and maintained by the **National Electrical Manufacturers Association (NEMA)** is the current standard, establishing the rules for storage and transmission of medical images, as well as protocols and standards for integration between devices such as image-capture scanners; data servers – which DICOM calls PACS (picture archiving and communication systems) – printers and several other network assets from multiple manufacturers, being widely adopted in hospitals, clinics, and other health institutions around the world.

Originated in the mid-1980s, with its first version published in 1985, DICOM became part of the ISO standards catalog as standard **12052:2017 "Health informatics – Digital imaging and communication in medicine (DICOM) including workflow and data management"** In 2017. The standard has gone through several revisions, additions, and updates. Its most current version, at the time of this writing, is **2021c** from 2021. The standard covers any branch of medicine where the use of imaging is predominant, also including veterinary and dentistry. Other standards such as **Health Level 7 (HL7)** and **Integrating the Healthcare Enterprise (IHE)** incorporate DICOM to specify aspects related to the storage and transmission of medical images.

As for IT interoperability and cloud-computing concerns, **DICOMWeb** – which is the DICOM standard for web-based medical imaging – is a set of RESTful services that enables the interoperability of healthcare images using industry-standard toolsets.

In other words, DICOM and DICOMWeb represent the current standard for medical-image management, enabling hundreds of service and product providers in the field to achieve interoperability between devices and IT services.

Initially drafted in 2003, DICOMWeb is considered a stable standard in its current incarnation, according to Genereaux et al. (2018), enabling the use of cutting-edge technologies, such as image analysis and machine learning, reducing the barrier for data storage, transmission, and retrieval. By preserving the DICOM information model, it makes the transition and evolution of legacy services and equipment smoother. Other models based on DICOM, such as the one proposed by Godinho et al. (2017) exist; however, they became obsolete with the incorporation of DICOMWeb to the current standard, as well as standardization efforts such as those described in Silva et al. (2017).

Finally, this chapter aims at providing an overview of current standards in use on healthcare technologies and services in the medical imaging field (also called diagnostic imaging), as well as identifying gaps and improvement opportunities pertaining to current standards in interoperability, use of cloud and service-oriented architectures, security, scalability, optimization, and ubiquity. Section 7.2 brings an overview of DICOM and DICOMWeb, Section 7.3 reviews ongoing work and discusses improvement opportunities, and Section 7.4 concludes while also commenting on possible future work.

7.2 DICOM and DICOMWeb

Digital imaging and communications in medicine (DICOM) is the standard for the communication and management of medical-imaging information and related data (ISO, 2017). According to Genereaux et al. (2018) – the work that describes the original proposal for the DICOMWeb standard – DICOM defines formats for images, video streams, waveforms, and derived data, enabling modalities such as computed tomography, magnetic resonance, X-ray, ultrasound, angiography, PET scan, microscopic image exams, exams with cameras, and ophthalmological devices, which can be formatted with objects of one or multiple frames, multidimensional volumes, or video loops. These can be associated with documents such as requisitions, consent forms, and reports. For each format, the standard defines which metadata is meaningful and should be provided as well (e.g., patient identification, demographics, parameters and workflow context).

DICOM is a worldwide standard that can be used in every locale. It provides mechanisms to handle data that support cultural requirements, such as different writing systems, character sets, languages, and structures for addresses and person names. It supports the variety of workflows, processes, and policies used for biomedical imaging in different geographic regions, medical specialties, and local practices (ISO, 2017). In terms of the information model, according to Genereaux et al. (2018), DICOM defines a logical hierarchy starting with the patient, as shown in Figure 7.1, where a patient can be a human or an animal (in case of veterinary practice) and has a collection of studies. Each study represents a set of images organized for a particular diagnosis and contains a collection of series. Each series represents a single acquisition event, on a single device (ie, an exam), and contains a set of instances. Each instance represents a single data object, which can be an image, a collection of images, or a document (measures, parameters, or report). Each instance has its own set of metadata (study, series, instance attributes), each with its own data type. As new imaging technologies for exams emerge, new types of data are defined.

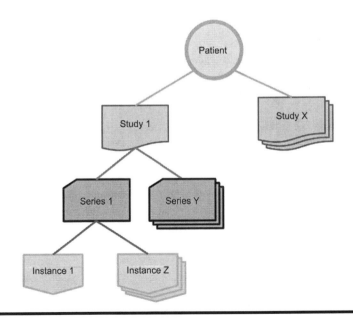

Figure 7.1 DICOM Information Model (Based on Genereaux et al. (2018)).

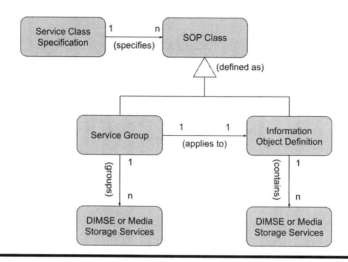

Figure 7.2   Information Object Description – IOD (Based on NEMA, 2021).

The DICOM standard defines that image-capture devices should communicate with a central service for storing images and their descriptor objects – called information objects. The service providers for storing and making available the images and their respective data are known as PACS – picture archiving and communication systems. The DICOM standard describes a generic framework for defining **information objects** – the **information object definition (IOD)** – as presented in Figure 7.2, which demonstrates in a generic way how to describe real-world entities.

Information objects are an abstraction of a real information entity (CT image, structured report, etc.), which is acted upon by one or more DICOM commands (ISO, 2017). Real-world entities are described according to the IOD model, as presented in the representation of a patient in Figure 7.3. It graphically describes operations (such as "to visit") and relationships that a patient has with other entities (such as "equipments," "studies," "exams").

The DICOM standard defines several service classes. A service class associates one or more information objects with one or more commands to be performed on those objects, determining requirements for command elements and how the resulting commands are applied to information objects, while also determining requirements for both service providers and users of communication services. DICOM also specifies how applications should build and encode data resulting from information objects and service classes, including support for more common image-compression standards, such as JPEG, and also establishes how data dictionaries should be defined. This is intended for the standardization of the innumerous types of exams and fields of application in which DICOM is to be used, with exam data ranging from 2D to 3D images, single-frame to multiple-frame exams, including video streams,

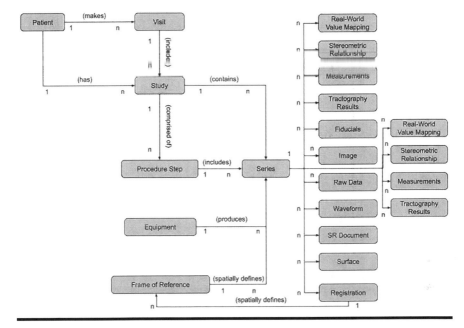

Figure 7.3 **Patient Information Object (Based on NEMA, 2021).**

point-cloud data, and other formats. Data dictionaries are used to categorize attribute fields, filters, parameters, and other aspects pertaining to exam metadata. On the upper boundary of a DICOM application, there are HTTP (DICOMWeb) and RTP services used for the network exchange of data. On the lower boundary of a DICOM application, there is a basic file service that communicates with physical storage devices for storage and retrieval of files. Figure 7.4 describes the general DICOM communication model.

The standard also defines the service and the protocol used to exchange messages (called **command streams** for the execution/calling of commands and **data streams** for data communication) using the so-called **DIMSE (DICOM message service element)**. In this context, "commands" are requests to operate on information across a network. "Command elements" provide encoding of a parameter of a command, which conveys this parameter's value, and "command streams" are the result of encoding a set of DICOM command elements using the DICOM encoding scheme (ISO, 2017). Data dictionary is the registry of DICOM data elements which assigns a unique tag, a name, value characteristics, and semantics to each data element. Data elements are units of information as defined by a single entry in the data dictionary. Data sets are exchanged information consisting of a structured set of attributes. The value of each attribute in a data set is expressed as a data element. Data streams are the result of encoding a data set using the DICOM encoding scheme, where data element numbers and representations are specified by the data dictionary (ISO, 2017).

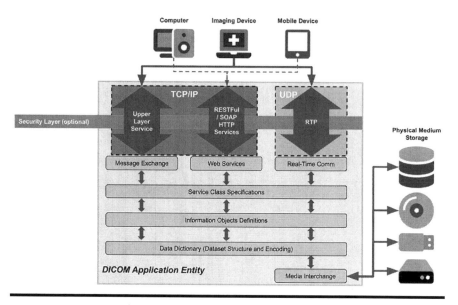

Figure 7.4   General DICOM Communication Model (Based on NEMA, 2021).

DIMSE, in turn, provides two types of information-exchange services: **notification services** and **transaction services**. Notification services are used in a publisher-subscriber manner, allowing observers to subscribe to subjects of interest and be notified of changes, and transaction services are used to store and modify data.

DICOM image format and protocols have a series of particularities, intrinsic to the needs of the medical field, in particular metadata whose absence can lead to incomplete information and serious errors with impacts on the health of patients (humans or animals). There are nuances associated with displaying medical images, including marker transformation, lifecycle management, scaling, and handling of large data sets. Even though IT systems and personnel are no strangers to concepts of image display, content upload and download, historically DICOM does not use the same technology standards found in other web applications. It should also be noted that the DICOM format is not recognized by Internet browsers and other agents commonly used in association with these systems, alerts Genereaux et al. (2018). Storing, retrieving, and displaying medical images, therefore, requires in-depth knowledge of the acquisition parameters and rules of the DICOM protocol. Storage, bandwidth, and latency issues are made more evident by image datasets that grow from gigs to terabytes. Extracting metadata for example requires traversing binary data rather than XMLs or JSONs. Scaling a PACS system also requires specialized knowledge that is not covered by cloud-computing infrastructure virtualization services.

With the latest technological advances, the needs of patients and healthcare professionals have also evolved. Consistent, device-independent, and remote access is a necessity and a reality that cannot be ignored. Application-development paradigms have pivoted to service-oriented architectures, as a result.

DICOMWeb is the current standard for image transmission in web-based environments, in regards to interoperability and architectural standards for web and cloud. It is composed of a set of RESTful services, allowing a direct implementation or to be used as a proxy for DIMSE services.

The following services are provided by DICOMWeb, as shown in Figure 7.5:

- Query (QIDO-RS – Query based on ID for DICOM Objects) – for querying DICOM objects
- Retrieve (WADO-RS / WADO-URI – Web access to DICOM persistent objects) – used for retrieval of DICOM objects. WADO-RS is used for collections of objects and WADO-URI for single instances
- Store (STOW-RS – STore Over the Web) – used for storage of DICOM objects
- Worklist (UPS-RS – Unified Procedure Step) – used for management of worklist items
- Capabilities – Service discovery

OBS: "RS" indicates a RESTful implementation, but there are also WS versions available that adhere to SOAP standards. The following sections (7.2.1 through 7.2.5) describe these services in detail, including available methods and related HTTP verbs, parameters, and header structures for each service.

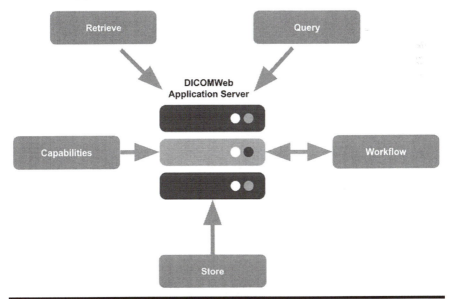

Figure 7.5   DICOMWeb Operations (Based on Genereaux et al. (2018)).

7.2.1 DICOMWeb Search Service (QIDO-RS – Query Based on ID for DICOM Objects)

ID-based queries for DICOM objects enable searches for studies, series, and instances by patient ID. Search parameters can be informed using pre-defined parameter IDs, as seen on the data dictionary section of the standard. For instance, as seen in Figure 7.6,

```
GET http://server.com/studies/?00100010=DOE^JOHN^
```

should retrieve all studies of the patient(s) named "John Doe," where 00100010 indicates the data element "PatientName" (subsection "Registry of DICOM Data Elements," tag "(0010,0010)"). The response can be provided as XML or JSON according to the server implementation support. Table 7.1 describes all QIDO-RS accepted methods, and Table 7.2 describes accepted search parameters. All request methods use the "GET" HTTP verb.

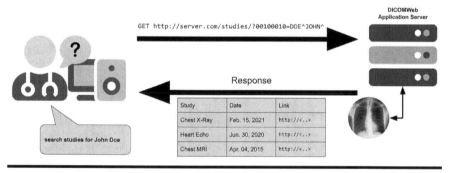

Figure 7.6 QIDO-RS (Based on NEMA, 2021).

Table 7.1 QIDO-RS Methods (Based on NEMA, 2021)

Path	Description
{s}/studies? ...	Searches for studies
{s}/studies/{study}/series? ...	Searches series of a study
{s}/studies/{study}/series/{series}/ instances? ...	Searches for instances of a series

Table 7.2   QIDO-RS Parameters (Based on NEMA, 2021)

Key	Value	Description
{attributeID}	{value}	Searches for elements of the given value
includefield	{attribute} | all	Includes informed attributes in the response
fuzzymatching	true | false	If fuzzy matching should be applied to the search
limit	{n}	Limit returned results
offset	{n}	Ignores a given number of leading results

7.2.2 DICOMWeb Retrieve Service (WADO-RS – Web Access to DICOM Persistent Objects)

WADO-RS (web access to DICOM persistent objects) is the service used for retrieving studies, series, and instances through a **UID (unique identifier)**. The returned response will contain a binary object containing the metadata and pixels. Images suitable for display in web browsers can be requested by specifying the media type as "image/jpg" or "image/png," for example. Images can be requested in a specific size or cropped to specific regions. An example request can be seen in Figure 7.7. Table 7.3 describes all WADO-RS accepted methods, Table 7.4 describes accepted search parameters for retrieval of rendered images, and Table 7.5 describes required and optional headers. All request methods use the "GET" HTTP verb.

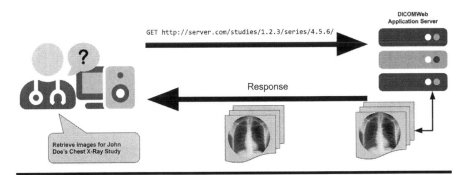

Figure 7.7   WADO-RS (Based on NEMA, 2021).

Table 7.3   WADO-RS Methods (Based on NEMA, 2021)

Path	Description
{s}/studies/{study}	Retrieves a complete study
{s}/studies/{study}/rendered	Retrieves a rendered study
{s}/studies/{study}/series/{series}	Retrieves a complete series object
{s}/studies/{study}/series/{series}/rendered	Retrieves rendered series
{s}/studies/{study}/series/{series}/metadata	Retrieves series metadata
{s}/studies/{study}/series/{series}/instances/{instance}	Retrieves instance objects
{s}/studies/{study}/series/{series}/instances/{instance}/rendered	Retrieves rendered instances
{s}/studies/{study}/series/{series}/instances/{instance}/metadata	Retrieves instance metadata
{s}/studies/{study}/series/{series}/instances/{instance}/frames/{frames}	Retrieves instance frames
{s}/{bulkdataURIReference}	Retrieves bulk data

Table 7.4   WADO-RS Search Parameters (Based on NEMA, 2021)

Key	Value	Description
annotation	"patient"/"technique"	Add burned-in demographics/procedure details
quality	{n}	Image quality (lossy factor)
viewport	vw,vh/sx,sy,sw,sh	Width, height, or crop to specific region
window	centre,width,shape	Center of the greyscale range in the image

7.2.3 DICOMWeb Storage Service (STOW-RS – STore Over the Web)

STOW-RS is a DICOMWeb service that allows storage of specific instances to the server. Unique identifiers should be provided for each **SOP** (**service object pair**) of study, series, instance, using the **UID** (**unique identifier**) field. It will also be

Table 7.5 Accepted Headers WADO-RS (Based on NEMA, 2021)

Category	Media Type	Support
Single Frame Image	image/jpeg	default
	image/gif	required
	image/png	required
	image/jp2	optional
Multi-frame Image	image/gif	optional
Video	video/mpeg	optional
	video/mp4	optional
	video/H265	optional
Text	text/html	default
	text/plain	required
	text/xml	required
	text/rtf	optional
	application/pdf	optional

necessary to specify the SOP class (among the fixed options determined by the standard, as per the "Data Dictionary" section). Data can be passed as XML or JSON. In response, the server returns a "receipt" of what was processed and what failed. It is possible for applications to upload a standard JPEG or PNG images to be stored as valid DICOM files, provided the mandatory metadata is informed as well. Figure 7.8 describes an example request for storing an imaging exam, and

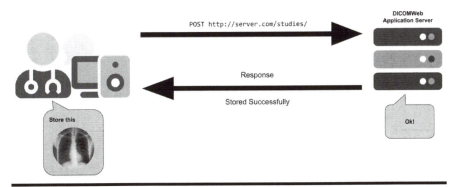

Figure 7.8 STOW-RS (Based on NEMA, 2021).

Table 7.6   STOW-RS Methods (Based on NEMA, 2021)

Path	Description
{s}/studies	Stores instances
{s}/studies/{study}	Stores instances

Table 7.6 describes available methods for storing exams. All request methods use the "POST" HTTP verb (which is the default HTTP verb used to send new data to a remote server).

7.2.4 DICOMWeb Worklist Service (UPS-RS – Unified Procedure Step)

UPS-RS is a DICOMWeb service which enables work item management. Also describes how notifications work (including subscriptions). Figure 7.9 describes an example request for retrieving a list of work items for a professional. Table 7.7 describes methods available to manage work items and subscriptions.

7.2.5 DICOMWeb Capabilities Service

The DICOMWeb capabilities service enables the discovery of supported services from a particular DICOMWeb endpoint. Using HTTP OPTIONS on an endpoint generates a **WADL (web application description language)** response that will be returned explaining the various supported options. Figure 7.10 describes an example request to discover the capabilities of a DICOMWeb server, and Table 7.8 describes the request syntax. The "OPTIONS" HTTP verb is used as determined by RESTful HTTP service standards.

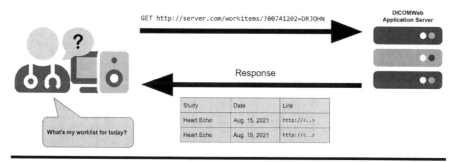

Figure 7.9   UPS-RS (Based on NEMA, 2021).

Table 7.7   UPS-RS Resources (Based on NEMA, 2021)

Verb	Path	Description
POST	{s}/workitems{?AffectedSOPInstanceUID}	create work item
POST	{s}/workitems/{instance}{?transaction}	Update work item
GET	{s}/workitems{?query*}	Search for work items
GET	{s}/workitems/{instance}	Retrieve a work item
PUT	{s}/workitems/{instance}/state	Change work item state
POST	{s}/workitems/{instance}/cancelrequest	Cancel a work item
POST	{s}/workitems/{instance}/subscribers/{AETitle}{?deletionlock}	Create a subscription
POST	{s}/workitems/1.2.840.10008.5.1.4.34.5/	Suspend subscription
DELETE	{s}/workitems/{instance}/subscribers/{AETitle}	Delete subscription
GET	{s}/subscribers/{AETitle}	open subscription channel
N/A	N/A	Send event reports

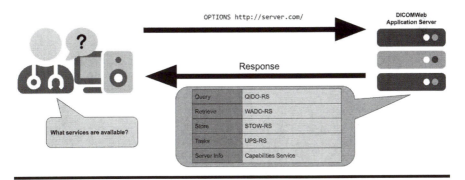

Figure 7.10   Capabilities (Based on NEMA, 2021).

Table 7.8   Capabilities Resources (Based on NEMA, 2021)

Path	Description
{s}/(any)	Returns service capabilities

7.3 Discussion

The DICOM standard continues to evolve, with revisions occurring more than once over the span of a year (in 2021 alone, three revisions of the standard have already been carried out at the time of this writing).

However, these revisions are more of incremental and corrective nature than evolutionary. The current interoperability standard is quite outdated in terms of communication and scalability concerns for the reality of cloud computing, still focusing on more basic communication issues at the network layer level and leaving a large vacuum in terms of architectural concerns and best practices at the application layer and interoperability level.

DICOMWeb, the current standard for interoperability that comes closest to cloud concerns, still focuses on the historical view of "web services," SOA versus REST, and does not address many of the issues relevant to the current standard of APIs such as those related to FOG and cloud computing, microservices, scalability, service discovery, resource scope, hierarchy, resource identification, state management, batch operations, filtering, versioning, access control, authentication, authorization and auditing, among other aspects commonly associated with cloud-computing solutions.

Furthermore, despite proposing a flexible descriptor format for the most varied types of exams in diverse areas of activity related to medical, veterinary, and odontological applications, the standard proposes a data dictionary with data elements represented and passed by encoded identifiers – which is not by any means developer-friendly – requiring constant use of reference material and conversion tables, instead of applying techniques of obfuscation of URLs and URIs or other security mechanisms on data transferred through endpoint requests.

Other criticisms include questions related to data ingestion. Due to the large number of possible optional fields, it's commonplace to have inconsistencies in the types of data inputted, due either to incompleteness (empty fields) or incorrect data (that does not conform to the field data type). Furthermore, it allows executable code, which raises security concerns due to the possibility of including malicious files (infected with malware and viruses).

Limitations such as these lead to initiatives as the one described in Spaltenstein et al. (2020), which disregards the DICOMWeb standard and proposes an architecture that allows support for DICOM and non-DICOM images in an integrated way, to be used in specific niches such as radiological imaging. There's also the one proposed by Hazarika et al. (2020), which explores the integration of the open-source viewer DICOM web viewer with DSpace, an open-source repository solution for storage and open access for academic and/or published content, also for the radiological imaging niche. Both, however, lack a broader abstraction of a cloud-based architecture. In Drnasin et al. (2020), an architecture is proposed based on WebRTC in the context of DICOM file sharing over P2P, as an alternative view for accessing images from a PACS central repository. Other initiatives, such as the one described by Liu (2020) focus on the problem of optimizing high-resolution images for devices via the web, which is another issue overlooked in the DICOMWeb standard (it is not uncommon to find exam files with a single capture comprising of gigabytes or even terabytes of data, depending on the application area).

Lebre et al. (2020) evaluate that, to better understand these issues, it's important to note the typical infrastructure in a standard DICOM usage scenario. Usually, it's composed of one or more PACS servers, serving acquisition modalities, distribution mechanisms, and visualization equipment in a single organizational domain, within an organizational intranet where authorized users have access to all resources within the repository. In this scenario, even basic security mechanisms such as permission-based access control like RBAC (rule-based access control) are often not required. However, this reality has also been changing with large organizations being divided into departments with different areas of activity, each with its own data infrastructure and organizational domains. Proprietary PACS solutions commonly provide some kind of authorization mechanism, but since those are not included in the DICOM standard, third-party solutions can gain access to data by ignoring these rules, warns Lebre et al. (2020). Traditionally, external clients can search and retrieve all DICOM objects stored on a server in PACS services without restrictions.

All other shortcomings and aspects concerning cloud architectures left out of the standard can be seen under the same light, as these are concerns that do not usually exist in a "on premises" model, where services are hosted on an organization's internal private infrastructure, while those concerns are most commonly associated with SaaS (Software as a Service), IaaS (Infrastructure as a Service) or PaaS (Platform as a Service) environments.

As a consequence of this focus on platforms hosted on local networks, there is a myriad of web-based viewers for the DICOM standard, many of which are open source and free, to the point where choosing a web-based viewer becomes a challenge in itself, as discussed by Wadali et al. (2020). Each solution has its strengths and weaknesses, but none apparently manages to cover the wide range of specific PACS solutions from the various suppliers involved.

On the other end, there's also a myriad of PACS with DICOMWeb features available. One of these available implementations is DICOMcloud (2021), which, despite its name, does not include any features that address a cloud-oriented architecture scenario. Figure 7.11 demonstrates DICOMcloud components.

Production-ready environments with cloud and edge-computing capabilities for processing, storing, and provision of medical images can be implemented through the use of current technologies, though. That, however, could be a very complex and difficult task in the current scenario, one with low reusability and scalability. Persons (2020) explores the results achieved through three attempts undertaken in this regard by different organizations: the first one in Ontario, Canada; the second, ELGA, in Austria; and the third, the RSNA Image Share Network, in the United States. According to Persons (2020), although the

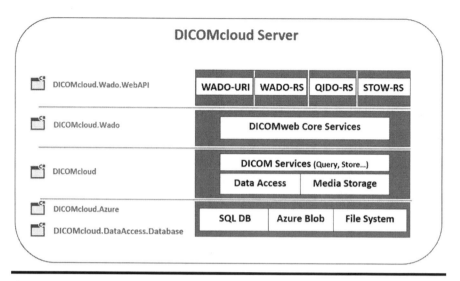

Figure 7.11 DICOMcloud Architecture.

Source: DICOMcloud, 2021.

current standard allows the exchange of images, it's not enough to establish that this occurs as a regular practice, bringing considerations beyond technological factors. It further establishes that the specification of the standards that must be used is critical to enable interoperability and highlights issues of information governance, the complex infrastructure required, as well as its cost of maintenance and implementation, concluding that governance and the establishment of a sustainable infrastructure are critical success factors. Furthermore, it establishes that interoperability is still the most critical factor in terms of allowing integrations with medical information services and patient registration (electronic medical records).

In this sense, works such as the one proposed by Lebre et al. (2020) describe necessary extensions and relevant future work to be incorporated into the standard. Lebre (2020) proposes a cloud-oriented, multi-user, and multi-archive architecture, with a multi-permissions policy seeking to provide additional layers of security. The proposal makes use of open-source platforms such as Dicoogle (2021), which has a modular architecture and uses an indexing system based on documents as a database. Among other possibilities, this platform enables specialized applications focused, for example, on **business intelligence** (**BI**) and **data analytics** (**DA**) using **ETL** (**extract, transform, load**) techniques such as the framework proposed in Godinho et al. (2019). Dicoogle's concept of plugins and provision of an SDK encourages developers and researchers to quickly develop new features, and it can be used to support three distinct scenarios, taking advantage of the modularized architecture: production, research, and teaching, providing a **vendor-neutral archive** (**VNA**) service. VNAs, concludes Lebre (2020), are fundamental for modern medical-image management environments as they use standardized data formats and interfaces, making images accessible to healthcare professionals regardless of the proprietary systems where they were produced.

According to Lebre et al (2020), some changes were introduced in the DICOMWeb implementation by Dicoogle to support RBAC mechanisms. Traditional PACS solutions generally provide some kind of proprietary authentication mechanism for their proprietary data-viewing client applications, but as said, they don't control third-party application access, using standard DICOM access mechanisms. In Dicoogle's implementation, the HTTP service must contain "Authorization" attributes in the headers to make use of the proposed system. Otherwise, the user is restricted to publicly available resources, or simply denied the service.

7.4 Conclusion and Future Work

DICOM and DICOMWeb are the de facto standard in use in the medical-imaging industry. But despite enabling integration with different devices and systems from different providers and enabling the use of web technologies, there are still multiple deficiencies and gaps that must be addressed for it to more adequately support the reality of cloud computing and IoT. Extensions and evolutions of the standard have been discussed but usually in a very biased view based on local solutions, private network infrastructures, and specific niches.

The standard lacks a broader vision that meets current standards for interoperability and scalability so that it can become consistent with the integrated, ubiquitous vision brought by the cloud and IoT. Issues related to latency and bandwidth also need to be considered, given the possibility of large datasets for exams. Basic security aspects such as access control, authentication, and authorization also urgently need to be included in the standard.

In a market described as oligopolistic, permeated by customized solutions that iterate over the DICOM standard adding proprietary tech to the complexities of interoperability, vendor-neutral initiatives should be encouraged. Just as well as the development of the standard toward better adherence to today's reality of ubiquitous and unobtrusive computing, accessible through convenient, continuous, and complete applications where anything is available anywhere, anytime, for anyone.

Moving in a different direction, due to its necessity to support a myriad of areas of expertise in diagnostic imaging, ranging from human medicine to veterinary medicine, from neurology to odontology, handling such different formats as single-frame, multi-frame, 2D, 3D imaging, video, and audio streams, point clouds, waveforms, and derived data, the DICOM standard has accumulated a great deal of complexity on its own specifications. Relevant work could be done in simplification and abstraction of some of that complexity, perhaps proposing lightweight derivations aimed at specific niches of application that could be bundled together to provide specializations or subdivisions – forks, or branches, if you will – from the main standard. For example, DICOM2D, DICOMVideo, and DICOM3D specializations could be described providing developer-friendly entry points to the main standard.

References

DICOMcloud. Available at: http://dicomcloud.com/. Accessed on 08/15/2021.

Dicoogle. Available at: https://dicoogle.com/. Accessed on 08/15/2021.

Drnasin, I., Grgic, M., & Gledec, G. (2020). Exploring WebRTC potential for DICOM file sharing. Journal of Digital Imaging, 33(3), 697–707. doi:10.1007/s10278-019-00305-0

Genereaux, B. W., Dennison, D. K., Ho, K., Horn, R., Silver, E. L., O'Donnell, K., & Kahn, C. E., Jr. (2018). DICOMweb™: Background and application of the web standard for medical imaging. Journal of Digital Imaging, 31(3), 321–326. doi:10.1007/s10278-018-0073-z

Global Market Insights (GVG) (2020). Medical Imaging Market Size By Product (X-ray Devices {Digital [Direct Radiography Systems, Computed Radiography Systems], Analog}, Magnetic Resonance Imaging (MRI), Ultrasound, {2D Ultrasound, 3D Ultrasound}, Computed Tomography, Nuclear Imaging, Mammography), By End-use (Hospitals, Diagnostic Centers), COVID-19 Impact Analysis, Regional Outlook, Growth Potential, Price Trends, Competitive Market Share & Forecast, 2021 – 2027. Available at: https://www.gminsights.com/industry-analysis/medical-imaging-market. Accessed on 08/15/2021.

Godinho, T. M., Lebre, R., Almeida, J. R., & Costa, C. (2019). ETL framework for real-time business intelligence over medical imaging repositories. Journal of Digital Imaging, 32(5), 870–879. doi:10.1007/s10278-019-00184-5

Hazarika, H. J., Handique, A., & Ravikumar, S. (2020). DICOM-based medical image repository using DSpace. Collection and Curation, 39(4), 105–115. doi:10.1108/CC-11-2019-0039

Intelligence Quotient for Innovation Research and Consultancy Pvt. Ltd. (IQ4I) (2015). Diagnostic Imaging Global Market. Available at: https://www.marketresearch.com/product/sample-8683588.pdf. Accessed on 08/15/2021

International Organization for Standardization (ISO) (2017). Health informatics—Digital imaging and communication in medicine (DICOM) including workflow and data management (ISO/DIS Standard No. 12052). Retrieved from https://www.iso.org/obp/ui/#iso:std:iso:12052:ed-2:v1:en. Accessed on 08/15/2021

Lebre, R., Silva, L. B., & Costa, C. (2020). A cloud-ready architecture for shared medical imaging repository. Journal of Digital Imaging, 33(6), 1487–1498. doi:10.1007/s10278-020-00373-7

Liu, L., Wang, L., huang, Q., Zhou, L., Fu, X., & Liu, L. (2020). An efficient architecture for medical high-resolution images transmission in mobile telemedicine systems. Computer Methods and Programs in Biomedicine, 187. doi:10.1016/j.cmpb.2019.105088

Marques Godinho, T., Lebre, R., Silva, L. B., & Costa, C. (2017). An efficient architecture to support digital pathology in standard medical imaging repositories. Journal of Biomedical Informatics, 71, 190–197. doi:10.1016/j.jbi.2017.06.009

National Electrical Manufacturers Association (NEMA). Digital Imaging and Communications in Medicine (DICOM). Current Edition. Available at: https://www.dicomstandard.org/current. Accessed on 08/15/2021.

National Health Service (NHS) England and NHS Improvement (2020). Diagnostic Imaging Dataset – Annual Statistical Release – 2019/20. Available at: https://www.england.nhs.uk/statistics/wp-content/uploads/sites/2/2020/10/Annual-Statistical-Release-2019-20-PDF-1.4MB.pdf. Accessed on: 08/15/2021.

National Health Service (NHS) England and NHS Improvement (2021). Diagnostic imaging network implementation guide. Available at: https://www.england.nhs.uk/wp-content/uploads/2021/04/B0030-Implementation-guide.pdf. Accessed on: 08/15/2021.

Persons, K. R., Nagels, J., Carr, C., Mendelson, D. S., Primo, H. R., Fischer, B., & Doyle, M. (2020). Interoperability and considerations for standards-based exchange of medical images: HIMSS-SIIM collaborative white paper. Journal of Digital Imaging, 33(1), 6–16. doi:10.1007/s10278-019-00294-0

Richards, M. (2020). Independent review: Diagnostics: Recovery and renewal. Available at: https://www.england.nhs.uk/wp-content/uploads/2020/10/BM2025Pu-item-5-diagnostics-recovery-and-renewal.pdf. Accessed on: 15/08/2021.

Silva, J. M., Marques Godinho, T., Silva, D., & Costa, C. (2017). Web validation service for ensuring adherence to the DICOM standard. doi:10.3233/978-1-61499-753-5-38 Retrieved from www.scopus.com

Spaltenstein, J., van Dooren, N., Pasquier, G., Roduit, N., Brenet, M., Pasquier, G., …Ratib, O. (2020). A multicentric IT platform for storage and sharing of imaging-based radiation dosimetric data. International Journal of Computer Assisted Radiology and Surgery, 15(10), 1639–1643. doi:10.1007/s11548-020-02179-y

Wadali, J. S., Sood, S. P., Kaushish, R., Syed-Abdul, S., Khosla, P. K., & Bhatia, M. (2020). Evaluation of free, open-source, web-based DICOM viewers for the indian national telemedicine service (eSanjeevani). Journal of Digital Imaging, 33(6), 1499–1513. doi:10.1007/s10278-020-00368-4

Chapter 8

Health Monitoring Based on the Integrated Offer of Cloud-IoT Sensing Services

Gabriel Neagu

National Institute for Research and Development in Informatics – I.C.I. Bucharest, Romania

Contents

8.1   Introduction 148
8.2   Specific HM Architectural Solutions – An Overview 149
8.3   Generic Sensing Service Scenario 150
8.4   Integrated Sensing Service Offer Approach 151
    8.4.1   Main Roles and Business Interactions 151
    8.4.2   Operation Rules 152
8.5   Service Offer Integrator Specificity 153
    8.5.1   SOI Business Model Specifications 153
    8.5.2   Core Entities of the SOI-MIS Data Structure 156
8.6   Implementation Scenarios for Integrated Sensing Service Approach 157
8.7   Conclusions 159
References 160

DOI: 10.1201/9781003145189-8

147

8.1 Introduction

The approaches based on cloud computing and Internet of Things (IoT) integration became popular when the limitation of storage and computing capacities of the IoT devices as compared with continuously increasing requirements regarding the volume of sensor-generated data and their complex analysis started to increasingly influence the performance level of provided solutions. Cloud computing has become a very attractive complementary solution to compensate these limitations due to its capacity to provide ubiquitous, convenient, on-demand network access to a shared pool of configurable computing resources (Mell and Grance 2011). Cloud-computing benefits include: flexibility to cope with dynamic data storage and processing requirements, anytime, anywhere, on any device secure access to patient data, advanced data governance, and disaster recovery solutions, cost-effectiveness generated by the pay-per-use principle (Strome 2015).

Complementarities between the IoT and cloud computing are obvious from many perspectives (Botta et al. 2016): computational and storage capabilities (limited vs. virtually unlimited), components involved (real world things vs. virtual resources), coverage (limited vs. ubiquitous), Internet usage (data concentration and transmission vs. service delivery). These complementarities generate obvious benefits in the case of their integration: scalable cloud capabilities and resources compensate for IoT technological constraints, while the IoT capability to interact with real-world things enables the diversification of cloud-based services (Perera et al. 2014).

The "cloud of things" concept was proposed to emphasize the importance of tight integration of cloud and IoT technologies. In (Aazam et al. 2014) major issues specific to this concept are identified: standardized protocols, energy efficiency, dynamic allocation of resources (depending on type, amount and frequency of data generation), identity management at the network level, service discovery for cloud managers or brokers, QoS provisioning considering the unpredictability of IoT environment, location of data storage for time-sensitive data, security and privacy, unnecessary communication of data. Another example of this integrated approach is provided by the Horizon 2020 BigClouT project dedicated to create distributed intelligence that can be implanted throughout a smart city network (BigClouT 2017). The solution is based on three key technologic enablers (IoT, cloud computing, and big data) and four-layer architecture: city entities, city IaaS, city PaaS, and city SaaS. This solution is a further extension of the former ClouT approach, aiming to help cities to face emerging challenges such as economic growth and development or efficient energy management by establishing an efficient communication and collaboration platform exploiting all possible information sources. The CloudThings architecture is oriented on deploying, operating, and composing IoT-based applications and services using cloud-specific services (Zhou et al. 2013).

In the context of demographic aging as an obvious trend with a significant economic and social impact, the ambient assisted living (AAL) concept has raised as a priority approach in healthcare, defining a system characterized by being connected, context-aware, pervasive, personalized, adaptive, and anticipative. According to the AAL Europe site (http://www.aal-europe.eu/), by 2060, almost 30% of the EU population will be over 65, as compared with almost 20% in 2017. For projects funded by the AAL programme, health monitoring (HM) is a central functionality, as it is illustrated by reported results of some recently finished ones: Pelosha (https://www.pelosha.eu/) – an integrated personalisable environment to address key aspects of older adult's health with specialized AAL services and applications; vINCI (https://vinci.ici.ro/) – an IoT framework for non-intrusive monitoring to assist caregivers and provide smart care for older adults at outpatient clinics and outdoors; FreeWalker (https://www.freewalker-aal.eu/) – a flexible and versatile solution for guiding and monitoring elderly or cognitive impaired persons in the outdoor environment and providing emergency information to recover disoriented persons safely.

With regard to HM requirements, the integration of IoT and cloud computing has a beneficial influence on improving the quality of life for elder people with chronic diseases (Gachet et al. 2012). Assisting medical staff in monitoring the treatment of elderly at home, developing personalized health services such as warnings or reminders for medication, providing personalized access to health information available on the Internet, supporting these social categories to do daily activities being aware in every moment about their health status are among these benefits.

The chapter is devoted to an HM solution centered on the integrated cloud-IoT sensing service offer. The intended contribution of this approach is to improve the sensing services accessibility and their fit with consumers' requirements.

The remaining part of the chapter is structured as follows: Section 2 provides an overview of specific HM architectural solutions adapted to the usage of IoT and cloud technologies. In Section 3, the generic sensing service scenario is introduced. Section 4 is devoted to the integrated sensing service offers approach, presenting the main roles, their business interactions, and the basic service operation rules. In Section 5, the specificity of the sensing service integrator, playing the central role in the proposed approach, is illustrated by its business model specifications and core entities of its managerial data structure. Section 6 presents two implementation scenarios of the integrated sensing service approach with the focus on the service integrator role. Some concluding remarks are presented in the final section.

8.2 Specific HM Architectural Solutions – An Overview

The BodyCloud SaaS approach is dedicated to collecting health-monitoring data (blood pressure, heart pulses, electrocardiogram, body movements) by sensor nodes in the body sensor network, and their real-time transfer to be stored, processed, analyzed, and visualized in a scalable fashion (Fortino et al. 2014). The architectural solution for a healthcare system based on the IoT devices, networking, and cloud technologies, proposed in (Zhang et al. 2017), is structured on three layers: (1) data collection (heterogeneous raw data in a variety of structures and formats, collected from a variety of sources and preprocessed before being transferred to the next layer), (2) data management (distributed heterogeneous data storage capabilities and advanced data processing and analysis methods), and (3) application service (access to visual data analysis results, open unified interface to data for development of user-centric applications and services). A six-layered solution for the smart hospital network system architecture detecting, locating, and monitoring smart objects is proposed in (Alharbe et al. 2015): data processing (collection real-time data using sensor-based technology), data integration (into appropriate databases), cloud computing (increase capacity of shared resources at the hospital level and in its interaction with the healthcare system), network (transfer data from different sources on one or multiple destination hubs), knowledge reasoning (data mining specific processing to support decision making responsibilities), and visualization (data representation to make it accessible to the user community). In (Plageras et al. 2016), the proposed three-layered framework for healthcare monitoring includes: home network to connect IoT devices and the local server, the gateway, and cloud resource for storing and analyzing data and video.

The MSI-MDD platform architecture for cloud-based monitoring services of seniors affected by dementia, presented in (Alexandru and Ianculescu 2017), takes advantage of the benefits generated by the integration of various assistive technologies, including cloud and IoT. A monitoring system proposed in (Li et al. 2017) is structured on data collection and data-transmission phases, to deal with real-time patient health information for heart diseases. An IoT-based health-monitoring system proposed in (Azimi et al. 2017) includes a management technique and a specific computing architecture to make possible autonomous adjustments to the patient status, while the IoT monitoring solution in (Pinto et al. 2017) is able to enroll vital information of patients and to activate alarms in emergency situations. In (Verma and Sood 2018), the proposed cloud-IoT m-health monitoring framework is used to trace potential diseases and rank their severity level. A recommender system for diabetes-specific prescriptions based on patient's body monitoring for identifying risks of foods and drugs is presented in (Ali et al. 2018). A comprehensive survey of HM solutions is provided in (Alsalibi et al. 2021).

8.3 Generic Sensing Service Scenario

The generic scenario of the sensing service is based on the interaction of four entities: the sensor owner, the sensor publisher, the extended service provider, and the sensor data consumer (Perera et al. 2014). The sensor owner might be a private or a public organization, a commercial sensor provider or an individual. In case the sensor owner decides that the data provided by its sensors will be available in the cloud, it has to define the access policy to these data that the potential sensor publisher should implement and potential users should comply with. A sensor sends data to a single sensor publisher, but subject to this policy, these data might be shared between several sensor publishers if necessary. The sensor publisher is a cloud provider that evaluates existing sensor owners' offers considering the potential sensor data consumers' interest in accessing these data. The extended service provider is a separate business entity specializing in advanced analysis and visualization of published sensor data.

The sensor data consumer has to identify and interact with all these providers to aggregate existing offers according to its needs. In case of HM, the medical staff is usually neither prepared nor interested and available for this effort. To avoid this inconvenience, the approach based on the integration of various sensing service contributors' offers is proposed, which implements the principle of "single-point-of-contact" in relation to the consumer side.

8.4 Integrated Sensing Service Offer Approach

8.4.1 *Main Roles and Business Interactions*

On the provider's side, the sensor device owner (SDO), sensor data publisher (SDP) and extended service provider (ESP) roles have a meaning similar with entities in the generic scenario presented above. SDO administrates and maintains a pool of devices that are available for sensing services, i.e., their data are published in cloud and are accessible for further use. SDP is a cloud-IoT platform administrator, which is publishing sensor generated data. ESP delivers value-added software solutions to process, analyze, and visualize sensor data published in the cloud, according to users' requirements. For example, in the case of real-time supervision and monitoring of mentally impaired or aging people, such high-quality services could be real-time analytics of monitoring data, risk assessment, fall, and crisis (seizure, stroke, heart attack) predictions.

On the customer's side, the integrated offer beneficiary (IOB) formulates the problem that has to be solved using sensing services, while the expertise to analyze the results provided by sensing services and to formulate recommendations to IOB belongs to the integrated offer user (IOU). In the HM context, IOB is the monitored patient and IOU is the medical unit providing HM services.

The sensing offer integrator (SOI) company plays the central role in this approach, as shown in Figure 8.1. After identifying a market opportunity, SOI analysis customer's requirements and starts negotiating the contributions to the integrated offer: (1) the sensor data publication in the cloud, (2) the availability of necessary sensor devices, and (3) the access to value-added services for sensor data analysis and visualization.

Next, SOI concludes the service provision contract with IOU that stipulates the configuration of the integrated service offer, the conditions of its activation, and the

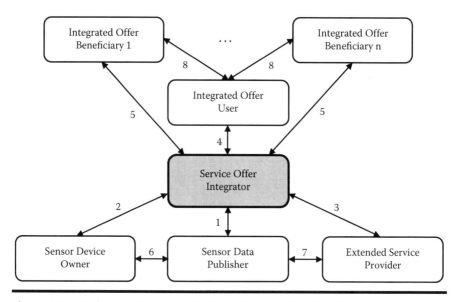

Figure 8.1 Business Interactions in the Integrated Sensing Service Approach.

access rights to the monitoring results (4). Based on provisions of the main contract, the interactions (1) to (3) are concluded by addendums to the framework agreement on SOI partnership, regarding concrete contributions to the concluded contract. Also, SOI negotiates a subsidiary contract with IOB on the provision, operation, and maintenance of sensor devices during the active monitoring sessions and on accessing the monitoring results according to the IOU's recommendations (5).

In addition to these main SOI interactions, the following supporting interactions are specific to this model, with the aim of implementing the service provision contract: (6) SDP and SDO decide on technical conditions to integrate identified sensor devices in the IoT platform; (7) SDP and ESP identify the requirements for installation and execution in cloud of selected value-added applications; (8) IOU stipulates the monitoring rules and IOB obligations during a monitoring session, as well as its access rights to available sensor data and value-added results.

(1) to (8) are called business interactions between entities playing those roles because they are governed by the provisions of the concluded contract. The model functioning involves also direct interactions between representatives of participating entities to solve various technical or procedural issues.

8.4.2 Operation Rules

The basic operation rules of HM service according to this approach are as follows:

(OR1) Sensors belonging to sensor devices accepted by the HM facility (IOU) are published sensors, i.e., they are eligible as monitoring data sources.

(OR2) An active sensor is a published sensor selected to be used as a data source during the patient's monitoring session.

(OR3) Within the contractual relationship between SOI and IOU, a treating doctor belonging to IOU formulates and negotiates with SOI representatives the integrated service configuration requirements for the benefit of the patient (IOB).

(OR4) After it, the doctor will activate the configured service as many times as necessary during the monitoring period by initiating a monitoring session.

(OR5) Each data instance collected by an active sensor during a monitoring session is stored and identifiable as a distinct value of a monitored parameter.

(OR6) Using the collected sensor data instances, each extended service accepted by IOU is available to generate instances of results from a predefined list.

(OR7) Each extended service result instance generated on request during a monitoring session is stored and identifiable as an output of the monitoring session.

(OR8) During the monitoring session, the session initiator (i.e. the doctor) has full access to the monitoring session data and result instances, and decides on their distribution to other stakeholders, according to their access rights.

(OR9) At the end of the monitoring session, all collected data and result instances will be archived to be available for later consultation, according to their archiving regime.

For (OR3), the service configuration requirements include:

■ the monitoring period;
■ the sensor devices allocated to the monitored patient;
■ the list of sensors on each allocated device, which are relevant during the monitoring period;
■ the selected value-added services for processing and visualization of collected sensor data;
■ the list of other interested parties that are allowed to access monitoring results (other doctors, assistive personnel, the monitored patient, caregivers) and their access rights;
■ the archiving regime for monitoring data and results.

8.5 Service Offer Integrator Specificity

8.5.1 SOI Business Model Specifications

A business model describes the rationale of how the value is created, delivered, and captured. The SOI business profile is close to the classical full service provider model, described in (Weill and Vitale 2001), where the aim is to provide total coverage of customer needs in a particular domain, via a single point of contact.

According to (Osterwalder and Pigneur 2010) a business model is structured in nine main building blocks, which are briefly specified in Table 8.1.

Table 8.1 Building Blocks of a Business Model (Adapted from Osterwalder and Pigneur 2010)

Name	*Definition*	*Details*
1. Customer segments	groups of people or organizations an enterprise aims to reach	Typology: mass market, niche market, segments with slightly/very different needs and problems
2. Value propositions	products and services that create value for a specific customer segment	Sources of value: novelty, design, performance, accessibility, price, usability, customization, cost reduction, risk reduction.
3. Channels	the way a company communicates with and reaches its customer segments to deliver a value proposition	Channel phases: rise awareness, help customers evaluate the proposed value, deliver a value proposition to customers, and provide post-purchase customer support.
4. Customer relationship	types of relationships a company establishes with specific customer segments	Typology: based on human interaction, no direct relationship (self-service), automated services (customized self-service), co-creation (creating value with customers), helping companies better understand their customers.
5. Revenue streams	various ways a company generates cash from each customer segment	Typology: asset sale, usage fee, subscription fee, lending/renting/leasing, licensing, brokerage fee (intermediation services), advertising fee.
6. Key resources	what assets are required by the business model	Typology: human and financial resources, physical assets (e.g., manufacturing facilities, distribution networks), intellectual resources (e.g., brands, proprietary knowledge, patents, copyrights).

(Continued)

Table 8.1 (Continued) Building Blocks of a Business Model (Adapted from Osterwalder and Pigneur 2010)

Name	Definition	Details
7. Key activities	what a company has to do according to its business model	Examples: production related activities, activities providing solutions to customers' needs, supporting activities (promotion, management, maintenance).
8. Key partnerships	suppliers and partners that are important for key resources and key activities of the business model	Main benefits: reduction of risk and uncertainty (strategic alliances), optimizing the allocation of resources and activities (e.g., outsourcing or sharing infrastructure), acquisition of particular/specific resources and activities.
9. Cost structure	operation costs for key resources, activities and partnerships (variable or fixed costs, economies of scale, economies of scope)	Main cost models: cost-driven model (low price value propositions and extensive outsourcing), value-driven model (oriented on value creation and highly personalized products and services).

Based on this structure, the proposed specifications for the SOI business model are as follows.

Customer segments: within the HM application domain the variant of "segments with slightly different needs and problems" is the most appropriate.

Value propositions: service availability, benefits of the cloud-IoT infrastructure, performance level of value-added services, accessibility, and usability of provided results are the main sources of value generation for its customers.

Channels: the right choice is the own and direct channel as efficient customer relationship management is a key success factor for this business profile. Also, considering the novelty of this approach on the market, the SOI channel should carefully implement and cover all channel phases, with specific attention paid to the first two ones.

Customer relationship: the priority goes to the direct, personal relationship with each customer. Another important critical success factor is the co-creation dimension, as this direct relationship is expected to provide relevant input for SOI itself in understanding specific needs and building a highly customizable offer.

Revenue streams: they are specific to the SOI business profile mentioned above, i.e. usage/subscription fees from the customers' side, advertising fees from third-party providers, fees for selling data about customers and membership fees from the providers' side.

Key resources: the cloud-IoT infrastructure, the human resource expertise of providing and integrating infrastructure services and advanced data analytics and visualization services, the licensed software.

Key activities: as specific to a service company, they are those dedicated to solving customer needs.

Key partnerships: they should be capable to provide complementary contributions to the integrated service offer and available for long-term collaboration to reduce risk and uncertainty.

Cost structure: it includes fixed costs for infrastructure operation, variable costs for sensor devices and value-added applications. The economy of scale is specific to this business model because of the better valorization of sensor data through their sharing between more interested users, which is a basic reason to adopt the cloud-IoT solution.

8.5.2 Core Entities of the SOI-MIS Data Structure

To ensure the effective implementation of the SOI business model, an efficient management information system should be in place, fully compliant with the basic operational rules of the SOI approach. To illustrate this request, the core entities of the database conceptual schema for the SOI-MIS are presented in Table 8.2.

Table 8.2 Core Entities of the SOI Managerial Data Structure

Name	Basic attributes
Sensor Device Owners	sdo-id, sdo-name, sdo-contact info
Sensor Device Statuses	sds-id, sds-name (available, active, defective)
Sensor Devices	sd-id, sd-name, sdo-id, sds-id, sds-date-time
Published Sensor Types	pst-id, pst-name (e.g., temperature, pressure, acceleration)
Published Sensors	ps-id, ps-name, pst-id, sd-id
Sensor Data Publishers	sdp-id, sdp-name, sdp-contact info
Extended Service Providers	esp-id, esp-name, esp-contact info

(Continued)

Table 8.2 (Continued) Core Entities of the SOI Managerial Data Structure

Name	Basic attributes
Extended Services	es-id, es-name, esp-id, sdp-id
Extended Service Results	esr-id, esr-name, es-id
Service Offer Integrator's Contracts	ctr-id, iou-id, ctr-start, ctr-end, ctr-value
Integrated Offer Users	iou-id, iou-name, iou-contractual info
Integrated Offer Beneficiaries	iob-id, iob-name, iob-contact info, iou-id
Contract-Sensor Devices	ctr-id, sd-id
Contract-Extended Services	ctr-id, es-id
Monitoring Session Initiators	msi-id, msi-name, iou-id
Monitoring Sessions	ms-id, ms-name, ctr-id, msi-id, iob-id, ms-start, ms-end
Monitoring Session-Published Sensors	ms-id, ps-id
Monitoring Session-Extended Service Results	ms-id, ers-id
Published Sensor Data Instances	ps-id, psdi-date-time, psdi-value
Extended Service Result Instances	esr-id, esri-date-time, esri-file-name

8.6 Implementation Scenarios for Integrated Sensing Service Approach

For most medical units and especially for small ones (clinics, general practitioners) that provide remote monitoring services specific to the outpatient treatment regime, the dominant scenario for implementing the integrated sensing service approach is to outsource it to a specialized provider, as a unique point of contact that takes full responsibility in implementing the service configuration requests, in service provision and operation, including administration of its results. This is mainly due to requirements generated by the quality metrics specific to this service, such as: high availability during the monitoring sessions, scalability to cope with inherent dynamics of monitoring volume (number of participants, duration of monitoring periods), intensity (number of monitored parameters, complexity level of data analysis), and health data security and privacy.

With regard to this last group of metrics, the main recommended solutions proposed in (EC-AIOTI 2017) include: data control by the user in any phase of the data life cycle, empowering the user to obtain sufficient knowledge on what its devices and related system are doing and sharing, encryption by default in communication and storage, life-time protection, trusted and transparent updates only by authorized parties, and identity protection by decoupling personal identity from device identity.

In addition, we should be aware that the medical staff is not available for the service operation effort. Their main interest is to have access to sensing data and results as decision support to solve patient problems.

Another scenario to implement the integrated service approach is specific to large medical facilities (hospitals) where the institutionalized patient setting is dominant. Depending on available financial, human, and technical resources, such medical unit may decide to implement the SOI role inside the unit.

The most significant specificity of this scenario is generated by the IT department capability to provide the functionality of IT infrastructure layers additional to cloud computing: edge and fog computing.

Edge computing is a complementary solution to currently dominating cloud computing where edge devices have more computing and storage capabilities, which improve their functionality and reduce the volume of data sent to the cloud. Being in line with requirements generated by many business models and applications, this computing paradim was pushed at the peak of the Gartner's hype cycle for cloud computing, 2018 (Smith and Anderson 2018).

Fog computing was initially defined as an extension of the cloud with the aim to provide networking, computing, and storage services between end devices and traditional cloud computing data centers (Bonomi et al. 2012). As compared with edge computing, the computing power and intelligence are in the local area network (Vermesan et al. 2018). This mid-infrastructure layer generates such significant advantages as minimizing the volume of data sent in the cloud, improving the privacy of sensitive data stored locally, limiting network communication impact on data latency and time-response performance, greater scalability for a variable number of connected devices and amount of data being generated and collected.

Under these circumstances, a three-layer infrastructure will be available, capable of providing decision support for:

■ time-critical decisions specific to risk evaluation in a real-time monitoring regime;
■ medical diagnosis based on current monitoring results and patient-related short- and medium-term historical data available in the local database;
■ predictive analysis, which is specific to personalized healthcare based on long-term data available in the cloud.

This infrastructure will impact on the interactions between SOI (IT department) and the other roles on the provider's side. In relation to the cloud provider, SOI will take over its responsibilities regarding sensor data publishing and will negotiate the necessary cloud resources to implement the long-term data storage and advanced analytics capabilities. In relation to SDO, SOI will negotiate conditions for integrating the sensor devices into the local edge-computing layer and, optional, the set up of a local buffer of the most critical and frequently used sensor devices. In relation to ESP, SOI will negotiate access to the extended services, which are specific to advanced data analysis for both diagnosis and predictive kind of decision support. In addition, the assimilation and in-house implementation of the most frequently used value-added services may be subject of these negotiations.

8.7 Conclusions

The advantages of combining cloud computing and IoT are generated by the complementarities between these two technologies. For traditional IoT applications, including HM, the cloud-IoT-based sensing service brings the advantages of improved efficiency in sensor data usage, scalable data storage and processing resources, facilities in data accessibility and sharing, advanced data governance and disaster recovery, and cost effectiveness. The chapter is dedicated to the integrated sensing service offer approach in HM, which provides the benefits of the single-point-of-contact principle in relation between medical units and service providers' side, simplifying their interaction, minimizing medical staff's effort to set up and operate the service, and improving service accessibility and its quality of operation. The provided information was structured with the aim to ensure the right understanding of the approach and favorable premises for its successful implementation and operation. First, the approach was described in terms of main roles, their responsibilities and interactions, as well as the basic service operation rules. Then, the specificity of the SOI company, playing the central role in this approach, was emphasized through its business model specifications and core entities of the managerial data structure. Two implementation scenarios were detailed for the integrated sensing service approach in case of medical units that provide HM services in outpatient and inpatient settings, respectively. In both cases, specific solutions for implementing the service offer integrator role were proposed.

In a larger context, the anonymised collected data and statistical results may be shared by an extended community of stakeholders, including research and academia, governmental institutions, and policy makers in healthcare.

As a final remark, the proposed approach might be of interest to any other application domain that could benefit cloud-IoT advantages. Nevertheless, the domain-oriented specialization of service companies implementing the SOI role is expected to have a significant influence on their efficiency and competitiveness on the market.

References

Aazam, M., I. Khan, A. Abdullah Alsaffar, and E-N. Huh. 2014. Cloud of Things: Integrating Internet of Things and cloud computing and the issues involved. In *Proceedings of the 11th International Bhurban Conference on Applied Sciences and Technology (IBCAST)*, 414–419, IEEE.

Alexandru, A., and M. Ianculescu. 2017. Enabling assistive technologies to shape the future of the intensive senior-centred care: A case study approach. *Studies in Informatics and Control* 26(3): 343–352.

Alharbe, N., A. S. Atkins, and J. Champion. 2015. Use of Cloud computing with wireless sensor networks in an Internet of Things environment for a smart hospital network. In *Proceedings of the 2015-the Seventh International Conference on eHealth, Telemedicine, and Social Medicine (eTELEMED)*, 52–58, IARIA.

Ali, F., S. R. Islam, and D. Kwak et al. 2018. Type-2 fuzzy ontology-aided recommendation systems for IoT-based healthcare. *Computer Communications* 119: 138–155.

Alsalibi A. I., M. K. Y. Shambour, M. A. Abu-Hashem, M. Shehab, and Q. Shambour. 2021. Internet of Things in health care: A survey. In: *Hybrid Artificial Intelligence and IoT in Healthcare*, eds. A. Kumar Bhoi, P. K. Mallick, M. Narayana Mohanty, and V. H. C. Albuquerque, 165–200, Springer.

Azimi, I., A. Anzanpour, A. M. Rahmani et al. 2017. HiCH: Hierarchical fog-assisted computing architecture for healthcare IoT. *ACM Transactions on Embedded Computing Systems (TECS)* 16(5s): 174. (1–20), ACM.

BigClouT. 2017. First BigClouT Architecture. Public deliverable 1.3, H2020 Project 723139 – Big data meeting Cloud and IoT for empowering the citizen clout in smart cities. https://ec.europa.eu/research/participants/documents/downloadPublic?documentIds=080166e5b312b41f&appId=PPGMS (accessed September 2, 2021).

Bonomi F., R. Milito, J. Zhu, and S. Addepalli. 2012. Fog computing and its role in the internet of things. In: *Proceedings of the 1st edition of the MCC workshop on Mobile cloud computing*, 13–16, ACM.

Botta, A., W. de Donato, V. Persico, and A. Pescapé. 2016. Integration of Cloud computing and Internet of Things: A survey. *Future Generation Computer Systems* 56: 684–700.

EC-AIOTI. 2017. Report on security & privacy in IoT. EC-AIOTI Workshop, January 13, 2017. https://ec.europa.eu/information_society/newsroom/image/document/2017-15/final_report_20170113_v0_1_clean_778231E0-BC8E-B21F-18089F746A650D4D_44113.pdf (accessed September 2, 2021).

Fortino, G., D. Parisi, V. Pirrone, and G. D. Fatta. 2014. Bodycloud: a SaaS approach for community body sensor networks. *Future Generation Computer Systems* 35: 62–79.

Gachet, D., M. de Buenaga, F. Aparicio, and V. Padrón. 2012. Integrating Internet of Things and Cloud computing for health services provisioning: The virtual Cloud carer project. In *Proceedings of 6th IEEE Int. Conference on Innovative Mobile and Internet Services in Ubiquitous Computing (IMIS)*, 918–921, IEEE.

Li, C., X. Hu, and L. Zhang. 2017. The IoT-based heart disease monitoring system for pervasive healthcare service. In *Knowledge-Based and Intelligent Information & Engineering Systems: Proceedings of the 21st International Conference, KES-2017*, Procedia Computer Science 112, 2328–2334, Elsevier.

Mell, P., and T. Grance. 2011. *The NIST Definition of Cloud Computing. Recommendations of the National Institute of Standards and Technology*, Special Publication 800–145.

Osterwalder, A. and Y. Pigneur. 2010. *Business Model Generation*. John Wiley & Sons.

Perera, C., A. Zaslavsky, P. Christen, and D. Georgakopoulos. 2014. Sensing as a Service model for smart cities supported by Internet of Things. *Transactions on Emerging Telecommunications Technologies* 25(1): 81–93.

Pinto, S., J. Cabral, and T. Gomes. 2017. We-care: An IoT-based health care system for elderly people. In *Proceedings of the 2017 IEEE International Conference on Industrial Technology (ICIT)*, 1378–1383, IEEE.

Plageras, A. P., K. E. Psannis, Y. Ishibashi, and B. G. Kim. 2016. IoT-based surveillance system for ubiquitous healthcare. In *Proceedings of IECON 2016–the 42nd Annual Conference of the IEEE on Industrial Electronics Society*, 6226–6230, IEEE.

Smith D., and E. D. Anderson. 2018. Hype Cycle for Cloud Computing, 2018. Gartner, ID: G00340420. https://www.gartner.com/en/documents/3884671 (accessed August 30, 2021).

Strome, T. 2015. A primer on healthcare Cloud computing. Healthcare Analytics.info. http://healthcareanalytics.info/2015/01/a-primer-on-healthcare-cloud-computing/#. VOYH1HJ6XQA (accessed August 28, 2021).

Verma, P., and S. K. Sood. 2018. Cloud-centric IoT based disease diagnosis healthcare framework. *Journal of Parallel and Distributed Computing* 116: 27–38.

Vermesan O., M. Eisenhauer, M. Serrano et al. 2018. The next generation Internet of Things–Hyperconnectivity and embedded intelligence at the edge. In: *Next Generation Internet of Things – Distributed Intelligence at the Edge and Human Machine-to-Machine Cooperation*, eds. O. Vermesan, and J. Bacquet, 19–102, River Publishers.

Weill, P. and M. Vitale. 2001. *We have moved place to space: migrating to e-business model.* Harvard Business School Press, Boston, USA.

Zhang, Y., M. Qiu, C-W. Tsai, M. M. Hassan, and A. Alamri. 2017. Health-CPS: Healthcare cyber-physical system assisted by cloud and big data. *IEEE Systems Journal* 11(1): 88–95.

Zhou, J., T. Leppanen, E. Harjula et al. 2013. Cloudthings: A common architecture for integrating the Internet of Things with Cloud computing. In *Proceedings of the IEEE 17th Int. Conference on Computer Supported Cooperative Work in Design (CSCWD)*, eds. W. Shen et al., 651–657, IEEE.

Chapter 9

Sleep-Stage Identification Using Recurrent Neural Network for ECG Wearable-Sensor System

Nico Surantha[1,2] and Vincent Valentine Jansen[1]

[1]*Department of Computer Science, Binus Graduate Program-Master of Computer Science, Bina Nusantara University, Jakarta, Indonesia*
[2]*Department of Electrical, Electronic and Communication Engineering, Tokyo City University, Faculty of Engineering, 1-28-1 Tamazutsumi, Setagaya-ku, Tokyo, Japan*

Contents

9.1 Introduction 164
9.2 Proposed Methods 166
    9.2.1 Data Collection of MIT-BIH Polysomnographic Dataset 166
    9.2.2 Pre-Processing of the Data 166
    9.2.3 First Algorithm: Long Short-Term Memory 168
    9.2.4 Second Algorithm: LSTM with Peephole Connection 169
    9.2.5 Third Algorithm: Gated Recurrent Unit 169
9.3 Results 169
    9.3.1 Model Training and Evaluation 169
    9.3.2 Pre-Processing 170
    9.3.3 First Algorithm: Long Short-Term Memory 170

DOI: 10.1201/9781003145189-9

9.3.4 Second Algorithm: LSTM with Peephole Connection................ 170
9.3.5 Third Algorithm: Gated Recurrent Unit..................................... 172
9.4 Conclusion... 172

9.1 Introduction

During good sleep, muscle and tissue rejuvenate. Memory consolidation also occurs. Therefore, maintaining the quality of sleep is crucial for human beings. Based on the survey of the National Sleep Foundation on 1,000 participants from the USA, 13% of the participants did not have enough sleep on non-workdays. The percentage was higher on workdays, in which 30% of the participants did not have enough sleep. The findings of this survey show that many people lack sleep, particularly on workdays. The lack of sleep may disturb individuals' lives by reducing productivity due to energy loss. Early detection of sleep-related disorders may prevent further sleep disorders in which evaluating sleep stages can be a good method for sleep study and early indication. According to the gold standard of sleep study, several stages of sleep can be classified as awake, REM, and NREM. The NREM contains several stages such as light sleep (stage 1 and 2) and deep sleep (stage 3 and 4).Classification of sleep stages can be done by visiting a sleep specialist. An experiment will be conducted for patients in the specific room to monitor their psychological conditions during sleep. Common devices such as electroencephalography and ECG can be employed for detecting brain waves and heart rates, respectively. For this work, ECG was chosen rather than EEG because it provides more comfort, where in EEG installation, EEG electrodes need to be placed on the patients. For ECG cases, a non-contact ECG sensor already exists. The ECG produces a signal as the result, as shown in Figure 9.1. Each data generated can be identified by sleep specialists. However, manual identification is very tedious and exhausting. Automatic identification of sleep stages will be very helpful for sleep research as the initial diagnosis. Recent developments of portable sensors, embedded system, cloud computing, and machine-learning algorithms have led to the emergence of big data analytics for healthcare. A sleep-monitoring system is developed using these technologies to allow patients to monitor their sleep condition regularly. The ECG signal collected using a portable ECG sensor can be aggregated in the data aggregator before being sent to cloud computing for signal processing. The sleep stage can be classified automatically by a machine-learning algorithm for early diagnostic. In the field of machine learning, artificial neural network has been known as a promising and emerging method that can be applied in many fields. One of the advantages of applying a neural network in the sleep study is that it has tolerance for some undesirable data or events with the ability to learn non-linear and complex relations. On the other hand, a neural network has some drawbacks, such as slow backpropagation learning, which can lead to local optima solution. LSTM is a type of recurrent neural network that

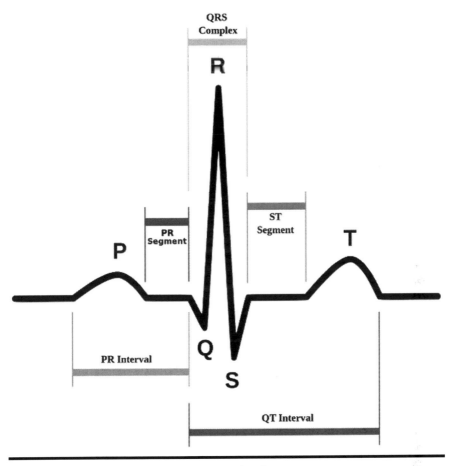

Figure 9.1 Several Components of ECG Signal.

addresses the vanishing gradient problem in vanilla RNNs through additional cells and input and output gates. Intuitively, vanishing gradients are solved through additional additive components, and forget gate activations, that allow the gradients to flow through the network without vanishing as quickly.

GRU is another commonly used RNN architecture, similar to an LSTM, but it only has two gates – a reset gate and an update gate – and notably lacks an output gate. Fewer parameters mean GRUs are generally easier/faster to train than their LSTM counterparts. The data features must be extracted in order to use RNN algorithm for identifying sleep stages. Features can be extracted based on heart rate variability from ECG. The HRV is one of physiological phenomena showing the continuous beating of the heart, which varies during sleeping. To extract the features of HRV, several methods can be employed, such as geometrical, time domain, poincare, as well as frequency domain. The study was conducted using several RNN architecture. The classification of sleep stages was conducted using

LSTM and GRU. The performance of LSTM and GRU were evaluated to obtain the optimum algorithm by calculating the accuracy percentage. The main contributions of this study is building a classifier model using RNN to achieve optimal accuracy in terms of sleep stages classification using HRV features obtained from ECG signal and evaluating the performance of each proposed RNN model compared to the previous research.

9.2 Proposed Methods

The methodology includes: 1) MITBPD collection, 2) pre-processing of data, 3) feature extraction of HRV, and 4) model building and evaluation. The algorithms used in this work were LSTM, LSTM with peephole connection and GRU. Performance comparison also was made.

9.2.1 Data Collection of MIT-BIH Polysomnographic Dataset

The data obtained contained recordings of physiological signal of the human body during sleeping. ECG, EEG, blood pressure, and respiration were included in MITBPD. The reason for using MITBPD dataset is because it is one of public ECG datasets that has labelled annotations and has been used by many previous researchers to make sure that the results of comparison carried out are fair. For simplicity, only an ECG signal was used, which was digitized with 12-bit per sample and sampling frequency of 250 Hz. The 18 files recorded during the sleeping period of 2 female and 16 male subjects were utilized. The participants' ages ranged from 32 to 56 years old ($x = 43$) with weight 89 –152 kg ($x = 119$ kg). Prior to pre-processing, 10,274 samples were retrieved in which each sample recording has a duration of 30 seconds. The MITBPD has class distribution of 17.79%, 38.28%, 4.76%, 1.78%, 6.89% and 30.5% for NREM1, NREM2, NREM3, NREM4, REM, and awake sleep stage.

9.2.2 Pre-Processing of the Data

Data annotation and RR interval were recorded and pre-processed. RR interval is a time delay between the current and previous heart beats. By calculating the time that elapsed between two consecutive R waves of ECG signal, RR interval was obtained. Data annotation was labelled by a sleep specialist, confirming the sleep stage for every 30 seconds. First, problematic data were removed. In this step, the annotation data and RR interval were synchronized. The problematic data refer to the missing timestamp that makes both data fail to synchronize. The data will be removed. Each annotation data may contain many RR intervals. If the annotation data did not match the scope of the research (such as awake, NREM, REM), then the data were removed. Then, feature extraction was performed to those set of RR interval from each annotation. For feature extraction of heart rate variability to track and interpret the electric activity of the heart, ECG can be used. There is a constant variation in the human heartbeat, which is recorded by ECG. The nervous systems, such as parasympathetic and sympathetic nerves, control the heart rate fluctuation. In this work, those variabilities were utilized to extract the 18 features, as shown in Table 9.1.

Table 9.1   The List of Features Extracted from HRV

No	Name of Feature	Method of Extraction	Explanation
1	SDNN	Time Domain	SDNN is the standard deviation of NN intervals $$SDNN = \sqrt{\frac{1}{N-1}\sum_{j=1}^{N}(RR_j - \overline{\overline{RR}})^2}$$
2	RMSSD	Time Domain	Root Mean Square of the Successive Differences $$RMSSD = \sqrt{\frac{1}{N-1}\sum_{j=1}^{N-1}(RR_{j+1} - RR_j)^2}$$
3	SDSD	Time Domain	standard deviation of the successive difference between adjacent R-R intervals
4	NN50	Time Domain	Total number of pairs of adjacent NN intervals differing by more than 50 ms $Count\ (|RR_{j+1} - RR_j|)$ where $|RR_{j+1} - RR_j| > 50$
5	pNN50	Time Domain	Percentage of adjacent NN intervals differing by more than 50 ms $pNN50 = \frac{NN50}{N-1} \times 100$
6	AVNN	Time Domain	AVNN is mean of all normal sinus to normal sinus of NN intervals $AVNN = \frac{1}{N}\sum_{j=1}^{N}RR_j$
7	HRV Triangular Index	Geometric al	total of RR interval / height of histogram of all RR intervals with 7.8125 ms bin
8	SD1	Poincare	standard deviation of perpendicular points to the line-of-identity $SD1^2 = \frac{1}{2}SDSD^2$

(Continued)

Table 9.1 (Continued)   The List of Features Extracted from HRV

No	Name of Feature	Method of Extraction	Explanation
9	SD2	Poincare	standard deviation of parallel points along the line-of-identity $$SD2^2 = 2SDNN^2 - \frac{1}{2}SDSD^2$$
10	SD1SD2 Ratio	Poincare	Ratio of SD1 dan SD2 $$SD1SD2\ Ratio = \frac{SD1}{SD2}$$
11	S	Poincare	Area of Ellipse $$S = \pi \times SD1 \times SD2$$
12	TP	Frequency Domain	Total Power
13	VLF	Frequency Domain	TP ranging from 0–0.04 Hz
14	LF	Frequency Domain	TP ranging from 0.04–0.15 Hz
15	HF	Frequency Domain	TP ranging from 0.15–0.4 Hz
16	LFHF Ratio	Frequency Domain	The ratio of LF to HF indicates the sympathovagal balance $$LFHF\ Ratio = \frac{LF}{HF}$$
17	LFnorm	Frequency Domain	Normalized LF value $$LFNorm = \frac{LF}{TP - VLF}$$
18	HFnorm	Frequency Domain	Normalize HF value $$HFNorm = \frac{HF}{TP - VLF}$$

9.2.3 First Algorithm: Long Short-Term Memory

In 1997, Hochreiter dan Schmidhuber introduce LSTM to solve the long-term dependencies problem. Like RNN, LSTM also consists of module-module with repeating process where each module used is a LSTM module. LSTM modules have different processes compared to normal RNN modules with the addition of cell state or memory cell that will be used to store information for long periods. The memory cell will decide what information what will be stored within the gate.

In LSTM, there are three gates: input gate, forget gate, and output gate. Each gate functions as a filter to store the information or not based on each gate's weight value.

9.2.4 Second Algorithm: LSTM with Peephole Connection

Gers et al. proposed LSTM with peephole connection, which is a variation from LSTM that has a weighted peephole connection. The purpose of the peephole connection is to connect CEC with other gates that are in the same block memory, allowing all gates to access the current cell state. In the original LSTM, every gate receives a connection from input and output units where when the output gates are closed, there are no gates that can access each CEC being controlled, which can led to decreased performance.

9.2.5 Third Algorithm: Gated Recurrent Unit

Chung et al. proposed a gated recurrent unit, which is a variation from LSTM that does not have an output gate. The purpose of GRU is to make each recurrent unit catch dependencies within different time scales with adaptives because not all information impacts the next step. Inside GRU, the component that organizes the information flow is known as gate, and GRU have two gates, the reset gate and the update gate. The reset gate on GRU will determine how to combine the new information input with past information, and the update gate will decide how much past information that will be stored.

9.3 Results

9.3.1 Model Training and Evaluation

The algorithms were used to classify four sets of data, which are 6, 4, 3, and 2 numbers of sleep stages in which the sets can be categorized as follows (1) six classes: awake, stage 1, stage 2, stage 3, stage 4, and REM, (2) 4 classes: awake, deep sleep, light sleep, and REM, (3) three classes: awake, NREM, and REM, (4) two classes: awake and sleep. The MITBPD has class distribution of 17.79%, 38.28%, 4.76%, 1.78%, 6.89%, and 30.5% for NREM1, NREM2, NREM3, NREM4, REM, and awake sleep stage. To validate the data, the 70% training and 30% testing data were implemented using stratified sampling where the training and testing data were used further for accuracy evaluation. The number of retrieved data was adjusted proportionally. The training and testing results data from train-test split are different from data that used in previous works.

9.3.2 Pre-Processing

The invalid data without annotation or irrelevant annotation, as well as incomplete RR interval, were taken out. The 1.17% of total data removed amounted to 120 data. The rest of the 98.83% data, 10,154 samples were synchronized with annotation data, data normalization, feature extraction, and RR interval.

9.3.3 First Algorithm: Long Short-Term Memory

The network takes 18 features as the input and for each EEG window "time step," the concatenated element vector is then fed to a stack of two (NLSTM layers) large recurrent LSTM layers with three units each. The two layers have 264 and 84 trainable parameters. The output layer is a small LSTM unit with softmax output activation, and it has 24 trainable parameters. The component output vector represents for each time step the class probabilities (or soft decisions) that the given 30 s input windows belong to sleep stages wake, REM, N1, N2, and N3, respectively. The experiments consisting of 100 LSTM iterations for each experiment were performed to evaluate LSTM algorithm. All 18 features were executed without a prior selection process. The mean accuracy of training data for six, four, three, and two classes were respectively 45.12%, 60.1%, 65%, and 71.07%. Consecutively, the mean accuracies of testing data for six, four, three, and two classes were 47.06%, 62.29%, 68%, and 72.92%. According to the accuracy evaluation, the difference of training and testing accuracy was significant in which the differences were 1.94%, 2.19%, 3%, and 1.85% for six, four, three, and two classes.

9.3.4 Second Algorithm: LSTM with Peephole Connection

The network takes 18 features as the input and for each EEG window "time step," the concatenated element vector is then fed to a stack of two (NLSTM layers) large recurrent peephole LSTM cell layers with three units each. The two layers have 264 and 84 trainable parameters. The output layer is a small peephole LSTM cell unit with softmax output activation, and it has 24 trainable parameters. The component output vector represents for each time step the class probabilities (or soft decisions) that the given 30 s input window belongs to sleep stages wake, REM, N1, N2, and N3, respectively. The experiments consisting of 100 LSTM with peephole connection iterations for each experiment were performed to evaluate LSTM with peephole connection algorithm. All 18 features were executed without a prior selection process. The mean accuracy of training data for six, four, three, and two classes were respectively 44.34%, 60.49%, 65.06%, and 71.28%. Consecutively, the mean accuracies of testing data for six, four, three, and two classes were 46.76%, 61.67%, 67.5%, and 72.27%. According to the accuracy evaluation, the difference of training and testing accuracy was significant in which the differences were 2.42%, 1.18%, 2.44%, and 0.99% for six, four, three, and two classes.

Table 9.2 Comparison with Previous Research

Author	Dataset	No. of Features	Classifier	Accuracy				
				2 Class	3 Class	4 Class	5 Class	
Xiao (2013)	SHRSV	41	Random Forest		**88.67%**			
Fonseca (2015)	PSG	80	Multi-class Bayesian Network		**80%**	69%		
Adnane (2012)	MIT-BIH	10	SVM	79.99%				
		12		79.31%				
Lesmana (2018)	MIT-BIH	18	ELM-PSO	**82.1%**	76.77%	71.52%	72.66%	
Yücelbaş (2018)	MIT-BIH	15	Morphological		**77.02%**			
Wei (2018)	MIT-BIH	11	DNN		77%			
Proposed	MIT-BIH	18	LSTM	72.92%	68%	62.29%	77.06%	
			LSTM with Peephole Connection	72.27%	67.5%	61.67%	76.76%	
			GRU	71.71%	67.42%	61.24%	76.50%	

9.3.5 Third Algorithm: Gated Recurrent Unit

The network takes 18 features as the input and for each EEG window "time step," the concatenated element vector is then fed toa stack of two (GRU layers) large recurrent GRU layers with three units each. The two layers have 264 and 84 trainable parameters. The output layer is a small GRU unit with softmax output activation, and it has 24 trainable parameters. The component output vector represents for each time step the class probabilities (or soft decisions) that the given 30 s input window belongs to sleep stages wake, REM, N1, N2, and N3, respectively. The experiments consisting of 100 GRU iterations for each experiment were performed to evaluate GRU algorithm. All 18 features were executed without a prior selection process. The mean accuracy of training data for six, four, three, and two classes were respectively 45.27%, 60.03%, 65.05%, and 71.24%. Consecutively, the mean accuracies of testing data for six, four, three, and two classes were 46.50%, 61.24%, 68%, and 72.56%. According to the accuracy evaluation, the difference of training and testing accuracy was significant in which the differences were 1.23%, 1.21%, 2.95%, and 1.32% for six, four, three, and two classes. The performance comparison of the proposed method and the existing methods is shown by Table 9.2.

9.4 Conclusion

In this research, sleep stage classification from heart rate variability of ECG signal was performed using three types of algorithms, four sets of classes, and two sets of features. Meanwhile, LSTM, LSTM with peephole connection, and GRU were used as algorithms. The set of classes are six, four, three, and two sleep stages in which the accuracy was compared. The study shows that LSTM exhibited the highest accuracy, followed by GRU and LSTM with peephole connection, respectively. It can be concluded that RNN model can be used to classify sleep stages with good accuracy results.

Chapter 10

Classification of Methods to Reduce Clinical Alarm Signals for Remote Patient Monitoring: A Critical Review

Teena Arora[1], Venki Balasubramanian[1],
Andrew Stranieri[1], Mai Shenhan[1], Rajkumar Buyya[2],
and Sardar M.N. Islam[3]

[1]*Federation University, Australia*
[2]*RMIT University, Australia*
[3]*Victoria University, Australia*

Contents

10.1 Introduction 174
    10.1.1 Remote Patient-Monitoring Application Architecture............. 176
    10.1.2 Alarms in RPM 176
    10.1.3 False-Positive Alarms 177
10.2 A Pentagon Approach 178
    10.2.1 Clinical Requirements 179
    10.2.2 Method Selection 179
    10.2.3 Design and Development... 180
    10.2.4 Clinical Trial and Analysis 180

DOI: 10.1201/9781003145189-10

173

      10.2.5 Feedback Loop 180

10.3 Classification Categories.. 181

      10.3.1 Physiological Data-Based Approach 183

            10.3.1.1 Customised Alarm Signals........................ 183

            10.3.1.2 Machine Learning 183

            10.3.1.3 Time Delay 184

            10.3.1.4 Integration of Techniques 184

            10.3.1.5 Coalition Game Theory 185

            10.3.1.6 Sensor Fusion 185

            10.3.1.7 Pattern Discovery 185

      10.3.2 Clinical Device-Centric Approach............................ 186

      10.3.3 Clinical Knowledge-Based Approach........................ 186

            10.3.3.1 Pattern Match 186

            10.3.3.2 Team-Based Method 186

      10.3.4 Clinical Environment-Based Approaches.................. 187

            10.3.4.1 Median Filters 187

            10.3.4.2 Dimension Reduction 187

10.4 Results and Discussion... 188

      10.4.1 Physiological Data 189

      10.4.2 Clinical Device-Centric 189

      10.4.3 Clinical Knowledge-Based 189

      10.4.4 Clinical Environment 189

10.5 Conclusions... 190

Notes 190

References 190

10.1 Introduction

The Internet of Things (IoT) has improved the quality of medical care processes using innovative technology [1]. For progressive nations, human health and well-being are imperative goals. Medical devices used by health professionals and doctors are essential for monitoring and preventing a patient's illness. IoT for patient monitoring provides several opportunities for researchers and developers to monitor patients remotely by using cloud- and fog-computing technologies [2,3]. The main characteristics of the IoT are [4]:

■ Interconnectivity: IoT provides interconnectivity of most devices for communication and information exchange.

■ Things-related services: The IoT can provide confidentiality and semantic consistency between physical and virtual things.

■ Heterogeneity: Devices used in IoT are heterogeneous as each integrated device in this network is manufactured by a different vendor. Deployed intelligent devices can also transfer and gather data over the Internet to reach their shared goal of providing the specialized service for which they are designed.

- Dynamic changes: The number of devices connected over the network, as well as their state of waking, active, sleeping, connected, and disconnected, is efficiently handled by the IoT.
- Enormous scale. The IoT handles data generated by many devices and their interpretation to generate useful information.
- Safety: This is one of the essential characteristics. The protection of our data, as well as the network endpoints, means creating a security paradigm.
- Connectivity: The connectivity network accessibility and compatibility of various things can be provided.

The IoT architecture consists of different technologies that safely deploy devices to deliver intelligent services. The sensors and actuators used in electronic devices are smart for communication and collection of data via network components. The collected data is transmitted to the storage servers for processing and then delivered as a service to the application users. Figure 10.1 shows how IoT communicates with other devices. All the recorded data is digital, which can be accessible by the end-users. The IoT architecture consists of the following four components:

- Smart devices: A smart device is an electronic gadget that can connect, share, and Interact with users and other smart devices. Although usually small in size, intelligent devices typically have the computing power of a few gigabytes.
- First Hope Network: The local network translates the device communication protocols to Internet protocols.
- The Internet: The Internet connects intelligent devices with backend servers.
- Back-ed server: These are primarily data centers or client applications.

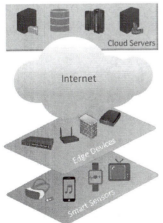

Figure 10.1   IoT Architecture.

With the advancement of technology, IoT is the opening opportunity for many innovative applications such as healthcare, transportation, robotics, automation, logistics, and industrial manufacturing. Remote patient monitoring (RPM) is one of the services provided by IoT that offers various benefits to both patients and physicians at anytime, anywhere, including continuous patient health monitoring and access to real-time health data through the Internet [5,6].

10.1.1 Remote Patient-Monitoring Application Architecture

Intelligent devices connected through networked systems can provide clinicians or caretakers with the patient's present and past health records in remote patient-monitoring (RPM) applications. The RPM application architecture mainly monitors the patient's health condition and a processing part to identify health-related issues. The typical vital signs such as heart rate, blood pressure, temperature, respiratory rate, and SpO_2 can be measured by Bluetooth-enabled sensors that collect a patient's health data, as shown in Figure 10.2. The sensed data are pre-processed and sent to the connected gateway, usually a smartphone or tablet, via Bluetooth, which runs an application that authenticates the patient's ID or other necessary information before transmitting to the cloud servers. After necessary authentication, the patients' real-time health data can be accessed using the cloud services from doctors or clinicians' personal computer or smartphones. The cloud services can have intelligent algorithms that can automatically raise alarms to clinicians for early intervention.

10.1.2 Alarms in RPM

The effectiveness of remote patient-monitoring systems depends on algorithms for automatically processing data to raise clinically significant alarms for the clinicians to make an informed decision and early intervention [7]. These clinical alarm needs to

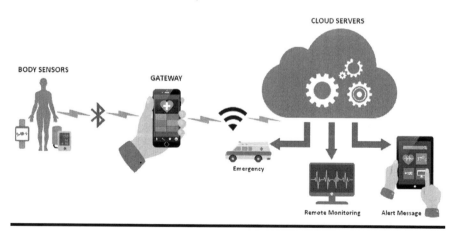

Figure 10.2   An Architecture for Remote Patient Monitoring (RPM).

be triggered "right on time" and accurate so that treatment can be commenced "well on time." Automated alarm signals play a pivotal role in increasing the quality of care and contributing to patients' good health, especially in remote patient monitoring, where clinicians or guardians are away from the patient.

Monitoring devices raise alarms with advanced data-processing algorithms for specific life-threatening situations when the life support devices are not working appropriately or when a patient's condition is forecast to deteriorate [8]. Therefore, an in-depth investigation of the patient's clinical needs and monitoring environment for efficient alarm generation is needed [7]. The capability of monitoring devices that detect a patient's clinical deterioration, depending on the algorithm used, results in frequent alarms. In most cases, most of these alarms may have crossed the pre-set parameter limits but have minimal or no clinical significance [9]. Due to frequent false positive alarms, clinicians can become less sensitive toward patients' alarms and neglect any possible dangerous situations [8], leading to alarm fatigue [8,10,11].

10.1.3 False-Positive Alarms

The literature in [12–14] has identified that most of the alarms in intensive care units (ICU) are non-actionable or false-positive, and only 5–13% of ICU alarms were actionable. One-quarter of monitored patients are responsible for two-thirds of all alarms [12]. In contrast, another study in [7] found that 2% of patients observed data in ICU contributed to 77% of false arrhythmia alarms. These studies show that only a few patients generate most false alarms.

Fewer false-positive alarms can be achieved in the ICU by applying the interventions to available medical devices such as changing the electrodes every day, with possible alarm delay, and the personalised widening of the alarm parameters as only < 26% of alarms found to be clinically significant [15]. Proper alarm settings, such as turning off duplicate alarms and considering alarm delay for alarm autocorrection and staff education on setting personalised parameter limits, are essential for reducing false alarms [16].

One of the significant issues with the current RPM application is the high sensitivity due to the advanced algorithm used in the medical devices, causing an increased number of false-positive alarms resulting in alarm fatigue, which decreases the quality of care [7,17]. And these current RPM applications, historically, do not have the sensitivity and specificity of the commercial-grade, non-mobile sensors that the hospital used. This problem will likely be exacerbated as we migrate to more aggregated sensors with arguably worse patient/sensor interfaces such as skin contact. Various other factors such as the lack of standard guidelines, pre-set threshold, patient's movements, a faulty device, low battery, data-processing algorithms contribute to an increased number of unnecessary alarm signals [18–20].

The contribution of this chapter is that it considers all the literature that builds upon medical devices and allows the researcher to translate the knowledge for futuristic RPM applications. The lack of standard guidelines for generating the alarm signal has been identified in the literature. Our proposed pentagon approach to developing a more efficient alarm signal will attempt to address this gap in the literature. Various causes for the origin of false-positive alarms have been identified from the literature. A classification has been done for multiple interventions used in the literature to reduce false-positive alarms based on four major approaches: clinical knowledge, physiological data, medical sensor devices, and clinical environments focusing on the causes of false-positive alarms. This review was conducted according to the critical review guidelines [21].

The rest of the chapter is organized as follows: Section 2 describes the proposed pentagon approach. Section 3 presents the classification categories. Section 4 presents the results, and the discussion, and conclusions are shown in the last section.

10.2 A Pentagon Approach

The literature does not address a general guideline to develop an effective alarm-signal generation strategy for clinical needs. This work proposes the "pentagon approach" for clinical alarm generation to guide researchers, clinicians, and developers to design an effective alarm-generation strategy for their needs. An effective alarm-generation strategy can help in reducing frequent false-positive alarm signals. The proposed guidelines in the pentagon approach (see Figure 10.3) provide a well-structured flow

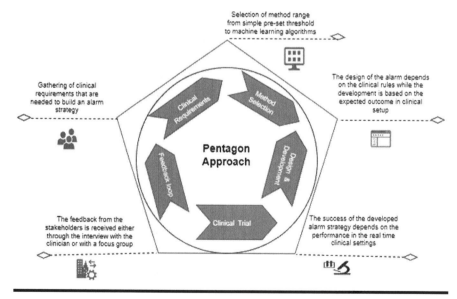

Figure 10.3 A Pentagon Approach to Building a Clinical Alarm Strategy.

of phases that help build an elegant solution at each level with clinical data verification. The guideline consists of the following five steps: the gathering of clinical requirements, selection of an appropriate method, application design and development, clinical trial, clinical analysis, and clinical response.

10.2.1 *Clinical Requirements*

This initial step in the guidelines includes gathering all the details required for the alarm strategy. A detailed list of clinical requirements should be made by interviewing the clinical staff and analysing the existing system. A few items on the clinical requirement list could be the scope for changes, the need for alarm, the expectation of patients and nurses, parameters to be observed, patient-centric alarm systems or generalised alarm systems, and the feasibility of the new systems, a scoring system to be used, medical devices to be used, architecture. Identifying the various causes that can affect the clinically recorded data value of the measured parameters is also essential for this phase. Studies show that some false-positive alarm signals are due to patient movement, smaller-sized sensors, or not appropriately placed sensors [22].

Selecting a suitable alarm strategy based on the gathered clinical requirements can help build an efficient system with fewer false-positive alarms. Literature [23] shows how identifying the causes and effects of unnecessary alarm signals is helpful for overall system quality. This paper-proposed method selection focused on the leading causes of the false-positive alarm in the current system. Identification of the leading causes for the origin of false-positive alarms has been discussed in Section 3 in detail. Therefore, selecting methods is the following step after gathering the requirements in building an effective alarm-signal strategy.

10.2.2 *Method Selection*

After gathering the clinical requirements and specifications, selecting the appropriate method to raise the alarm signal is imperative. The clinical needs and specifications list will input the proper alarm-strategy phase. Method selection should be made to reduce the unnecessary alarms focusing on the clinical requirements. However, the literature does not identify various methods focusing on the alarm causes. A critical review has been done to identify and categorise the multiple methods used in the literature, focusing on the causes in this study to fill the gap. The critical review has been discussed in Section 3. This categorisation will help researchers further identify the possible methods for the categories' causes.

The simplest and most widely used methods are customisation of the pre-set threshold value [24–27], machine-learning techniques [28,29], pattern-matcher method [30], and median filter [31]. The time delay method of the sensor value received at the destination by the clinician or a caretaker in RPM using the time-critical parameter is a proper technique to lessen the anomalies in the alarm signal [32,33].

10.2.3 Design and Development

Once the method is selected in the previous phase, the next step is to design and develop the alarm strategy. The design behind an alarm-signal strategy depends on the clinical rules, algorithms, and necessary features. The development of the alarm-signal strategy is carried out based on the expected outcomes, the risk associated with the alarm signals, security, and privacy of the clinical environment. In the case of remote patient monitoring, the design and development of the alarm signal, the strategy included networking technologies such as ZigBee, Bluetooth, and cellular networks [34,35].

10.2.4 Clinical Trial and Analysis

The design and development from the previous phase for a required clinical setup take the form of software, smart device, or other tangible means. The developed solution is then implemented technically in the relevant clinical environments for the trial. Clinical trials are done to check the feasibility of the developed alarm signal strategy according to precise clinical requirements. The following aspects need to be considered for the clinical trial and analysis:

- various problems encountered
- alternate methods
- quality of applied methods
- reliability of the alarm
- validation of the alarming outcome
- performance measures
- limitation of the designed system in real-time
- software or hardware bugs
- improvements needed for various clinical needs

The literature shows that the developed alarm-signal strategy is more effective if tested in the clinical setting before actual deployment [34,36]. The reasoning alarm system designed for remote patient monitoring is more productive by testing the alarm system on various mobile devices and observing their response time [34]. The prototype of the developed fuzzy logic-based alarm system for automated anesthesia level controller has proven beneficial in literature [36].

10.2.5 Feedback Loop

After the clinical trial, the deployment of the alarm-signal strategy is performed in relevant clinical settings. The feedback for these life-critical alarm systems is most effective through direct interviews with the clinicians, a questionnaire, or a focus group of the stakeholders [37,38]. Quantitative and qualitative approaches have a firm agreement and can be used as an effective tool for collecting feedback for these alarm systems. Key factors to be considered for this phase are as follows:

- Culture
- Ease of use
- Clinical staff perspective
- Patient perspective
- Security of data
- Performance
- Quality of results

Based on the collected feedback, the necessary steps are planned to make the system work better in the clinical environment. The motivation behind implementing the feedback is to maintain the implemented strategy for various new requirements using the pentagon approach. The following section describes the classification categories of multiple causes of false alarms.

10.3 Classification Categories

The first phase of the pentagon model is to identify the clinical requirements. Identifying the causes of false-positive alarms is one of the essential clinical requirements. The unusual movement of the patient [39], the vibration of the sensors, use of incompetent clinical knowledge, inappropriate medication, erroneous sensor placement on the body of the patient, time of the measurement, use of incorrect parameter values, incorrect threshold settings [40], false interpretation of the alarms, software bugs, and hardware malfunction [41] are the few identified causes from the literature.

The identified causes are categorised based on the nature of the cause of the false-positive alarm under knowledge, data, device, and environment, as shown in Figure 10.4. As one of the main contributions of this work, we classified the causes

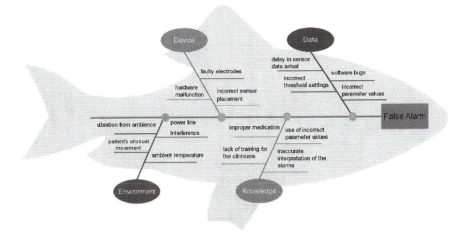

Figure 10.4 False Alarm[1] Causes in a Clinical Setup.

into four broader categories. Our study of various alarm-strategy methods in the literature convincingly falls under any one of these more general categories. Also, we have found that the causes of the alarm are related to one of these categories. The following gives a brief description of the categories and the nature of the causes of false-positive alarms.

- *Data:* The false-positive alarms that arise due to incorrect parameter values, delay in data arrival of sensor data, in case of remote patient monitoring, incorrect threshold settings, and software bugs that directly affect the interpretation of the vital signs of the patient falls under the data category.
- *Device:* Device or technically related false positive alarms include faulty electrodes, erroneous sensor placement on the patient's body, and hardware malfunction that falls under the device category.
- *Environment:* False positive alarms can be triggered due to the unusual movement of the patient, external noise, power-line interference, ambient temperature, and vibration from the ambience that originate in the clinical setup come under the environment.
- *Knowledge:* The knowledge category consists of those false positive alarms caused due to human error, such as lack of training for the clinicians, inaccurate interpretation of the alarm signals, incorrect parameter values, and drastic changes in vital signs due to improper medication.

The motive behind categorising the causes of false-positive alarms is to identify the methods that can overcome the causes. The methods that are related to the causes are collated under approaches. The naming of the approaches is derived from the identified categories, as shown in Figure 10.5, and are based on the suitable method one can choose to reduce the effect of causes responsible for frequent false positive alarms.

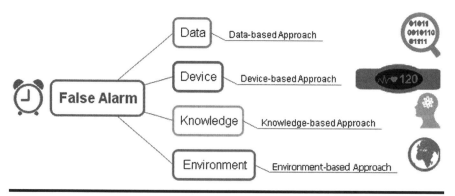

Figure 10.5 Classification of False-Positive Alarm[2] Artefacts and Approaches.

Our literature review is based on the significant publications in the clinical and biotechnology field and further refined for the clinical trials. The literature review has shown the following methods used to reduce the number of false positive alarms: pattern match, changing electrode, machine learning, time delay, median filter, dimension reduction, sensor fusion, integration, coalition game theory, and team-based. Figure 10.5 shows the approaches consist of different types of methods that are similar and related to the approach and are related to the approach type that can be used to solve the causes of the false-positive alarm. The classification of the approaches and the methods is helpful in the second phase of the pentagon model, which is method selection, and will facilitate the third phase of the pentagon model, the design and development of the alarm-signal strategies, depending on the nature of the false alarm. A detailed description of the approach and the methods are given in the following section.

10.3.1 Physiological Data-Based Approach

In physiological data-based approaches, the observed vital signs data is the leading cause of false alarms. The identified methods used to reduce clinical false alarms focusing on the physiological data are discussed below.

10.3.1.1 Customised Alarm Signals

The customised alarm signals are those alarm signals that are set manually based on user requirements and differ based on the user's physiology and medical condition. Studies show that personalised alarm-signal parameters and set manual limits for physiological monitoring reduced false-positive alarms by 43% from the baseline [24]. For instance, 89% reduction in the total mean weekly alarm signals were measured by self-reset alarm signals for bradycardia, tachycardia, and heart rate (H.R.) limits where low H.R. is et to 45 bpm and high H.R. is set to 130 bpm [25]. Adapting parameter limits of SpO_2 monitors also results in fewer warnings per day and improved "nurses" satisfaction with the less frequent and effective alarm signals [26]. Notable improvements were achieved by implementing procedure-specific vital signs settings for cardiac patients by considerably reducing 80% of false-positive alarms [27].

10.3.1.2 Machine Learning

In machine-learning methods, alarm-signal systems learn about a clinical event that needs to be detected with the help of customised algorithms and datasets. Multivariate approaches in ICU alarm signals can achieve higher accuracy than using different algorithms for different alarm signals. These approaches can extract hundreds of relevant features to capture the characteristics of all alarm signals from arterial blood pressure (ABP) and electrocardiogram (ECG). The comparison study [28] found a 13.96% false-positive alarm suppression rate against feature-based false-positive alarm detection.

Srivastava [29] shows that feature extraction based on data segments has been used for machine learning. Based on this method, two models using random forest classifiers (RFC) and thresholds have been developed to assess the data. K-fold cross-validation has been applied for the evolution of RFC due to less than 750 records from the physio-net database. Simple association rules have been used on two designed models using the two subsets of data for arrhythmia and predicted 95.56% of reliable alarm signals.

The machine-learning algorithm was applied to 4107 "experts" labeled data extracted from 114 quality signals of ECG, PPG, and ABP waveforms. The false-positive alarm-suppression rate for the extracted dataset is 86.4% for asystole, 100% for extreme bradycardia, and 27.8% for severe tachycardia with no suppression of any true-positive alarms. The suppression of true-positive alarm means that reliable alarm signal or clinical usefulness was not suppressed. While for the ventricular tachycardia alarm signals, the false-positive alarm suppression performance was 30.5%, with a true-positive alarm suppression rate below 1% [42].

10.3.1.3 Time Delay

The time delay method uses some delay time before triggering the alarm signal. This delay proved helpful in false-positive alarm reduction. Decreasing the alarm limit of SpO2 to reduce false-positive alarms may increase more episodes of hypoxemia. However, a delay of 15 seconds between crossing the threshold value and triggering the alarm signal would reduce the false-positive alarm by 60% [15]. A minimal threshold variation of short durations of a 14-second delay in an ICU reduced false-positive alarms by 50%, while a 19-second delay reduced alarms by 67% [43].

Over 12 months, 316,688 alarms were recorded for 6,701 patients in trauma resuscitation. It was found that a 2-second delay in alarm signal would reduce incidents by 25%, and 5 seconds would reduce the alarm signals by 49% [44].

10.3.1.4 Integration of Techniques

The integration of techniques uses sensor fusion, time delay, feature extraction, etc., to reduce false-positive alarms. For example, the algorithm derived from the features and timings of the ABP signals used to reduce ECG arrhythmia alarm signals on an average of 47% for 447 adult patient records in the MIMIC II database [45].

Suppressing ICU alarm signals using automated features and engineering using ABP signals, coupled with machine-learning algorithms such as vector machines, random forest, and extreme random tree classifier, suppressed 90.3% of the false tachycardia alarm signals. And only 0.54% of the true-positive alarms were incorrectly suppressed [17].

10.3.1.5 Coalition Game Theory

Coalition game theory works by grouping the agents in the game together. A similar way for a patient monitoring system based on this theory has been developed, which considers inter-feature dependencies on the PhysioNet's MIMIC-II database also resulted in an improved classification of the alarm signals [46]. Inter-feature's mutual information helps in the accuracy of the classification of the alarm signals. This method has been applied to collect data from hospitals for arrhythmias, including asystole, extreme bradycardia, extreme tachycardia, ventricular tachycardia, ventricular flutter/fibrillation, arterial blood pressure (ABP), and photoplethysmogram (PPG). And observed features such as mean, variance, median, kurtosis, and entropy resulted in the successful suppression of 75% of false-positive alarms [47].

10.3.1.6 Sensor Fusion

Different physiological sensor information is fused in sensor fusion. This information was then fed into the customised algorithm to predict true-positive alarms. A set of algorithms using heart-rate variability (HRV) index, Bayesian inference, neural networks, fuzzy logic, and majority voting has been proposed in [48] to fuse the ECG, arterial blood pressure, and PPG. Upon fusion, three kinds of information are extracted from each source. Namely, heart rate variability, the heart rate and difference between sensors, and the spectral analysis of low and high noise of each sensor are fed as an input to the algorithms. The results are validated with 20 sets of recordings from the MIMIC database, which showed that neural networks fusion had the best false-positive alarm reduction of 92.5%. In contrast, the Bayesian technique decreased by 84.3%, fuzzy logic was 80.6%, majority voter was 72.5%, and the heart rate variability index showed a 67.5% reduction [48].

A Bayesian approach has been used to fuse electrocardiogram, arterial blood pressure, and PPG from physiological sensors to create robust heart estimations. The HRV index and majority voter technique are then compared using 20 selected records from the MIMIC II database. Results showed that Bayesian fusion presents a lower error rate of 23%. In comparison, the other evaluated techniques give an error rate of 35% (ECG only), 40% (ABP only), 41% (PPG only), 37% (HRV index), and 31% (majority voter) [49].

10.3.1.7 Pattern Discovery

Pattern discovery identifies various signal patterns by observing physiological data features, time, the relationship between alarm-signal categories, etc., which are responsible for alarm signals. Heuristic techniques to extract inter-alarm signal relationships include identifying the presence of alarm-signal clusters, the pattern of transition from one alarm signal category to another, temporal association, and prevalent sequence have developed. Desaturation, bradycardia, and apnea constitute 86% of alarm signals, and by inhibiting a category further, the 30s/60s alarm signal reduced by 20% [50].

10.3.2 Clinical Device-Centric Approach

Artefacts[3] caused due to device-related issues falling under clinical device-centric approaches. The approaches for the solution should be device-based for causes such as faulty devices, device malfunction, defective device parts, and aged devices. Literature shows that few studies have focused on devices to reduce false-positive alarms. Changing the electrodes daily on cardiac monitors results in average alarm signals per bed being reduced by 46% [51]. A two-adult nursing unit was examined by changing the electrocardiographic electrode for two intervention periods – the change of electrodes showed the cardiac monitor alarm events were decreased by 20.6% and 71.0% in the first and second intervention periods [52].

10.3.3 Clinical Knowledge-Based Approach

An erroneous assessment of the patient's condition or incorrect interpretation of the false-positive alarm falls under clinical knowledge-based approaches. The approaches that use the knowledge gained from experience or research to interpret the alarm signal fall under this category.

10.3.3.1 Pattern Match

The clinician uses pattern matching to match patterns from the observed data or signals. A knowledge-based approach, based on pattern match, for neonatal intensive care unit for probe change has been conducted in [53] and shows that 45 probe changes with the accuracy to identify 89% of false-positive alarms. The clinician marks up features of interest on the monitor data. Then their knowledge is used as a pattern matcher over a particular set of intervals for a new collection of raw data [54].

10.3.3.2 Team-Based Method

Grouping various methods based on clinician knowledge can be done, which acts as a team to reduce false-positive alarms. A team-based method to reduce cardiac monitor alarms has been developed. This method has four steps:

- Setting up age-appropriate parameters
- Daily electrode changes

■ Individual monitor assessment
■ Procedure to stop monitoring

The results show compliance increased from 38% to 95%, and the median number of alarms decreased from 180 to 40, which is a 77.78% decrease in false alarms [55].

10.3.4 Clinical Environment-Based Approaches

In this approach, artifacts are due to the surrounding environment in which the patient monitoring setup resides. The causes, such as power-line interference, electrode malfunction, floor vibrations, wobbly connections, and any other artefacts caused due to multiple sources that may or may not be related to other sources fall under this category.

10.3.4.1 Median Filters

A median filter removes short-term noise in the measurement signal without manipulating the baseline signal. Some literature studies use this method to remove interference caused by sources like power lines, noise, subject movement, etc. Due to power sources in the ECG signal, interference could be reduced using the notch filter in the monitors, a band-stop filter with a narrow stopband is used [56].

An effective combination of a "short" (15 seconds) and a "long" (2.5 minutes) filter in a database of 10 cardiac surgery patients has been evaluated. The result showed that therapeutic consequences increased from 12 to 49%, with no relevant alarm signal missed [31].

The artificial neural network (ANN) based algorithm has been developed for removing non-linear time-varying noise characteristics of ECG to detect QRS complex. The noise removal using a linear whitening filter for MIT/BIH arrhythmia database records 97.5% and band-pass filtering records 96.5% [57].

10.3.4.2 Dimension Reduction

Dimension reduction reduces the number of input variables used to evaluate the output, as more inputs make the processing task more complicated. Continuous and non-invasive B.P. monitoring problems have been addressed with a proposed methodology of de-noising, feature extraction, and various regression stages using dimension reduction. For dimension reduction, the study reduced the length of the original feature vectors using principal component analysis (PCA) to reduce the feature-length from over 190 to 15. Using this methodology, the cumulative error percentage for threshold 15mmHg comes from diastolic blood pressure (DBP)

95.7%, mean arterial pressure (MAP) 93.1%, and systolic blood pressure (SBP) 72.7%, which is less as a comparison to British hypertension society standards [58].

10.4 Results and Discussion

We have reviewed the various methods and techniques to reduce false-positive alarms in patient-monitoring systems. The leading causes of false-positive alarms in these methods and techniques lack analysis of the sources of false-positive alarms. There are various artefacts like movement, vibration, and noise in the clinical setup. These artifacts are the reason for false-positive clinical alarms [59]. The recorded artefacts can lead to changes in physiological recorded patient data or misinterpret the algorithm used for monitoring patient's conditions, resulting in higher numbers of false-positive alarms.

We have categorised various approaches based on the nature of the causes that have been identified in the literature to reduce false-positive alarms. The graph in Figure 10.6 has been plotted for suppressing false-positive alarm rates in the proposed approaches by various methods and techniques in these approaches. It is not feasible to collate all the methods that use the same sample size and clinical setup. Therefore, this paper considers all those methods that conducted clinical trials rather than simulations.

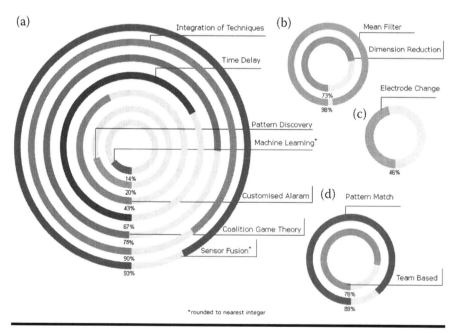

Figure 10.6 Suppressed False-Positive Alarm Rate for (a) Physiological Data (b) Clinical Environment, (c) Clinical Device Centric, and (d) Clinical Knowledge-Based Approaches.

10.4.1 Physiological Data

The chart shows that most false-positive alarms are due to the vital signs data. Subsequently, many methods suppress the same, such as customised alarm parameters, machine learning, time delay, coalition game theory, integrating various methods, sensor fusion, and pattern discovery. These listed methods focus on patient data to reduce false-positive alarms using multiple ways.

10.4.2 Clinical Device-Centric

Interestingly, the number of false-positive alarms due to the device is minimal. Subsequently, daily electrode change is the only method found in the literature to suppress the false-positive alarm caused due to device-centric issues. The apparatus used for remote patient monitoring is getting more reliable and efficient. Changing the electrode daily effectively suppressed false-positive alarms for device-related problems by 46%.

10.4.3 Clinical Knowledge-Based

Similarly, fewer clinical false-positive alarms are found due to incomplete clinical knowledge. The pattern match is one of the methods under clinical false-positive alarms with the suppress false-positive alarm rate of 89%. Clinicians use their knowledge to identify the patterns in the recorded patient data to predict the patient's condition. Another method under clinical knowledge is the team-based method, which suppresses a false-positive alarm rate of 78%. Clinicians use their knowledge to use various methods such as customised parameters or electrode changes to suppress the false-positive alarm. This clarifies minimum human error in the healthcare environment and the importance of regulatory measures followed in the device certification.

10.4.4 Clinical Environment

Although the clinical setup also contributes toward the false-positive alarms and the related methods to reduce them are median filters, which filter the signal for noises or disturbances, the false-positive alarm suppresses rate found to be 96%. Dimension-reduction methods were found to suppress the false-positive alarm rate by 73%.

We have found that most artefacts causing false-positive alarms affect clinical recorded data with the overall observation. Many effective methods have been listed under a clinical data-based approach that focuses on clinical data to suppress false-positive alarms. Under clinical data-based approaches, sensor fusion and integration of various techniques have been found effective as they could suppress false-positive alarm rates of more than 90%. The clinical devices became more efficient and reliable using updated hardware and software, causing fewer false-positive alarms. On the other hand, when the clinician uses their knowledge to match the pattern to reduce the false-positive alarm, they suppress the false-positive alarm rate by 89%. As fewer clinical alarms are recorded in the clinical setup, the mean filter is one of the effective methods to suppress false-positive alarms.

10.5 Conclusions

The presented pentagon clinical alarm-generation approach gives the guidelines with five phases that will be highly useful for the applied researchers and developers to create an efficient clinical-alarm signal strategy for patient monitoring. Significant factors to suppress false-positive alarms in the alarm strategy are highlighted in the pentagon approach. A critical review of various interventions from literature for false-positive alarms has been done to categorise them based on physiological data used, clinical device involvement, use of clinical knowledge, and the setting up of the clinical environment. These approaches are classified based on the source for various artefacts responsible for the false-positive alarms. This classification will act as a catalog for the researchers to view multiple interventions used in literature focusing on the artefacts for the false alarms. Our proposed work articulated that the methods used to reduce false clinical alarms without analysis of artefacts are significant sources of frequent false-positive alarms. For our future research direction, better physiological data-based approaches with the help of data-mining techniques will be designed to reduce the number of false alarms in an RPM.

Notes

1. False alarm and false-positive alarm terms used in the paper signify the same meaning.
2. False alarm and false-positive alarm terms used in the paper signify the same meaning.
3. Artefacts are anomalies introduced into digital signals because of digital signal processing.

References

[1] Fernandes, C.O. and C.J.P. de Lucena. *An Internet of Things Application with An Accessible Interface for Remote Monitoring Patients.* 2015. Cham: Springer International Publishing.
[2] Sharma, S. and V. Balasubramanian. *A biometric based authentication and encryption Framework for Sensor Health Data in Cloud.* In Proceedings of the *6th International Conference on Information Technology and Multimedia.* 2014.
[3] Whaiduzzaman, M., et al., *A privacy-preserving mobile and fog computing framework to trace and prevent COVID-19 community transmission.* IEEE Journal of Biomedical and Health Informatics, 2020. **24**(12): pp. 3564–3575.
[4] Patel, K.K., and S.M. Patel, *Internet of things-IOT: definition, characteristics, architecture, enabling technologies, application & future challenges.* International Journal of Engineering Science and Computing, 2016. **6**(5).

[5] Desai, F., et al., *HealthCloud: A system for monitoring health status of heart patients using machine learning and cloud computing.* Internet of Things, 2022. **17**: p. 100485.

[6] Malasinghe, L.P., N. Ramzan, and K. Dahal, *Remote patient monitoring: a comprehensive study.* Journal of Ambient Intelligence and Humanized Computing, 2019. **10**(1): pp. 57–76.

[7] Hravnak, M., et al., *A call to alarms: Current state and future directions in the battle against alarm fatigue.* Journal of Electrocardiology, 2018. **51**(6, Supplement): pp. S44–S48.

[8] Bell, L., *Monitor alarm fatigue.* American Journal of Critical Care, 2010. **19**(1): p. 38.

[9] Chambrin, M.C., *Alarms in the intensive care unit: how can the number of false alarms be reduced?* Critical Care, 2001. **5**(4): pp. 184–188.

[10] Christensen, M., et al., *Alarm setting for the critically ill patient: a descriptive pilot survey of nurses' perceptions of current practice in an Australian Regional Critical Care Unit.* Intensive and Critical Care Nursing, 2014. **30**(4): pp. 204–210.

[11] Sendelbach, S. and M. Funk, *Alarm fatigue: a patient safety concern.* AACN Advanced Critical Care, 2013. **24**(4): pp. 378–386; quiz 387-8.

[12] Casey, S., G. Avalos, and M. Dowling, *Critical care nurses' knowledge of alarm fatigue and practices towards alarms: A multicentre study.* Intensive and Critical Care Nursing, 2018. **48**: pp. 36–41.

[13] Cho, O.M., et al., *Clinical alarms in intensive care units: Perceived obstacles of alarm management and alarm fatigue in nurses.* Healthcare Informatics Research, 2016. **22**(1): pp. 46–53.

[14] Ruppel, H., M. Funk, and R. Whittemore, *Measurement of physiological monitor alarm accuracy and clinical relevance in intensive care units.* American Journal of Critical Care, 2018. **27**(1): pp. 11–21.

[15] Paine, C.W., et al., *Systematic review of physiologic monitor alarm characteristics and pragmatic interventions to reduce alarm frequency.* Journal of Hospital Medicine, 2016. **11**(2): pp. 136–144.

[16] Cosper, P., et al., *Improving clinical alarm management: guidance and strategies.* Biomedical Instrumentation & Technology, 2017. **51**(2): pp. 109–115.

[17] Lameski, P., et al., *Suppression of intensive care unit false alarms based on the arterial blood pressure signal.* IEEE Access, 2017. **5**: pp. 5829–5836.

[18] Wilken, M., et al., *Alarm fatigue: Causes and effects.* Studies in Health Technology and Informatics, 2017. **243**: pp. 107–111.

[19] Baker, K. and J. Rodger, *Assessing causes of alarm fatigue in long-term acute care and its impact on identifying clinical changes in patient conditions.* Informatics in Medicine Unlocked, 2020. **18**: p. 100300.

[20] Plesinger, F., et al., *Taming of the monitors: reducing false alarms in intensive care units.* Physiological Measurement, 2016. **37**(8): p. 1313.

[21] Grant, M.J. and A. Booth, *A typology of reviews: an analysis of 14 review types and associated methodologies.* Health Information & Libraries Journal, 2009. **26**(2): pp. 91–108.

[22] Kalid, N., et al., *Based real time remote health monitoring systems: A review on patients prioritization and related "big data" using body sensors information and communication technology.* Journal of Medical Systems, 2018. **42**(2): pp. 1–30.

[23] Hueske-Kraus, D., M. Wilken, and R. Röhrig, *Measuring Alarm System Quality in Intensive Care Units Work in progress.* 2018.

[24] Graham, K. and M. Cvach, *Monitor alarm fatigue: standardizing use of physiological monitors and decreasing nuisance alarms.* American Journal of Critical Care: An Official Publication, American Association of Critical-Care Nurses, 2010. **19**: pp. 28–34; quiz 35.

[25] Whalen, D.A., et al., *Novel approach to cardiac alarm management on telemetry units.* Journal of Cardiovascular Nursing, 2014. **29**(5): pp. E13–E22.

[26] Ketko, A.K., et al., *Balancing the tension between hyperoxia prevention and alarm fatigue in the NICU.* Pediatrics, 2015. **136**(2): pp. e496–e504.

[27] Schmid, F., M.S. Goepfert, and D.A. Reuter, *Patient monitoring alarms in the ICU and in the operating room.* Critical Care, 2013. **17**(2): p. 216.

[28] Wang, X., et al. *A Machine Learning Approach to False Alarm Detection for Critical Arrhythmia Alarms.* in *2015 IEEE 14th International Conference on Machine Learning and Applications (ICMLA).* 2015.

[29] Srivastava, C., S. Sharma, and A. Jalali, *A novel algorithm for reducing false ar-rhythmia alarms in intensive care units.* Conf Proc IEEE Eng Med Biol Soc, 2016. **2016**: pp. 2525–2528. doi:10.1109/embc.2016.7591244

[30] Shurkhovetskyy, G., et al., *Data abstraction for visualizing large time series.* Computer Graphics Forum, 2018. **37**(1): pp. 125–144.

[31] Au-Yeung, W.-T.M., et al., *Reduction of false alarms in the intensive care unit using an optimized machine learning based approach.* NPJ Digital Medicine, 2019. **2**(1): pp. 1–5.

[32] Balasubramanian, V. *Critical time parameters for evaluation of body area Wireless Sensor Networks in a Healthcare Monitoring Application.* In *2014 IEEE Ninth International Conference on Intelligent Sensors, Sensor Networks and Information Processing (ISSNIP).* 2014.

[33] Balasubramanian, V. and A. Stranieri. *Performance evaluation of the dependable properties of a Body Area Wireless Sensor Network.* in *2014 International Conference on Reliability Optimization and Information Technology (ICROIT).* 2014.

[34] Minutolo, A., M. Esposito, and G. De Pietro, *Design and validation of a light-weight reasoning system to support remote health monitoring applications.* Engineering Applications of Artificial Intelligence, 2015. **41**: pp. 232–248.

[35] Lynn Campbell, J., *A Mixed-methods Approach to Evaluating the Usability of Telemedicine Communications.* in *Proceedings of the 38th ACM International Conference on Design of Communication.* 2020.

[36] Mirza Mansoor, Gholamhosseini Hamid, Harrison Michael, A Fuzzy Logic-based System for Anaesthesia Monitoring. *Conference proceedings : Annual International Conference of the IEEE Engineering in Medicine and Biology Society. IEEE Engineering in Medicine and Biology Society Conference,* 2010. **2010**: pp. 3974–3977. doi:10.1109/IEMBS.2010.5627987

[37] Morgan, D.L., *Focus Groups.* In: Annual Review of Sociology, 1996. **22**(1): pp. 129–152.

[38] Lambert, M.J., *Clinical measurement and patient feedback systems.* In: J. J. Magnavita (Ed.), Using technology in mental health practice. 2018. pp. 145–162. American Psychological Association. doi:10.1037/0000085-009

[39] Ostojic, D., et al., *Reducing false alarm rates in neonatal intensive care: a new machine learning approach,* In: Ryu, P.D., LaManna, J., Harrison, D., and Lee, S.S. (eds). *Oxygen Transport to Tissue XLI.* 2020, Springer. pp. 285–290.

[40] Pliego Marugán, A. and F.P. García Márquez, *Advanced analytics for detection and diagnosis of false alarms and faults: A real case study.* Wind Energy, 2019. **22**(11): pp. 1622–1635.

[41] Sahoo, T., et al., *Quality improvement initiative for reduction of false alarms from multiparameter monitors in neonatal intensive care unit.* Journal of Education and Health Promotion, 2019. **8**: p. 203.

[42] Li, Q. and G.D.J.J.o.e. Clifford, *Signal quality and data fusion for false alarm reduction in the intensive care unit,* Journal of Electrocardiology. 2012. **45**(6): pp. 596–603.

[43] Cvach, M., *Monitor alarm fatigue: an integrative review.* Biomedical Instrumentation & Technology, 2012. **46**(4): pp. 268–277.

[44] Colton, K., et al., *Full of sound and fury, signifying nothing: burden of transient noncritical monitor alarms in a trauma resuscitation unit.* Journal of Trauma Nursing, 2013. **20**(4): pp. 184–188.

[45] Saeed, M., et al., *Multiparameter Intelligent Monitoring in Intensive Care II (MIMIC-II): a public-access intensive care unit database.* Critical Care Medicine, 2011. **39**(5): p. 952.

[46] Afghah, F., A. Razi, and K. Najarian, *A Shapley Value Solution to Game Theoretic-based Feature Reduction in False Alarm Detection.* 2015. https://doi.org/10.48550/arXiv.1512.01680

[47] Afghah, F., et al. *A Game Theoretic Predictive Modeling Approach to Reduction of False Alarm.* 2016. Cham: Springer International Publishing.

[48] Borges, G. and V. Brusamarello, *Sensor fusion methods for reducing false alarms in heart rate monitoring.* Journal of Clinical Monitoring and Computing, 2016. **30**(6): pp. 859–867.

[49] Borges, G.D.M. and V. Brusamarello. *Bayesian fusion of multiple sensors for reliable heart rate detection.* In *2014 IEEE International Instrumentation and Measurement Technology Conference (I2MTC) Proceedings.* 2014.

[50] Joshi, R., et al., *Pattern discovery in critical alarms originating from neonates under intensive care.* Physiological Measurement, 2016. **37**(4): pp. 564–579.

[51] Cvach, M.M., et al., *Daily electrode change and effect on cardiac monitor alarms: an evidence-based practice approach.* Journal of Nursing Care Quality, 2013. **28**(3): pp. 265–271.

[52] Smith, D.H., *Impact of daily electrocardiographic electrode changes upon technical related cardiac monitor alarm events.* 2017.

[53] Hunter, J. and N. McIntosh. *Knowledge-Based Event Detection in Complex Time Series Data.* 1999. Berlin, Heidelberg: Springer Berlin Heidelberg.

[54] Stell, A., L. Moss, and I. Piper. *Knowledge-driven inference of Medical Interventions.* in *2012 25th IEEE International Symposium on Computer-Based Medical Systems (CBMS).* 2012. IEEE.

[55] Dandoy, C.E., et al., *A team-based approach to reducing cardiac monitor alarms.* Pediatrics, 2014. **134**(6): pp. e1686–e1694.

[56] Nizami, S., J.R. Green, and C. McGregor, *Implementation of artifact detection in critical care: A methodological review.* IEEE Reviews in Biomedical Engineering, 2013. **6**: pp. 127–142.

[57] Raj, S., K.C. Ray, and O. Shankar, *Development of robust, fast and efficient QRS complex detector: a methodological review.* Australasian Physical & Engineering Sciences in Medicine, 2018. **41**(3): pp. 581–600.

[58] Kachuee, M., et al., *Cuffless blood pressure estimation algorithms for continuous healthcare monitoring.* IEEE Transactions on Biomedical Engineering, 2017. **64**(4): pp. 859–869.

[59] Cunningham, S., A.G. Symon, and N. McIntosh, *The practical management of artifact in computerised physiological data.* International Journal of Clinical Monitoring and Computing, 1994. **11**(4): pp. 211–216.

Chapter 11

Cloud Computing in Medical Imaging, Healthcare Technologies, and Services

Arushi Ananthakrishnan[1], Arya Agrawal[2], Asmi Dhull[1], Manan Gupta[2], Dhanush Srikanth[3], Shreemanto Lahiri[4], Divyansh Srivastava[3], and Utkarsh Chadha[3,5]

[1]School of Electronics Engineering, Vellore Institute of Technology, Vellore, Vellore, Tamil Nadu, India
[2]School of Computer Science and Engineering, Vellore Institute of Technology, Vellore, Vellore, Tamil Nadu, India
[3]School of Mechanical Engineering, Vellore Institute of Technology, Vellore, Vellore, Tamil Nadu, India
[4]School of Information Technology and Engineering, Vellore Institute of Technology, Vellore, Vellore, Tamil Nadu, India
[5]Department of Materials Science and Engineering, Faculty of Applied Sciences and Engineering, School of Graduate Studies, University of Toronto, St George Campus, Toronto, Ontario, Canada

Contents

11.1 Introduction to Cloud Computing..196
    11.1.1 Essential Characteristics 196

DOI: 10.1201/9781003145189-11

195

11.1.2 Service Models...197
11.1.3 Deployment Models 197
11.1.4 Introduction to Cloud Computing in Healthcare..................197
11.2 The Benefits of Cloud Computing in the Healthcare Domain...........199
11.3 Looking at the Past of Cloud Computing in Healthcare 200
11.4 The Present Trends in Cloud-Computing Dynamics..........................202
11.5 Analysis 205
11.5.1 Comparison 208
11.5.2 How Can It Move Forward?...210
11.6 Conclusion and Future Scope...211
References 213

11.1 Introduction to Cloud Computing

The "cloud" refers to a set of services, i.e., storage, database management, networking, etc., that exist on the Internet and are not hosted locally by the user. Organisations providing this service are called cloud providers for Microsoft and Amazon, and they usually charge for their services after a certain threshold is crossed; otherwise, it is provided free of cost in most cases [1,2].

It is a model for providing omnipresent, convenient, on-demand network access to a shared configurable computing resource that can be rapidly provisioned and released with minimal management effort or interaction from service providers. This cloud model is made up of five essential features, four deployment types, and three service models [3,4].

11.1.1 Essential Characteristics

First is on-demand self-service, which is provided to the customer as desired. There is no need for any physical contact between the customer and the provider; thus, it reduces time and increases efficiency of the whole transaction. Additionally, it provides access to a lot of capabilities via networking by using thick or thin client platforms.

Resource pooling, which compiles resources to serve customers via a multi-tenant method. There are unique virtual and physical resources dynamically assigned and reassigned based on consumer demand. The consumer has minimal control over or understanding of the exact location of the provided resources, but they may be able to define the location at another level, like country, state, or data centre. Capabilities may be provided, and in some cases, in response to demand, to grow outward and inward. Provisioning capabilities usually look infinite to the client, and they may be employed at a particular instance. Measurable customer service regulates and optimises resource utilisation; cloud systems employ a metering capability at some level of abstraction apt for the kind of service like storage, processing, bandwidth, among others. Transparency is achieved on both ends as every usage by the user and provision given by the provider [1].

11.1.2 Service Models

Software as a service (SaaS) makes use of apps created by the cloud-service provider accessible via thin client interface, which is usually web based. The consumer is free to use multiple devices to employ the service but is unable to control the cloud infrastructure. The consumer may however be allowed to make changes to the user-specific applications in terms of configuration.

With Platform as a Service (PaaS), the customer after gaining authorization develops applications that utilize the cloud platform, i.e., the libraries and tools already present in the infrastructure. The consumer cannot make changes to the core infrastructure itself; however, they can change the installed applications.

Infrastructure as a Service (IaaS) is a type of cloud (IaaS). Customers are given the ability to supply processing, storage, networks, and other basic computer resources, allowing them to deploy and run any software, including operating systems and apps. Although customers have no control over the cloud infrastructure itself, they do have control over operating systems, storage, and installed applications, as well as possibly limited control over some networking components.

11.1.3 Deployment Models

Private cloud. It is an infrastructure designed for the use of a single entity from which many clients may branch out. It is owned and operated by a separate third entity.

Community cloud. This infrastructure is designed by a group of entities with a common goal. It is managed and operated as a community and not a single organization (Figure 11.1).

Public cloud. Anyone who wishes to use the cloud infrastructure can do so. It might be owned, managed, and controlled by a corporation, a university, a government body, or a combination of these institutions. It is located on the cloud provider's premises [6,7].

11.1.4 Introduction to Cloud Computing in Healthcare

Cloud computing is here to stay, as large IT behemoths such as Amazon, Google, Microsoft, and others are substantially investing in it by creating vast data centres to support it and assist companies in using it. They're developing medical-record-keeping services with their healthcare partners [8–14]. On Microsoft HealthVault applications, Microsoft and Kaiser Permanente collaborated. Its primary purpose is to consolidate health and fitness data in one location so that it may be easily

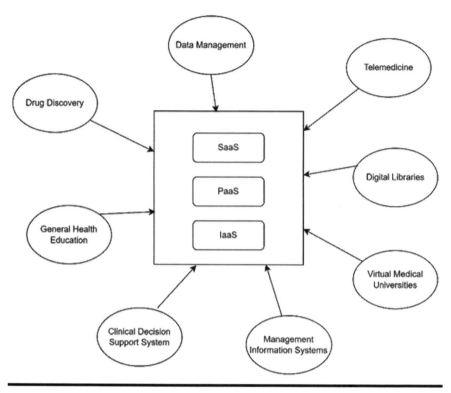

Figure 11.1   Cloud-driven Healthcare Services [5].

formatted and shared with healthcare organisations, including patients. Google Health obtains health records from Cleveland Clinic's MyChart software via cloud services [15–21]. Many healthcare organisations are already reevaluating their present business strategies, including risks and benefits, to see how they can utilise the cloud because of its cost-effective methods [22–28]. The sooner these businesses use the cloud, the more efficient they will be and the more sharing opportunities they will provide for healthcare organisations and patients. According to research and a survey conducted by marketsandmarkets.com (M&M), approximately 32% of healthcare organisations are already using cloud-based applications. Around 75% of businesses that do not already use any cloud apps stated they plan to do so in the future three to five years.

The analysis conducted by the same reached the conclusion that the public model will be the first picked by their strategic firms, eventually leading to the adoption of hybrid and finally private cloud models. This seems to be consistent with the poll conducted in 2010 by Accenture, Furthermore they add that the ones who will have an edge in the future are the ones who adopt this technology as fast as possible (Wan, Greenway, Harris, & Alter 2010) [2,8] (Figures 11.2 and 11.3).

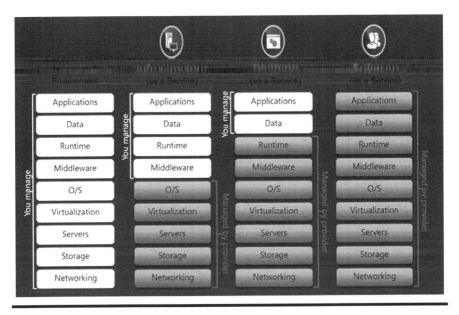

Figure 11.2 Infrastructure vs Platform vs Software.

Figure 11.3 The Topology for the IoT Framework for Healthcare Includes the Publisher, Broker, Subscriber, and the Technologies that Connect Them [29].

11.2 The Benefits of Cloud Computing in the Healthcare Domain

Both patients and healthcare organisations benefit from the use of the cloud in medical services would result in significant improvements in patient-service quality, a collaboration between healthcare organisations and cost savings in healthcare IT. The cloud network enables the sharing of data across IT, and this particular feature is used in medical organisations to better the customers' experience. Data is shared among hospitals, imaging centres, clinics, pharmacies, and insurance companies so that prescription information, test results, etc., can be combined and compiled so that no time is wasted in parsing this information. All of this information would be utilised to make judgments, gain better diagnoses and treatments to generate better outcomes, schedule physician visits, expedite insurance acceptance, and so on, all of which greatly enhances a patient's quality of care. When shifting to the cloud, one of the most important benefits for healthcare organisations is the reduction in IT expenditures. If the cloud model is implemented, all IT operations will be shifted to a remote cloud-computing infrastructure where they will be executed and stored. The new "pay-as-you-go" model allows businesses to only pay for what they use, eliminating the previous need to invest in costly hardware infrastructure or software licensing, as well as retain in-house employees for maintenance, security, and replications, because cloud-computing providers handle it all. The value of human life is priceless, and medical resources are scarce (Wang, 2010). As a result, cloud-based healthcare services provides us with a cost-effective concept in which patients and health organisations benefit from this new technology by improving patient quality of service through a systematic and integrated platform (Wang, 2010), coordinating medical processes, and reducing IT infrastructure maintenance costs, all of which contribute to a better healthcare environment [2].

11.3 Looking at the Past of Cloud Computing in Healthcare

Technology has been an integral part of many domains of healthcare, and the four most recent innovations have been electronic health records (EHR), mobile health applications, 3D printing, and telemedicine. Electronic health records first gained ubiquity in the 1960s. However, its adoption grew enormously between 2007 and 2012, increasing from 34.8% to 71%, as researched by the Centers for Disease Control and Prevention. The healthcare IT budget in the United States escalated under George W. Bush's presidency, a National Health Information Coordinator sub-cabinet position was created, and an industry-wide mandate making it compulsory for healthcare providers to implement electronic health record systems by 2014 was issued.

Congregation of data such as medical records in one system can benefit patients, staff, and hospitals in numerous ways. It can expedite the diagnosis and allow quicker access to the experts. It also has a benefit for the environment, by reducing power consumption and also allowing for reduced paperwork. Cloud computing not only helps medical staff and patients but also the human resources element of healthcare infrastructure. Costs can be transferred to infrastructure-management companies that can use economies of scale to keep the system and upgrade it over time. They can then provide their services and hardware as a pipeline service to organisations [30].

By introducing the American Recovery and Reinvestment Act of 2009, Obama backed this project (ARRA). Healthcare professionals that embraced EHR systems by 2014 received additional cash and incentives under the ARRA. It also imposed sanctions on those who did not comply.

MEDLINE was searched in July 2013 and December 2014 for papers using the terms "cloud computing" and "cloud-based." Two researchers separately categorised and summarised each journal and conference publication before combining their findings [31].

The research concluded that out of the 102 publications that were analyzed, six major themes emerged. They were telemedicine/teleconsultation, medical imaging, public health, patient self-management, hospital administration and information systems, therapy, and secondary data utilisation. The research also emphasizes the aspects of wide area network connectivity to enable accessing and sharing data and having quick flexibility to spontaneously adapt to computing demands. According to the research, eight articles advocate for cloud-computing services that are pay-per-use, removing the need for upfront investment. Meanwhile only 14 articles have showcased successful implementation, despite the fact that 22 articles illustrate the importance of cloud computing in the healthcare industry, and 66 articles focus on either conceptual or prototypes of these projects. Furthermore, cloud computing often viewed parallel to Internet/web-based data exchange in many papers fails to explain the specific technologies highlighted in them. The research concluded that regardless of the elevated interest in cloud computing and its applications in healthcare, there aren't enough effective implementations. Many studies and articles just use the term "cloud" to relate to "virtual machines" or "web based" without highlighting its benefits. Involving third-party cloud partners also shines a light on the issues relating to data integrity and security that hamper its adoption in the healthcare industry. Inspite of these drawbacks, they still highlight cloud computing's scalability, flexibility, pay-per-use, and broad network access.

Cloud computing is an infrastructure system presented as an IT service that allows customers to connect to a shared pool of customizable and optimized computing resources such as servers, and data centers on-demand through the Internet. The IT services enabled by CC are web-based and can be quickly deployed with little administrative and maintenance effort. While focusing on the distinctions of cloud computing with traditional IT infrastructures, CC comes through as "a fundamental change" in how IT services are evolved, established, preserved, upgraded, and paid for. If implemented in the right ways, CCSs can benefit numerous companies in the healthcare field that furnish healthcare-associated commodities and assistance. CC allows healthcare organisations with less-equipped IT resources to effortlessly access essential aforementioned services via a grid based on a pay-as-you-go pricing model. CC permits healthcare companies with a shortage of employees in IT industries to quickly distribute said resources to address rapidly-changing medical demands while imposing just a minimal effort of their own IT staff. As a result, CC complements traditional health infrastructure and adds significant value to healthcare enterprises. In the healthcare industry, specialists have urged for a major acceleration of CC implementation.

According to a recent poll, an escalating number of healthcare organisations want to use CCSs, and through that, reduce the costs by utilizing the benefits of CC (HIMSS, 2016) [32].

Shifting to cloud infrastructure and congregating data can help data specialists and doctors to analyze the overall health of the population and identify early signs of problems that might affect a huge subset of the population. This data can also be used to analyze certain regions and isolate geo-factors that might affect that specific area. This can help institutions in making timely well-planned decisions for specific areas and curb them before they reach critical mass.

During times of crisis or natural/man-made disasters, access to personnel information of other healthcare organisations can increase collaboration between them. This can benefit patients who can be guided to treatment and experts more quickly.

During times of crisis or natural/man-made disasters, shared infrastructure may collapse; therefore, data redundancy and local backups of the data are important in such a system. Data integrity and security are of utmost importance when dealing with local backups of data of such confidential nature.

11.4 The Present Trends in Cloud-Computing Dynamics

The integration of cloud computing with health information management has been observed as an ongoing trend worldwide. The agencies need to automate and boost up to get entry into the clinical statistics to offer "withinside the cloud" services and products to patients, doctors, and institutions. For example, the American Occupational Network and HyGen Pharmaceuticals are finessing patient care by employing the use of digital medical records and using the cloud to update the clinical processes. The investors are not just limited to pharmaceutical companies, but companies like Google and Microsoft are closely engrossed "withinside the cloud" as well. Their new services for the clinical reports are in tandem with Microsoft's newly introduced HealthVault and Google's Health program. While nonetheless in beta testing, these MNCs have partnered with massive pharma companies for their ventures, Microsoft collaborating with Kariser Permante and Google, on the other hand, working with The Cleveland Clinic. Microsoft and Google are distinguished examples of many different business enterprise services that can be following the accelerating fashion of putting formerly neighbourhood and personal fitness statistics "withinside the cloud." This overflowing data can be saved in large statistics facilities and could offer access to prime facilities to all the concerned stakeholders [33] (Figure 11.4).

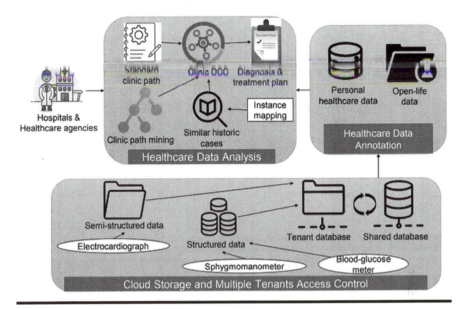

Figure 11.4   3 Layers of Cloud Storage on the Cloud's m-Health Monitoring [29].

These trends are driving the healthcare market dynamics in today's time:

1. The growth and need for consumerism:
   The consumerist market trend shifted the market demand from volume-based to the value-based need for healthcare. Stakeholders are not ranked on the scope of the service required but on the value achieved by the consumer. The service fee module has long been awarded to doctors and hospitals for providing the necessary treatments. Value models try to commend professional providers and organisation providers based on care cabin and clinical results. This implementation is enabled by variable-on-demand IT resources so that the process becomes cost-efficient.
2. Health regulations and financial risks involved:
   Healthcare reforms and regulations are changing the state of healthcare. Regulations affect the market structure and lead to integration both vertically and horizontally. Healthcare regulations are rapidly growing m-Health by trading clinical spaces for wellness spaces. All these factors affect the need for cloud-native applications that are designed and developed to meet the rapidly changing consumer demands along with keeping in mind the stipulations.
3. Digitalization:
   The information holes that arose from pre-existing systems have been significantly brought down with the advent of digitalization and the increasing number of "learned" consumers. Medical management is transitioning to a delivery model that is focused on being an information-providing module,

being open to collaboration. The new-age technology provided by the cloud lowers initial outlays in the capital that was initially being paid by healthcare via long-term licensing.

4. Preventative practice of medicine:

Any consumer in today's time has the advent of interest in acquiring the best aftercare and giving back to the community as well. Wearable tech through digitalization, IoT promotion, and m-Health is thus a part of the new trends being observed worldwide. Furthermore, the delivery of required services is becoming more decentralised, giving patients a broader range of institutions from which to seek treatment [6].

A few resources available in this field [34]:

- Centres for Disease Control and Prevention (CDC)
  The CDC Information Innovation Consortium (CHIIC) was launched for the population to discover and get information about the surveillance shortcomings and their solutions for the health services available to them.
- IBM Explorys
- eClinicalWorks
  PRISMA creates a timeline for any patient by having a database from stakeholders ranging from primary healthcare providers to hospitals.
- McKesson
  ProPBM™ manages design control and provides the necessary content to analysts.
- Cerner
  Social risk factor determinator along with pointing on to vulnerabilities in the community, focusing on the socially affected factors concerning the patients.
- IBM Phytel Population Health Management

Here are a few trends in the present-day applications in the healthcare field [29]:

1. Ambient Assisted Living (AAL)

The AAL is a fairly young IT course in which tech items are placed in the surrounding environment that acts as an assistant to senior citizens so that they can live independently. Recent advances in sensor-based tech, as well as the availability of smart healthcare gizmos, have caused a significant increase in AAL research.

Furthermore, an increasing number of AAL applications use cloud computing to refine data, use it for analysis, and provide real-time monitoring and effects mitigated.

2. Internet of m-Health Things (mIoT)

The use of mIoT through mobile computing and medical sensors to monitor patients and telecommunications and software-defined networks have been on the rising curve. Data retrieval, diagnosis, and practice of medicine become more effective and efficient. As a result, it provides completely integrated functions and has the potential to become more inventive in the future.

3. Wearable Technology

In the IoT healthcare context, wearable devices are more pocket friendly and bring many benefits to the concerned parties. These devices can corroborate with any wearable accessory, the in-built sensors capture and monitor health and environment, later uploaded to a database or fog layer for real-time processing. In addition, these wearable devices are supported by all gadgets that analyse collected data and send it to cloud computing-based frameworks for data processing.

4. Cognitive IoT (CIoT)

The rise of sensor technology will lead to the prices rising significantly, but that will come along with upgradation of the technology being used and the level of sensors being used. As part of today's new IoT concept, cognitive computing refers to brain-mimicing features to analyse data and patterns, using CIoT. As a result, the sensor's processing power increases and it adapts automatically to the environment.

Technology ensures efficient collaboration between different institutions, a feature beneficial for the future.

11.5 Analysis

E-health or e-healthcare is the use of modern technology, such as electronic and communication over the Internet, mobile phones, and computers, to make healthcare and treatment more accessible and also contactless. These days, e-healthcare uses a variety of technologies, resulting in a wide range of services being provided in areas such as being able to look up information and advice from the Internet with respect to healthcare, booking appointments online, or even getting on video calls with healthcare professionals, which results in problems being diagnosed in patients without physically being present. Additionally, no travelling would be necessary to meet the concerned personnel, which saves time and money [35].

5. Healthcare for the Community

Establishing IoT and cloud-computing networks in the context of public clinics, residential suburbs, or healthcare servicing the countryside. Community-based healthcare systems allow you to connect different networks to build a structure that is collaborative in nature.

6. Blockchain and Healthcare

An issue that impedes connective healthcare (sharing of data between stakeholders of healthcare) is data fragmentation. In recent times, the development of blockchain technology has made fundamental progress in solving the problem of data fragmentation. Blockchain, due to its feasibility, is also being promoted in developing countries with the inclusion of both the urban and rural populations. This can also prove to be a boon for the rural areas where services for healthcare are limited due to the lack of standard medical professionals.

The implementation of this system may also be difficult due to unfamiliarity with information and communication technology or ICT, and additionally, the non-prevalence of the infrastructure involved to implement the same. Although it may be seen as difficult now, countries both developed and developing are rapidly deploying these infrastructures. The pandemic caused by COVID-19 resulted in a number of people becoming familiar with e-healthcare, with people needing to book their vaccination slots and interacting with healthcare professionals online. A large part of the population is familiarised and involved with the use of e-healthcare services and also prefers it over traditional involvement with medical professionals due to its viability. To implement this on a larger scale, cloud computing may be the most efficient way to bring this about [35]. As of now, cloud computing would prove to be a great advantage for developing countries. This would aid the implementation of advanced technologies and bring about modernization to such countries due to its low funding during its beginning processes [36].

Some key characteristics that are considered for implementing cloud computing in healthcare are: 1) Registration, 2) Symptom checking, 3) Appointment online, 4) Diagnosis on call, 5) Messaging real-time 6) E-prescription, and 7) Manager for notification. Table 11.1 shows the required tools and their usage in the proposed model for implementing cloud computing in healthcare [51].

Table 11.1   Implementation Tools Required for the Proposed Model [35]

S.no.	Tools	Usage
1	HTML, CSS, JavaScript	To bring about the frontend development
2	Bootstrap, jQuery	To bring about responsive web pages
3	MongoDB	Data storage in a cloud
4	Node.js and Express.js	For backend implementation
5	Socket.IO, Redis PubSub	Messaging between doctors and patients
6	WebRTC	Doctors and patients on video call

Theme 1
That cloud computing is a very important topic and can provide a lot of benefits to different sectors. However, challenges like culture, infrastructure as well as security may stand in the way
Theme 2
The private solution should be deployed since in the case of sensitive and governmental solutions, security and privacy are major concerns which can be satisfied with the private solution.
Theme 3
Risk Management and Management support as well as healthcare actors support are one of the main challenges in Egypt and a plan to overcome those must be put in place first.
Theme 4
There is a lack of knowledge, national mission and vision regarding the security of data. Besides, there is the lack of infrastructure.
Theme 5
there are some hospitals that have a healthcare information system to keep their patients' records like some private hospitals and in public like the hospitals related to ministry of interior affairs and ministry of defence or the educational hospitals.

Figure 11.5 The Scope of Research in Cloud Computing with Respect to Healthcare [33].

Taking a look at this model would give a better insight into the expectation and possible implementation of cloud computing. In addition to cloud computing, AI can also be integrated into the system for better and personalised results. Cloud computing has a lot of advantages, some of them being the ability to constantly exchange medical information and bring ease of use to the entire system. Some companies that own public cloud-service providers are Dell, Amazon, and IBM. These clouds give users no control whatsoever and raise privacy concerns. Private clouds are those restricted to a certain organisation and data isn't shared. In these types of clouds, the data may be hosted internally or externally. There exists another type of cloud known as a hybrid cloud, which integrates the features of both a private cloud and a public cloud. Some clouds known as community clouds are primarily used by smaller companies. These clouds are shared by multiple organisations within a community that shares certain needs [36] (Figure 11.5).

The cloud infrastructure would involve both software and hardware components [37]. For healthcare to begin its transition into cloud-based systems, the applications with respect to it must be finalised. Clouds are an alternative being considered instead of the infrastructure involved with networking due to its ability to reduce cost, and the time involved and bring about an increase in efficiency and flexibility. With a reduction in costs, healthcare systems can implement these funds in areas such as expenditure needs and staff budget. The additional advantages would exclude the need for effort with respect to system management. The cloud also is not required to be backed up and is available on a demand basis [38].

Some important characteristics of cloud computing are as follows:

- Network access of a broad range
- Immediate flexibility
- Pooling of resources
- Measure of services [37]

11.5.1 Comparison

Cloud computing is defined as using the Internet to supply services such as the computing of various devices, cloud databases and servers, data storage and backup, networking, and a lot more. It has resulted in the change in the operation of applications driven by IoT. The integration of medical healthcare systems and cloud computing would result in a lot of advantages and an increase in efficiency with respect to traditional healthcare systems. Some major benefits would be centralized and seamless data storage; medical professionals would have easy access to patient information and data. The execution of such technologies would enable a significant increase in healthcare use. Although the systems of e-healthcare in developed countries are better than those in undeveloped countries, those undeveloped countries are definitely trying to implement these systems more efficiently [35].

The introduction of cloud computing to healthcare services would also require powerful computing systems with the ability to carry and process a large amount of data. Plenty of research is being done to better implement cloud computing due to the awareness of what these servers could achieve. In spite of the extensive research being done about cloud computing, the medical field is not ready to adopt these systems primarily because of privacy concerns with cloud computing. The medical data set consists of sensitive information that can be accessed only with the permission of the patient involved [39].

Cloud computing is being sought after for e-healthcare, but there are certain challenges the medical community faces regarding its implementation:

- The first and foremost challenge would be the risk regarding information security. The data stored must be continually monitored to prevent the leaking of data. Additionally, the company hosting the cloud should have a good communication system. There are major issues with security over cloud computing since it may result in patients having no control over their sensitive data. This lack of control may be the absence of adequate security over the kernels that store the relevant information.
- The conversion and integration of cloud computing into an extensible and reliable infrastructure would be hard to implement. Additionally, problems concerned with encryption, latency, and data transfer would need to be

resolved. This also poses a difficulty to developing countries trying to execute in developing countries because problems with migration and finances become involved [36].

Researchers are aware of the privacy issues concerned with cloud computing and are hence working on its better implementation for e-healthcare. Now cloud computing is being used extensively in the fields of both science and business; it is also being used for personal use. When it comes to cloud computing, the commitment is less with respect to the infrastructure involved with storage and computational processing. Companies can change their scalability as they wish and don't have to commit to being either small-scale or large-scale. This is essential for organisations of small or medium sizes as they significantly lower costs involved in maintaining and buying the necessary hardware. There are companies that rent out their resources for data storage and managing the servers involved with cloud computing. Some important and large-scale cloud-computing software are Amazon, Microsoft, Google, and Alibaba [40].

We now look at how using cloud computing in healthcare organisations will provide an advantage for traditional data storage:

1. Implementation of cloud computing would ease the ability to migrate data more easily and effectively.
2. It would ease the workload on healthcare-related organisations and would allow better focus on issues involving strategizing.
3. The cost-effective platform can be used for system hosting. Additionally, it makes hosting manageable across an organisation.
4. It can also easily be modified with upcoming programs with continuous changes in technology and demands [41,42].

An expert in the field agreed in an interview on the implementation of e-healthcare and cloud computing that its usage would prove to be convenient but current infrastructure in developing countries makes its usage difficult and requires extensive development. The present infrastructure in a lot of developing countries needs to be renovated to give way to up-and-coming technologies, such as cloud computing. The implementation of these infrastructures would additionally be a burden on government budgets. The first and foremost is to implement the infrastructure pertaining to cloud computing in hospitals. This implementation would bring about a massive change in the management within organisations involved with healthcare. Since management plays a major role in the functioning of an organisation, it would definitely be a major change in the working environment. The security concerns involved with the implementation have been confusing with respect to the cloud models and hence require extra supposition to bring about more structure to the policies pertaining to data management. The management of identities and access seems to be another concern due to computing resources being common. This in turn involves concepts such as authentication, information security, and functionality. Another aspect these experts made a comment about is the legal factor involved. They believe that there would be a need for a new set of laws concerning this new advancement. They additionally think that this aspect is neglected quite often [43].

The healthcare industry depends on reliability and availability when it comes to information and can even prove to be a threat otherwise. These systems must also be able to survive unavoidable circumstances such as disasters. Performance is also another factor being involved in the slow implementation of cloud computing in industries involved with healthcare [44].

11.5.2 How Can It Move Forward?

In a lot of developing countries, the ratio between doctors and patients is very low; hence, these countries don't have an elaborate healthcare system. According to research, a large portion of the demographic is ready for the implementation of ICT (information communication and technology). Additionally, a significant number of people actually preferred cloud-based solutions that provided characteristics such as getting diagnosed by doctors over video streaming or even the production of an e-prescription. An evaluation done by these researchers showed that the users find that using these was quite easy with navigation and usage being very comfortable [35] (Table 11.2).

This evaluation further indicated some insight into the future application of cloud-based healthcare systems. Bringing about these changes could prove to make a massive change in data storage. It could also help in developing smarter, safer, and more efficient healthcare using cloud computing. Cloud computing is continuously evolving as people have started to exploit this field because of its potential usage [38].

Table 11.2 This is the Final Evaluation Result Comparing Traditional Healthcare Systems and a Proposed Cloud-Based e-Healthcare Model [35]

Feature	Square Hospital	Evercare Hospital	United Hospital	Proposed System
Symptom checker	N	N	N	Y
Online appointment	Y	Y	Y	Y
Patient record management	N	N	N	Y
Text messaging	N	N	N	Y
Video call service	N	N	N	Y

According to a research paper, risk management is a feature that is neglected quite frequently when considering cloud computing, and preparation for any kind of risk is additionally essential. They also think that studying the trends would help in the improved implementation of these features. The issues regarding safety must be discussed on a large scale and hence would enable better utilisation [43].

Cloud computing is playing a major role in our lives and revolutionising them at a very rapid rate [44]. Its use in our day-to-day life is increasing at an exponential rate. Several areas of the potential implementation of cloud computing in healthcare are slowly being utilised. Their role could help in a better relationship between healthcare professionals and patients. This would also significantly reduce the costs required to treat patients [6]. Although the issues pertaining to security persist, research is making slow but steady progress, which would bring about a revolution in the healthcare industry.

11.6 Conclusion and Future Scope

In this study, based on the medical organisational specifications and requirements for storing and collaborating data, insights into what cloud computing stands for have been provided. Integrating cloud computing into healthcare has been on the agenda for many documents, so we aimed to explain the actual process, how this trend has been accepted and integrated into the market, and how it may evolve in the upcoming future. Healthcare is a very broad domain and this paper focuses on reviewing the correlation between healthcare and cloud computing to benefit multiple domains. Cloud computing and its applications have been on the rise for many years now. Its benefits stretch far and wide and include quicker, efficient, and more transparent access for everyone. Governments can also benefit by having consolidated access to the data and making decisions that affect several broad areas of society at a time.

E-healthcare uses various technologies to better the healthcare industry as a whole by using and providing a diverse set of services. Some key characteristics to consider implementing cloud computing in healthcare are:

1) Registration, 2) Symptom checking, 3) Appointment online, 4) Diagnosis on call, 5) Messaging real-time 6) E-prescription, and 7) Manager for notification.

The first and foremost challenge would be the risk regarding the security of the information; the next would be the difficulty to implement the conversion and integration of cloud computing into an extensible and reliable infrastructure over such an extensive domain.

In early future work, this study will be extended by looking for new developments in the field of IoT and how it can collaborate further with healthcare to make the healthcare industry completely self-sustaining and futuristic. The goal of proving medical services to remotely located patients and the concept to measure the medical information continuously is yet to be achieved but is definitely the future aim.

The past, present, and future of this domain have been analysed and presented, and it is hoped that the audience gets a gist of this vast field, still yet to be completely unveiled.

After going through various research papers, we could comment that there is a certain aperture in the literature review of cloud computing in the healthcare industry. Various types of literature lie within the reach of this topic. Some of them are related to the espousal of cloud-computing technology in the medical industries, while some are related to the application of information technology(IT) in healthcare industries. Even though these two are closely related to our topic of research, there is a major difference in the implementation of IT in contrast to cloud computing because the nature of the cloud-computing technique is far too abstract. The major limitation or constraint in the application of cloud computing in healthcare is privacy and security issues [45]. Shifting the standard healthcare systems to the cloud overcomes the geographical barrier between health providers and patients. So far the solution for security concerns of the stored data mainly has been the usage of the AES algorithm and data encryption methods [46]. With the development of hybrid cloud computing, there will be an extension in studies related to this field, and its main goal would be to provide medical services remotely to the patients, as well as measure the medical information simultaneously [47]. After scanning research papers and content available on various reliable websites, we found out that the hospitals in countries like the United States, Australia, Canada, and a few others, due to the federal law (regulations like HIPAA) and their own policies face restrictions on using cloud-computing technologies to store patient's data [48]. The strict restrictions and regulations of HIPAA (Health Insurance Portability and Accountability Act of 1996) regarding accessing patients' data make numerous cloud providers hesitant to sign contracts with the medical industries. Modular software development in cloud computing is considered the foundation that can take the future of cloud-computing technology in a constructive direction as the security and accessibility of features upgrade when code becomes modular [49]. If cloud computing continues to evolve, the use of hardware will be limited and most of the work will be done by the application of cloud computing and virtualization. The hardware cost will decrease, and the data that gets stored in the cloud would get analysed by machines themselves, resulting in no human involvement [50,51]. With respect to the future, we want to standardise the cloud-computing application in the medical industries of various countries. For further perusal, our priority would be to explore novel solutions regarding security concerns, virtualisation, and the public nature of cloud computing.

References

[1] Cloud, H. (2011). The NIST definition of cloud computing. *National Institute of Science and Technology, Special Publication,* 800(2011), 145.

[2] Alrowaijri, S. M. (2020). An architecture to improve the security of cloud computing in the healthcare sector. In Rashid Mehmood, Simon See, Iyad Katib, and Imrich Chlamtac (eds.), *Smart Infrastructure and Applications* (pp. 249–266). Springer, Cham.

[3] Mamdiwar, S. D., Akshith, R., Shakruwala, Z., Chadha, U., Srinivasan, K., & Chang, C.-Y. (2021). Recent Advances on IoT-Assisted Wearable Sensor Systems for Healthcare Monitoring. *Biosensors,* 11(10), 372. doi:10.3390/bios11100372

[4] Gupta, P., Krishna, C., Rajesh, R. et al. (2022). Industrial internet of things in intelligent manufacturing: a review, approaches, opportunities, open challenges, and future directions. *International Journal on Interactive Design and Manufacturing (IJIDeM).* doi: 10.1007/s12008-022-01075-w

[5] https://www.linkedin.com/pulse/cloud-service-model-understand-types-characteristics-peerzade/

[6] Ahuja, S. P., Mani, S., & Zambrano, J. (2012). A survey of the state of cloud computing in healthcare. *Network and Communication Technologies,* 1(2), 12.

[7] Kumar, V., Jangirala, S., & Ahmad, M. (2018). An efficient mutual authentication framework for healthcare systems in cloud computing. *Journal of Medical Systems,* 42(8), 1–25.

[8] Ashtari, S., Eydgahi, A., & Lee, H. (2015). Exploring cloud computing implementation issues in the healthcare industry. *Transactions of the International Conference on Health Information Technology Advancement,* 49. https://scholarworks.wmich.edu/ichita_transactions/49

[9] http://www.cdc.gov/epiinfo/cloud.html

[10] Sajid, A., & Abbas, H. (2016). Data privacy in cloud-assisted healthcare systems: state of the art and future challenges. *Journal of Medical Systems,* 40(6), 1–16.

[11] http://www.ibm.com/watson/health/explorys/

[12] https://www.eclinicalworks.com/

[13] http://www.mckesson.com/health-plans/population-health/

[14] https://www.ibm.com/watson/health/population-health-management/resources/phytel-solution

[15] https://www.cerner.com/solutions/population-health-management

[16] Lorido-Botran, T., Miguel-Alonso, J., & Lozano, J. A. (2014). A review of auto-scaling techniques for elastic applications in cloud environments. *Journal of Grid Computing,* 12(4), 559–592.

[17] Doukas, C., Pliakas, T., & Maglogiannis, I. (2010). Mobile healthcare information management utilizing Cloud Computing and Android OS. In *2010 Annual International Conference of the IEEE Engineering in Medicine and Biology,* pp. 1037–1040. IEEE.

[18] Darwish, A., Hassanien, A. E., Elhoseny, M., Sangaiah, A. K., & Muhammad, K. (2019). The impact of the hybrid platform of internet of things and cloud computing on healthcare systems: opportunities, challenges, and open problems. *Journal of Ambient Intelligence and Humanized Computing,* 10(10), 4151–4166.

[19] Devadass, L., Sekaran, S. S., & Thinakaran, R. (2017). Cloud computing in healthcare. *International Journal of Students' Research in Technology & Management,* 5(1), 25–31.

[20] Guo, Y., Kuo, M. H., & Sahama, T. (2012, December). Cloud computing for healthcare research information sharing. In *4th IEEE International Conference on Cloud Computing Technology and Science Proceedings* (pp. 889–894). IEEE.

[21] Calabrese, B., & Cannataro, M. (2015). Cloud computing in healthcare and biomedicine. *Scalable Computing: Practice and Experience, 16*(1), 1–18.

[22] Desai, F., Chowdhury, D., Kaur, R., Peeters, M., Arya, R. C., Wander, G. S., ... & Buyya, R. (2022). HealthCloud: A system for monitoring health status of heart patients using machine learning and cloud computing. *Internet of Things, 17,* 100485.

[23] Chiregi, M., & Navimipour, N. J. (2016). Trusted services identification in the cloud environment using the topological metrics. *Karbala International Journal of Modern Science, 2*(3), 203–210.

[24] Myers, J. E. Data Modeling for Healthcare Systems Integration: Use of the MetaModel. Source: https://metadata.com/whitepapers/myers1.pdf

[25] Rajabion, L., Shaltooki, A. A., Taghikhah, M., Ghasemi, A., & Badfar, A. (2019). Healthcare big data processing mechanisms: The role of cloud computing. *International Journal of Information Management, 49,* 271–289.

[26] Shahzad, A., Lee, Y. S., Lee, M., Kim, Y. G., & Xiong, N. (2018). Real-time cloud-based health tracking and monitoring system in designed boundary for cardiology patients. *Journal of Sensors, 2018,* 15 pages. doi:10.1155/2018/3202787

[27] Wukkadada, B., & Saiswani, V. P. (2000). Online Healthcare System Using Cloud Computing and Artificial Intelligence. *IOSR Journal of Computer Engineering, 20,* S40–S43.

[28] Annie Alphonsa, M. M., & Amudhavalli, P. (2018). Genetically modified glow-worm swarm optimization based privacy preservation in cloud computing for healthcare sector. *Evolutionary Intelligence, 11*(1), 101–116.

[29] Dang, L. M., Piran, M., Han, D., Min, K., & Moon, H. (2019). A survey on internet of things and cloud computing for healthcare. *Electronics, 8*(7), 768.

[30] Kurdi, R., Aljehani, M., Subasi, A., & Qaisar, S. M. (2017, November). Cloud computing-based healthcare information systems: a proposal for the Kingdom of Saudi Arabia. In *2017 International Conference on Electrical and Computing Technologies and Applications (ICECTA)* (pp. 1–5). IEEE.

[31] Griebel, L., Prokosch, H. U., Köpcke, F., Toddenroth, D., Christoph, J., Leb, I., ... & Sedlmayr, M. (2015). A scoping review of cloud computing in healthcare. *BMC Medical Informatics and Decision Making, 15*(1), 1–16.

[32] Gao, F., & Sunyaev, A. (2019). Context matters: A review of the determinant factors in the decision to adopt cloud computing in healthcare. *International Journal of Information Management, 48,* 120–138.

[33] Shimrat, O. (2009). Cloud computing and healthcare. *San Diego Physician. org,* 26–29.

[34] Ali, O., Shrestha, A., Soar, J., & Wamba, S. F. (2018). Cloud computing-enabled healthcare opportunities, issues, and applications: A systematic review. *International Journal of Information Management, 43,* 146–158.

[35] Integrating Cloud Computing in E-healthcare: System Design, Implementation and Significance in Context of Developing Countries – Md Ishak1, Raiyan Rahman2, and Tahasin Mahmud3.

[36] Challenges of Deploying Cloud Computing in eHealth – Nermeen Mekawiea*, Kesmat Yehiab.

[37] Designing framework for better healthcare using cloud computing – Dr. Ranjana Rajnish.

[38] What's the Forecast for Cloud Computing in Healthcare? – Jeff Kabachinski.

[39] Privacy Preserving k-Nearest Neighbor for Medical Diagnosis in e-Health Cloud Jeongsu Park and Dong Hoon Lee.

[40] Biometrics-as-a-service: Cloud-based Technology, Systems, and Application – Silvio Barra, Kim-Kwang Raymond Choo, Michele Nappi, Arcangelo Castigolione, Fabio Narducci, Rajiv Ranjan.

[41] REPORT on the use of cloud computing in health – Jeremy Thorp, Greg Fletcher, Jurgen Wehnert, Christof Gessner, Luc Nicolas.

[42] Cloud Computing for Interoperability in Home-Based Healthcare – Yan Hu.

[43] Multiscale not Multicore: Efficient Heterogeneous Cloud Computing – Anil Madhavapeddy, Richard Mortier, Jon Crowcroft, Steven Hand.

[44] Study of Cloud Computing in HealthCare Industry – G. Nikhita Reddy, G.J. Ugander Reddy.

[45] Ashtari, S., Eydgahi, A., & Lee, H. (2015). Exploring Cloud Computing Implementation Issues in Healthcare Industry.

[46] Siam, A. I., Almaiah, M. A., Al-Zahrani, A., Elam, A. A., El Banby, G. M., El-Shafai, W., Abd El-Samie, F. E. and El-Bahnasawy, N. A. (2021). Secure Health Monitoring Communication Systems Based on IoT and Cloud Computing for Medical Emergency Applications. *Computational Intelligence and Neuroscience*, vol. 2021, 23 pages. doi:10.1155/2021/8016525

[47] https://azure.microsoft.com/en-in/overview/what-is-hybrid-cloud-computing/#:~:text=A%20hybrid%20cloud%E2%80%94sometimes%20called,to%20be%20shared%20between%20them

[48] https://yalantis.com/blog/hipaa-vs-healthcare-laws-in-other-countries/

[49] https://data-flair.training/blogs/future-of-cloud-computing/

[50] https://www.flexmind.co/cloud-computing/future-of-cloud-computing/

[51] Nigam, V. K., & Bhatia, S. (2016). Impact of cloud computing on health care. *International Research Journal of Engineering and Technology*, 3(5), 2804–2810.

Chapter 12

An Insight into Image Steganography for Medical Informatics

Asha Durafe[1,2] and Vinod Patidar[1]

[1]School of Engineering, Sir Padampat Singhania University Bhatewar, Udaipur, Rajasthan, India
[2]Department of Electronics Engineering, Shah & Anchor Kutchhi Engineering College Chembur, Mumbai, Maharashtra, India

Contents

12.1   Introduction 218
12.2   Medical Image Steganography 219
12.3   Classification of Image Steganography Based on
        Embedding Domain 219
        12.3.1   Spatial Domain Steganography 220
        12.3.2   Transform Domain Steganography 222
        12.3.3   Hybrid Domain 224
        12.3.4   Steganography Based on AI Approaches 228
12.4   Image Steganography with Encryption 229
12.5   Spread-Spectrum (SS)-Based Image Steganography 230
12.6   Performance Evaluation 233
12.7   Statistical and Analytical Measures Used 234
12.8   Conclusion 236
Funding 236
References 236

DOI: 10.1201/9781003145189-12

217

12.1 Introduction

In this era of digital-image transmission over the Internet, privacy and security of the shared data have become of utmost concern. The most extensive destruction ever caused was by the WannaCry ransomware attack, which infected computers in 150 countries, cancelling patient surgeries and medical reports and causing communication channels to became inaccessible [1]. In view of this, security, confidentiality, and integrity have become the primary requirements of an electronic health record (EHR) system. Accordingly, medical centers need to exchange personal patient information in the form of medical radiology images, medical history, patient's age and weight, immunization records, and lab test data. As the amount of data exchanged between the hospitals and medical centers for research, education, or consultation has increased exponentially, the secrecy of patient data has become a significant challenge for the security experts. Medical image steganography offers a solution to this problem by hiding the patient's sensitive data inside a cover image, which will be invisible and not easily extracted by an unknown user. Cryptography is another term associated with data hiding in which a secret key is shared between the sender and the receiver. Alternatively, confidential information is transmitted in an encrypted form. This encrypted data can easily create suspicion to the third party about the existence of secret information; it is prone to prying the intruders who can try several decryption algorithms to recover the hidden information. Therefore, steganography has been preferred and widely used from ancient times to camouflage private and confidential data. As indicated in Figure 12.1, the process of steganography generates a stego-image in which the secret medical data can be embedded inside a cover media. The embedding process should be executed in such a way that the stego-image produced will be a replica of the cover image with the secret data shielded inside the cover. This chapter presents a comprehensive literature survey of the various image-steganography algorithms developed to assure privacy and secrecy in the field of medical informatics. It also highlights the statistical and analytical measures used for the performance evaluation of image steganography and suggests some guidelines to improvise the current research trends in the existing techniques.

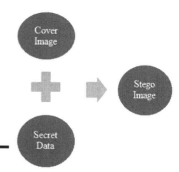

Figure 12.1 Image Steganography Process.

12.2 Medical Image Steganography

Medical image steganography can be effectively utilized to implement a secure e-health system that can speed up diagnosis and further treatment. Sensitive medical data such as patient's name, email address, residential address, workplace address, e-card details, mediclaim details have to be protected from the cyber-criminals who may misuse it. In the medical informatics field, it is essential to handle this sensitive information by carefully obfuscating it inside a suitable cover media. Furthermore, image steganography can also be used to secure the DICOM (digital imaging and communications in medicine) standard, which is widely used for storage, printing, and transmission of medical images. Figure 12.2 shows the medical image steganography process, which can be used to securely transmit patients' confidential details as secret images hidden inside a cover image. This secret information can be extracted by the authorized medical experts at the other end for further diagnosis, research, or treatment.

12.3 Classification of Image Steganography Based on Embedding Domain

Image steganography is generally classified based on the domain used for the embedding process. Figure 12.3 shows the classification of existing different types of image-steganography algorithms.

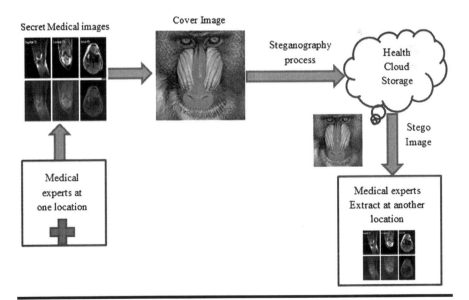

Figure 12.2 Medical Image Steganography.

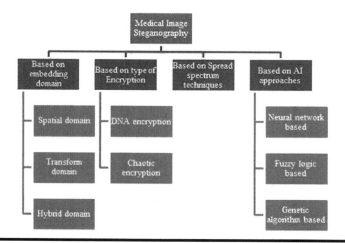

Figure 12.3 Classification of Image Steganography.

12.3.1 Spatial Domain Steganography

These are the substitution-based methods that undeviatingly modify the pixels to conceal the secret data. These are simple to implement and have low complexity and high imperceptibility. However, these spatial domain techniques suffer from some drawbacks, such as limited robustness, and they are less immune to cyberattacks.

■ LSB substitution methods: Direct LSB substitution structures are quite possibly the most traditional methods of concealing impressively huge confidential messages without presenting numerous noticeable mutilations. It is a process in which the LSB pixels of the image are customized. The biggest advantage of the LSB substitution method is the simplicity. However, LSB substitution falls as easy prey to factual image-processing attacks and possible damages [2]. Chang et al. [3] developed an LSB substitution-based steganography algorithm using a DES encryption algorithm for online transmission of real-time secret images. The existing greedy algorithm was modified for rapid generation of the substitution matrix. Zhou et al. [4] proposed a steganography method that embeds digital signature and electronic patient record (EPR) into a medical image. This algorithm applies the LSB substitution method to secure the signature.

■ Pixel value differencing (PVD): To tackle the visual quality issue of LSB coding, another steganographic approach based on pixel difference value is used. The difference value between two neighboring pixels is used to decide how many secret bits should be embedded. In this method, a cover image is partitioned into two non-overlapped consecutive pixel blocks in a zigzag direction. Further, in each block, the difference value between two pixels is calculated to decide the embedding size of bits, where difference values are grouped into a number of ranges. Finally, the difference value is modified with the new difference value, along with the secret data. The PVD method embeds a larger secret data into images with higher visual imperceptibility as compared with the LSB substitution method. Al-Dmour et al. [5] proposed a steganography algorithm to conceal patients' sensitive information to recognize contrast regions in the image and a hamming code that inserts three secret message bits into four bits of the cover image. Wu et al. [6] developed a PVD-based algorithm to hide patients' confidential data by enlarging the embedding rate and imperceptibility of the stego-image.

- Histogram-based methods: Policy of histogram-preserving algorithm is to reduce the histogram discrepancy between the cover image and the stego-image. When the histogram distribution is well preserved, the stego-image has increased immunity against steganalysis attack. Cheng et al. [7] introduced histogram-preserving steganography based on block (HPSB) in which a secret image is encapsulated inside the cover image based on histogram profit-loss settlement. Yang et al. [8] proposed histogram-based reversible data-hiding method with two interleaving predictive stages. Pixel prediction can be done with column-based and chessboard-based approaches.

- Mapping-based methods: In these methods, the cover and secret images are separated into M × N blocks, where the highest similarity of blocks between the cover and secret images are searched. It is followed by compressing the index information of matched and unmatched blocks and inserted through allocated LSB to obtain a less disfigured image [9]. Husainy [10] introduced a method to secure the digital text of a confidential message inside a cover image. In this, a mapping table is used to create substitution and transportation operations by mapping a character in the message to more than one value of 7-MSBs of the pixel. Roy and Changder [11] presented a method to map a secret image as a longest common subsequence (LCS) of a given cover image. The cover image has a large amount of randomness and a huge length contrast with the secret image; the length of the LCS between them is relied upon to be near the length of the binary string equivalent of the secret image. Joshi et al. [12] presented a technique in which the seventh bit of the chosen pixel and the next pixel are utilized to conceal and extract the secret data.

- Pixel/block indicator based methods: In these methods, one of the RGB channels is used as an indicator, and other channels are kept as data channels. Adnan [13] proposed a technique in which two LSBs in one RGB channel are used to indicate the existence of data in the remaining RGB channels. This method avoids the dependency on a separate key. Tiwari and Shadiliya [14] introduced the Triple-A concealment technique to secure confidential information. Two separate keys are used to increase the randomization thereby increasing the level of security.

- Pixel-value prediction-based methods: To enhance the visual imperceptibility and payload capacity of spatial domain methods, pixel-value predictors are used that predict the pixel intensities rather than directly modifying the pixel values. Yu et al. [15] discussed prediction-based image hiding in which compression codes were used to hide the confidential information. To enlarge the embedding rate, Jafar et al. [16] developed a multiple predictors-based data embedding, which was the extension of the prediction error approach to embed the secret data without adding any predictor overhead. However, this approach was not judged with any steganalysis test. In [17] Yip et al. proposed a bijective mirror-mapping approach to embed the secret data with the help of multiple predictors. However, this method needed manual tuning of the system parameters to obtain the best possible efficiency. Table 12.1 indicates the statistical measures evaluated by various steganographers using spatial domain techniques in the previous decade. It can be inferred that LSB substitution methods have offered better PSNR values as compared to the other methods mentioned in Table 12.1.

12.3.2 Transform Domain Steganography

At the cost of high complexity, these methods offer increased robustness against cyberattacks and have high payload capacity as compared to the spatial domain methods. Transform techniques insert the message by modulating coefficient in a transform domain inside significant areas of a cover media. Embedding in the DWT domain shows promising results and outperforms DCT embedding, especially in terms of compression survival. A steganographer should use foresight when embedding the transform domains particularly; however, DWT aims to be suppler than DCT [27]. Depending on the user requirement and need of the application, transforms other than discrete wavelet can also be used, and each one offers advantages over the others. Curvelet transform, framelet transform, slantlet transform, and dual-tree DWT are some of the other types of transformations that can be used in particular applications [28].

■ DWT (discrete wavelet transform)/IWT (integer wavelet transform) based methods: The first and foremost aim of medical-image steganography is to keep up secret communication among the authorized users. To attain this objective, DWT/IWT-based steganography has demonstrated noteworthy robustness as compared to the spatial domain techniques. DWT performs down sampling of the cover image, and the resulting coefficients can be modified to hide the secret image. IWT is a type of non-linear transform, which is of interest to the steganographer to obtain efficient lossless compression [29]. Parul et al. [30] proposed a modified secure and high-capacity-based steganography algorithm to conceal a large size confidential image into a cover image occupying lesser memory space. Arnold transformation is used to create the confusion matrix related to the secret image. Discrete wavelets

Table 12.1 Year-Wise Development in the Spatial Domain Techniques

Sr. No.	Authors	Year	Approach used	Statistical measures	Significant characteristics
1	Kaur et al. [18]	2020	Reversible data hiding with pixel-value ordering	Avg. embedding capacity 37233 bits	Increased embedding rate and high visual quality
2	Gandharba [19]	2018	LSB+PVD	Avg.PSNR 38.34	Undetectable with RS steganalysis
3	Cheng et al. [7]	2018	Histogram based	Avg.PSNR 52.53	High PSNR, low relative entropy
4	Kim & Park [20]	2017	Layered PVD based	Avg.PSNR 36.52	Embedding capacity improved by a factor of 1.3
5	Pradhan et al. [21]	2016	Seven pixel value difference method	Avg.PSNR 39.81	Increased embedding capacity
6	Singh & Singh [22]	2015	LSB based on colour wavelengths	PSNR 55.93 MSE 0.164	Low noise and highly secure image transfer
7	Champakamala et al. [23]	2014	LSB based method with ARM 7 and GSM	Avg. PSNR 68	Robust against histogram attack but hidden data easily recoverable
8	Juneja et al. [24]	2013	Two component based LSB	Avg. PSNR>52	LSB based on two components
9	Sharmila et al. [25]	2012	Edge regions are used for embedding with LSB	MSE 0.013168 PSNR 66.96	Increased security & high payload capacity
10	Medeni et al. [26]	2010	Based on PVD	PSNR 42.68	less difference between original and stego image of 40017 bits

are utilized to transform both the images in frequency domain, and subsequently, alpha blending operation is performed. Then the inverse discrete wavelet transformation (IDWT) is applied to get the stego image. Integer wavelet transform (IWT) was applied to camouflage MRI medical images into a cover image. Arnold transform was used and a shuffled secret image was attained. The shuffled secret image was secured into the cover image, and inverse IWT was applied to obtain the stego image [31].

■ DCT (discrete cosine transform)-based methods: DCT is one of the main elements of JPEG compression in which the secret information is distributed evenly over the entire cover image, making the technique robust against intruders. Algorithms F5 and Outguess are the most reliable methods of frequency-domain steganography. Both utilize DCT embedding. Since the cosine coefficients cannot be measured accurately, DCT is called a lossy compression transform. Also recurring computations using limited precision numbers instigate rounding errors into the ultimate outcome. Variances between initial coefficients and restored coefficients depend on the technique used to calculate DCT. JpegJsteg is a steganography tool that implements the compression algorithm by using DCT for hiding secret data. It generates a JPEG stego-image from the input of information to be hidden and a lossless cover image. Arunkumar et al. [32] proposed a method using RIWT and DCT where embedding was performed on the singular values. Logistic encryption was utilized to make the system more robust for transmission of medical images.

12.3.3 Hybrid Domain

These methods combine the advantages of both the spatial as well as transform domain to build a highly secure data hiding technique, but they are distinctly rigid and difficult to implement. Gunjal and Jha [33] have developed a new technique that has combined LSB and DCT embedding algorithms with blowfish encryption, which creates the cipher text to be embedded in the LSB of DCT coefficients of cover image.

■ SVD (singular value decomposition) & DWT-based methods: SVD-based hiding methods are susceptible to false-positive errors since S components of secret image are hidden inside S components of cover image, and the remaining matrices U and V are used as keys to extract the secret image [34]. Figure 12.4 shows the embedding of secret data inside a cover image using SVD.

SVD has been used extensively as an effective data analysis tool in various applications like image compression and image hiding [34]. If SVD is applied on an image I with size $M \times N$, *and* then three matrices called U with left singular values

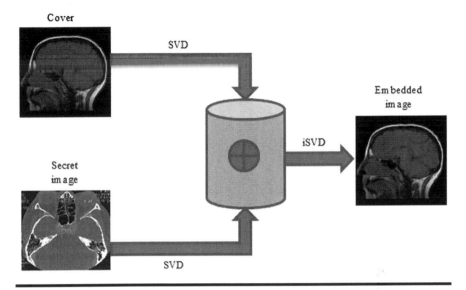

Figure 12.4   Singular Value Decomposition.

V with right singular values and *S* with the diagonal elements are created as given in (12.1) below,

$$I = U \times S \times V^T \tag{12.1}$$

SVD implemented along with other frequency domain techniques has shown excellent results with respect to visual quality and robustness as compared to pure SVD transforms. In SVD-based embedding, the singular values *S* of the secret image are inserted into the singular values *S* of the cover image as shown in Figure 12.4. Whereas the left and right singular vectors *U* and *V^T* are utilized as key components on the receiver side. However, this method of insertion may result in false-positive error and to avoid it, the entire secret image can be indirectly inserted into *U* and *V* components of cover image [35].

- Singh et al. [36] investigated the outcome of using various error-correcting codes like BCH code, R-S code, Hamming code on the robustness of image steganography to be used in telemedicine. Mandy et al. [37] represented a method of singular-value replacement. First DWT was used to transform the cover image into frequency domain, and then secret image was inserted using SVD. As illustrated in Figure 12.5, cover image and secret image are decomposed into LL, LH, HL, and HH planes using DWT, which are further transformed into U, S and V matrices using SVD, and then a stego image is obtained by implementing inverse DWT.

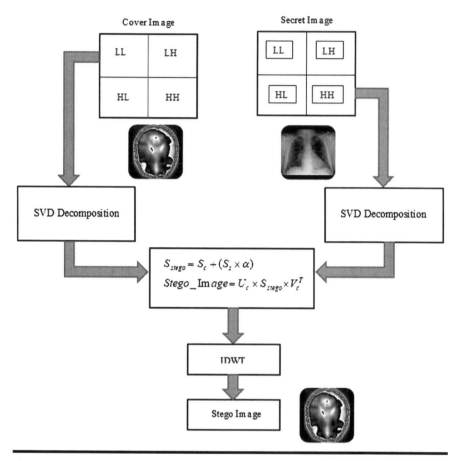

Figure 12.5 DWT+SVD-Based Medical Image Steganography ("Medical images are taken from MedPix image database").

- IWT (integer wavelet transform) & SVD-based methods: Durafe and Patidar [35] presented a technique to create a unique stego image by hiding the secret color image inside a fractal cover image. The embedding of the secret image was implemented using DWT-SVD combination and was compared with IWT-SVD combination. The statistical analysis proved that the IWT-SVD method is faster than DWT-SVD and is also easy for hardware implementation. Singh et al. [38] proposed a scheme based on SVD and IWT to strengthen the security and imperceptibility. The results were compared with DCT and redundant DWT, which showed that SVD-IWT combination served more robustness against common types of image-processing attacks.

The statistical measures to indicate imperceptibility metric of various transform domain techniques are listed in Table 12.2, below which highlights that a blend of transform domain approach and SVD contributes increased visual quality.

Table 12.2 Year-Wise Development in the Transform Domain Techniques

Sr. No.	Authors	Year	Approach used	Statistical measures	Significant characteristics
1	Durafe & Patidar [35]	2020	SVD+DWT & SVD+IWT	Avg. PSNR 64dB	Large payload capacity with less computational time
2	Murugan et al. [39]	2020	DWT	PSNR 54dB	Performance with different fusion factors is analysed.
3	Subhedar & Mankar [40]	2020	SVD+Framelet transform	Avg. PSNR 69.52dB	Avg stego detection accuracy is 63%
4	Thanki et al. [41]	2017	SVD-DCT	PSNR>60dB	Security enhanced with CS encryption
5	Thakkar & Shrivastava [42]	2017	SVD+DWT	PSNR 43dB	Successful extraction under various types of noise attacks
6	Jero et al. [43]	2014	SVD+DWT	PSNR 69.13dB	BER is 0% for dynamic location selection
7	Xiao et al. [44]	2015	SVD+Framelet	Avg. PSNR 37dB	Can resist compression and cropping attacks
8	Prabhakaran et al. [45]	2013	Dual transform based on DWT & IWT	PSNR 35-54dB	combination of cryptography and steganography based on concept of double staging
9	Huang et al. [46]	2011	3 level 2D-DWT with 9/7 wavelet filter	PSNR of 31.41 dB for 36 710 bits of embedding capacity	maintains imperceptibility of stego-image
10	Xu et al. [47]	2004	Invertible 2D wavelet transform is used that lays out integer to integer	PSNR>39dB	For totally errorless recuperation, the data ought to be preprocessed by a convolution encoder prior to implanting.

12.3.4 Steganography Based on AI Approaches

Steganalysis, i.e., the art of detecting hidden data inside a stego image, can become a severe challenge to most of the privacy-preserving algorithms. To counter this threat, artificial intelligence (AI) is incorporated in image-steganography methods. Among the most favored algorithms implemented in artificial intelligence are GA (genetic algorithms), which are used to enhance the embedding capacity, and NN (neural networks) and FL (fuzzy logic) are focused to create high robustness. As shown in Figure 12.6, a cover image in the form of X-ray can be used to carry confidential CT scan reports of a patient by using an NN/GA/FL-based embedding approach.

■ Neural networks/Deep neural network-based methods: NN-based steganography models use neural networks to find appropriate locations in the cover image to hide the secret information. Zhang et al. [48] proposed a convolutional neural network (CNN) based method where a secret image can be hidden only in Y channel of cover image using generative

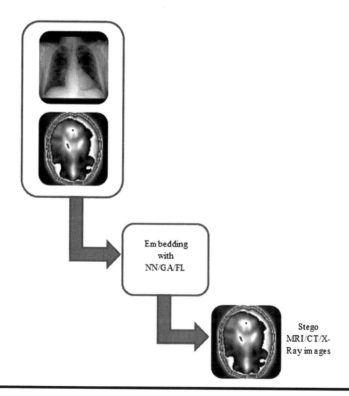

Figure 12.6   AI-Based Medical Image Steganography (MIDAS, Medpix medical image database).

adversarial networks to increase the security. Baluja [49] presented a deep-learning-based method in which the steganography system was divided into three networks as secret image prep network, hiding network, and reveal network, which are trained to extract the secret image. Duan et al. [50] implemented deep neural-network-based image steganography using StegNet, which is a fully convolutional neural network. It consists of an encoder, decoder, and a pixel-level classification layer to create a segmentation map.

- Genetic algorithms (GA) based methods: GA is an optimization method that struggles to find such values of its input so as to obtain the best output. Wang et al. [51] developed a method that incorporates the genetic algorithm to search the nearest optimal replacement of LSB for better perceptual quality. Wu et al. [33] proposed an image-hiding algorithm based on LSB substitution and GA to generate global and local optimal substitution strategy, which enhances the image quality while imparting high payload capacity.

- Fuzzy-logic–based methods: Fuzzy logic is a robust decision-making tool that can be used as a pixel-merging method or implemented as an edge-detection tool in medical-image steganography. Karakis et al. [52] proposed a method to hide electroencephalogram (EEG) inside an MR (magnetic resonance) image using non-sequential LSBs of image pixels and fuzzy logic. Karakis et al. [53] used FL algorithm to select LSBs of image pixels. These selected LSBs of the cover image pixels are used to hide bits of the secret data. Vanmathi et al. [54] presented a fuzzy-logic–based edge-detection method to define the degree to which a pixel has a place with an edge.

12.4 Image Steganography with Encryption

An additional layer of security to the image steganography can be introduced by encrypting the secret data before embedding into cover media. Since time is an important factor in healthcare applications, the steganographer should take care of the encrypting and decrypting complexities. Figure 12.7 depicts the process of encrypting the secret image before embedding it inside the cover image. Jain et al. [55] presented medical-image steganography to hide patients' secret data using chaotic standard map, linear feedback shift register, and Rabin public-key cryptography. Durafe [56] proposed an image-steganography method to hide the secret images using LSB and RSA encryption algorithm implemented using Raspberry-Pi and GSM modules. Prem Navas et al. [57] introduced a medical-image security system using LSB embedding, and the medical image to be hidden was encrypted with a logistic map.

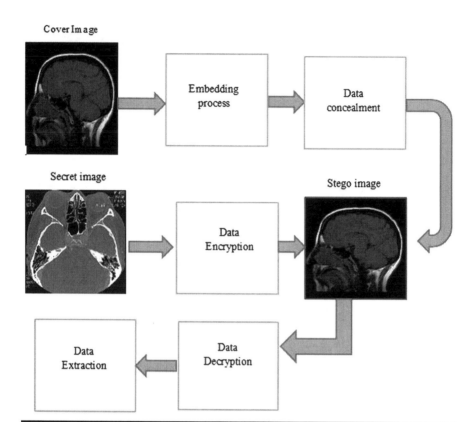

Figure 12.7 Medical Image Steganography with Encryption.

12.5 Spread-Spectrum (SS)-Based Image Steganography

In spread-spectrum-based methods, the frequency domain of the cover image is treated as a communication channel, and the secret image is treated as a signal that is transmitted through the channel. The secret image is spread throughout the entire spectrum of the cover image, making its presence unnoticeable [58]. Eze et al. [59] proposed an SS-based image hiding scheme for secure transmission of medical images in teleradiology. This blind SS-data-hiding method has improved payload capacity up to 6 bits per sample.

The comparative analysis of all the prevailing steganography techniques is listed in Table 12.3 from which it can be inferred that each individual technique has some pros and cons. Hence, to avail maximum benefits from these techniques, it is advisable to amalgamate the features of these methods depending on the application requirements.

Table 12.3 Comparative Analysis

Authors	Medical image used	Embedding domain	Embedding method	Payload capacity	Statistical measures
Zhou et al. [4]	Mammography	Spatial	LSB of random pixels	6720 bits	33dB-42dB
Memon et al. [60]	CT,X-ray,MRI	IWT	Hybrid	128 character	58dB
Nipanikar et al. [61]	MRI +Mammogram	DWT	wavelet coefficients +edge transformation	8100 bits	61.1dB-72.7dB
Karakis et al. [52]	EEG+MR	Hybrid	LSB+Fuzzy logic	9438516 bytes	Avg. 56dB
Navas et al. [62]	MRI	IWT	LSB	3400 characters	44dB
Liao et al. [63]	MRI	Transform	DCT	embedding payload 0.4 bpnzAC.	Not checked
Orooba [64]	CT scan	spatial	LSB	Not checked	35dB
Pareek & Patidar [65]	X-Ray, MRI, CT	AI based	Genetic Algorithm	Not checked	Avg. Correlation coeff. 0.035

(Continued)

Table 12.3 (Continued) Comparative Analysis

Authors	Medical image used	Embedding domain	Embedding method	Payload capacity	Statistical measures
Sampaio & Jackowski [66]	DICOM images	spatial	LSB	Not checked	Max. absolute difference of $5.29 * 10\mp 4$
Prabhakaran et al. [66]	MRI	IWT	Arnold transform	Not checked	Avg. PSNR 46dB
Stoyanov & Stoyanov [67]	CT scan	AI based	Nuclear spin generator	0.74 BPP	Avg. PSNR 113.2dB
Eze et al. [59]	DICOM images	Spread spectrum based	Constant Correlation Compression Coding Scheme	24,576 bit max.	Avg. PSNR 71.43dB

12.6 Performance Evaluation

The performance of an image steganography system is measured with the following specifications:

1. Embedding capacity – Total number of bits that can be secreted in the cover image.
2. Robustness – Capability of embedding algorithms to store embedded data, even after going through the process of compression and decompression of a file.
3. Tamper resistance – Difficulty in change of secret data whenever it has been implanted in some cover medium.
4. Complexity (computational cost): A metric that decides the degree to which a data-hiding system is expensive and time consuming to conceal and retrieve the secret data. For a perfect image-hiding scheme, computational cost should be minimum.
5. Imperceptibility: Decides the quality of the stego image and is measured with the statistical measures like MSE (mean square error) and PSNR (peak signal to noise ratio).

As seen in Figure 12.8, the performance parameters discussed in section 1.6 can be assembled in a pyramid structure, and, depending upon the application requirements, the appropriate method of medical-image steganography can be chosen. Also it can be inferred that it is not possible to design a steganography model that satisfies all the requirements of an ideal system, and hence, a trade-off has to be made always among the different performance parameters. However, it is observed

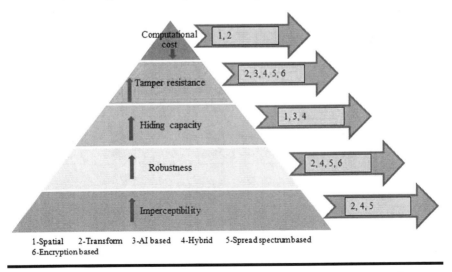

Figure 12.8 Performance Pyramid for Various Methods of Medical Image Steganography.

that hybrid steganography models have achieved maximum performance efficiency till now in the literature.

12.7 Statistical and Analytical Measures Used

The metrics used measure the visual quality, payload capacity, robustness, undetectability, and computational efficiency of an image-steganography system, are listed in Table 12.4.

Table 12.4 Statistical and Analytical Measures

Measure used	Formula	Purpose
MSE (Mean Square Error)	$MSE = \frac{1}{M \times N} \Sigma_{i=1}^{M \times N} ((C_i - S_i) * (C_i - S_i))$ M and N represent the height and width of the cover image with pixel value C_i along stego pixel value S_i	Visual quality check metric to measure the difference between cover image and stego image. Ideally, it should be zero.
PSNR (Peak Signal to Noise Ratio)	$PSNR = 10 \log_{10} \left(\frac{P_{max}^2}{MSE} \right)$ P_{max} is the maximum pixel value which is 255	Visual quality check metric, which measures the imperceptibility of the stego image. Ideally, it should be above 28dB [58]
SSIM (Structural Similarity Index Measure)	$SSIM(C, S) = \frac{(2\mu_c\mu_s + C_1)(2\sigma_{cs} + C_2)}{\left(\mu_c^2 + \mu_s^2 + C_1\right)\left(\mu_c^2 + \mu_s^2 + C_2\right)}$ in which μ is mean, σ is variance and σ_{cs} is the covariance of cover image C and stego image S with $C_1 = (0.01 * R)^2$ and $C_2 = (0.03 * R)^2$	Perceptual quality metric to measure the difference between cover image and stego image. Ideally, it should be 1.
	with dynamic pixel range R	
BRISQUE score (Blind/ reference less image spatial quality evaluator	$f(x; a, \sigma^2) = \frac{a}{2\beta \Gamma (1/a)} \exp\left(-\left(\frac{|x|}{\beta}\right)^n\right)$	It is a spatial feature extraction model utilizing image pixels to assess image features. Ideal range is 30 to 40, which indicates high perceptual quality [56].

(Continued)

Table 12.4 (Continued) Statistical and Analytical Measures

Measure used	Formula	Purpose
NCC (Normalized Cross Correlation	$NCC = \frac{\sum_{i=1}^{M \times N}(C_i \times S_i)}{\sum_{i=1}^{M \times N}(C_i)^2}$	Used to measure robustness by assessing the similarity and differences between original and extracted secret images [58]. Ideally, it should be 1.
BER (Bit Error Rate)	$BER = \frac{Number\ of\ bits\ in\ error}{Total\ bits\ transmitted}$	It is an image-quality metric to assess imperceptibility.
RMSE (Root Mean Square Error)	$RMSE = \sqrt{MSE}$	Indicates degree of similarity between cover image and stego image on a pixel-by-pixel basis.
Payload capacity (BPP)	$BPP = \frac{B_s}{C_i}$ where B_s indicates secret image bits and C_i indicates cover image pixels	It indicates the amount of secret payload that can be hidden inside a cover image. Measured in bits per pixel (BPP)
TC (Time complexity)	TC = Time of embedding + Time of extraction	It denotes the computational time required for the complete process of steganography and should be as low as possible.
IF (Image Fidelity)	$IF = 1 - \left(\frac{\sum_{i=1}^{M \times N}(C_i \times S_i)^2}{\sum_{i=1}^{M \times N}(C_i)^2}\right)$	It is an image-perceptual quality metric that defines the degree of exactness in the reconstructed secret image.

12.8 Conclusion

This chapter presents a comprehensive survey of the various methods of image-steganography methods used in the field of medical informatics. Right from the basic structure of medical-image steganography to various available methods used, their advantages and pitfalls are analyzed and tabulated aptly to offer a complete foresight to a new researcher in this field. Furthermore, the available statistical and analytical metrics are discussed to highlight their significance. The upcoming steganographers who are keen to probe security in healthcare applications may benefit with the following recommendations based on the aforementioned review.

- Validate the design with available steganalysis tools and image-processing attacks. Steganalysis is the process of detecting secret information from a stego-image floated in a network. This validation will prove the robustness of the designed steganography scheme against the existing detection tools and attacks.
- Blend Steganography with encryption to reinforce security aspects in a way that, even if the stego-image is detected by any steganalysis tool, then also the intruder is left with another challenge of decrypting it.
- Adopt a suitable cover-image selection method to embed maximum secret data in it, thus enhancing the hiding capacity. Furthermore, it is also important to select the locations carefully since high-fidelity textured and edge regions selected for embedding makes the detection crucial. Focus on 2D space rather than going for 3D cover images for maximum throughput and undetectability.
- Amalgamate the features of spatial and transform domain making a hybrid model that can be trained with artificial intelligence or machine-learning-based algorithms. This approach can attain maximum ideal requirements of a steganography system.

Funding

One of us (VP) received the MATRICS grant (MTR/2018/000203) from the Science and Engineering Research Board (SERB), Department of Science and Technology (DST), Government of India.

References

[1] Cyber attacks on medical imaging systems, OpenMedscience, https://openmedscience.com/medical-device-cyber-security/
[2] Wu M. N., Lin M. H., Chang C. C. (2004). A LSB Substitution Oriented Image Hiding Strategy Using Genetic Algorithms. In: Chi C. H., Lam K. Y. (eds) *Content Computing. AWCC 2004. Lecture Notes in Computer Science*, vol 3309. Springer, Berlin, Heidelberg. 10.1007/978-3-540-30483-8_27

[3] Chang C. C., Lin M. H., Hu Y. C. (2002). A fast and secure image hiding scheme based on LSB substitution. *International Journal of Pattern Recognition and Artificial Intelligence* 16(04):399–416.

[4] Zhou X., Qu H., Huang H., Ku, Liu S. L. (2001). Authenticity and integrity of digital mammography images. *Medical Imaging, IEEE Transactions on* 20(8): 784–791.

[5] Al-Dmour H., Al-Ani A., Nguyen H. (2014). An efficient steganography method for hiding patient confidential information. 36th Annual International Conference of the IEEE Engineering in Medicine and Biology Society, Chicago, IL, pp. 222–225, doi: 10.1109/EMBC.2014.6943569

[6] Wu D. C., Tsai W. H. (2003). A steganographic method for images by pixel-value differencing. *Pattern Recognition Letters* 24(9):1613–1626.

[7] Cheng J., Chen Z., Yang R. (2018). An efficient histogram-preserving steganography based on block. *Journal on Image and Video Processing* 2018:74. 10.1186/s13640-018-0306-6

[8] Yang C.-H., Tsai M.-H. (2010). Improving Histogram-based Reversible Data Hiding by Interleaving Predictions. *IET Image Processing* 4(4):223–234.

[9] Wang R.-Z., Chen Y.-S. (2006). High-payload image steganography using two-way block matching. *IEEE Signal Processing Letters* 13(3):161–164. doi:10.1109/lsp.2005.862603

[10] Al-Husainy M. A. F. (2009). Image steganography by mapping pixels to letters. *Journal of Computer Science* 5(1):33–38. ISSN 1549-3636, doi:10.3844/jcs.2009.33.38

[11] Roy R., Changder S. (2014). Image realization steganography with LCS based mapping. 2014 Seventh International Conference on Contemporary Computing (IC3). doi:10.1109/ic3.2014.6897176

[12] Joshi K., Gill S., Yadav R. (2018). A new method of image steganography using the 7th bit of a pixel as indicator by introducing the successive temporary pixel in the grayscale image. *Journal of Computer Networks and Communications* 1–10. doi:10.1155/2018/9475142

[13] Abdul-Aziz Gutub A. (2010). Pixel indicator technique for RGB image stegano-graphy. *Journal of Emerging Technologies in Web Intelligence* 2(1):56–64.

[14] Tiwari N., Shandilya M. (2010) Secure RGB image steganography from pixel indicator to triple algorithm-an incremental growth. *International Journal of Security and its Applications* 4(4):53–62.

[15] Yu Y. H., Chang C. C., Hu Y. C. (2005). Hiding secret data in images via predictive coding. *Pattern Recognition* 38:691–705.

[16] Jafar I. F., Darabkh K. A., Al-Zubi R. T., Al Na'mneh R. A. (2015). Efficient Reversible Data Hiding Using Multiple Predictors. *The Computer Journal* 59(3):423–438. doi:10.1093/comjnl/bxv067

[17] Yip S. K., Au O. C., Wong H. M., Ho C. W. (2006). Generalized lossless data hiding by multiple predictors. Proceedings IEEE Int. Symp. Circuits and Systems, Island of Kos, Greece, May 21–24, pp. 1426–1429. IEEE.

[18] Kaur G., Singh S., Rani R. (2020). A high capacity reversible data hiding technique based on pixel value ordering using interlock partitioning. 7th International Conference on Signal Processing and Integrated Networks (SPIN). doi:10.1109/spin48934.2020.9071330

[19] Swain G. (2017). High capacity image steganography using modified LSB substitution and PVD against pixel difference histogram analysis. *Multimedia Security: Novel Steganography and Privacy Preserving* 2018 Article ID 1505896, 10.1155/2018/1505896

[20] Kim J., Park H. (2017). Image steganography using layered pixel-value differencing. Eighth International Conference on Graphic and Image Processing (ICGIP 2016). doi:10.1117/12.2266342

[21] Pradhan A., Sekhar K. R., Swain G. (2016). Digital image steganography based on seven way pixel value differencing. *Indian Journal of Science and Technology* 9(37):1–11. doi:10.17485/ijst/2016/v9i37/88557

[22] Singh A., Singh H. (2015). An improved LSB based image steganography technique for RGB images. 2015 IEEE International Conference on Electrical, Computer and Communication Technologies (ICECCT). doi:10.1109/icecct.2015.7226122

[23] Champakamala B., Padmini K., Radhika D. (2014). Least significant bit algorithm for image steganography. *International Journal of Advanced Computer Technology* 3(4):34–38.

[24] Juneja M., Sandhu P. S. (2013). A new approach for information security using an improved steganography technique. *Journal of Information Processing Systems* 9(3):405–424.

[25] Sharmila B., Shanthakumari R. (2012). Efficient adaptive steganography for colour images based on LSBMR algorithm. *ICTACT Journal on Image and Video Processing* 2(03):387–392.

[26] Medeni M. B. O., Souidi E. M. (2010). A generalization of the PVD steganographic method. *International Journal of Computer Science and Information Security* 8(8):156–159.

[27] Cheddad A., Condell J., Curran K., Kevitt P. M. (2009). Digital image steganography: Survey and analysis of current methods. *Signal Processing* 90:727–752.

[28] Subhedar M. S., Mankar V. H. (2014). Current status and key issues in image steganography: A survey. *Computer Science Review* 13–14:95–113. doi:10.1016/j.cosrev.2014.09.001

[29] Reichel J., Menegaz G., Nadenau M. J., Kunt M. (2001). Integer wavelet transform for embedded lossy to lossless image compression. In *IEEE Transactions on Image Processing*, 10(3):383–392. doi: 10.1109/83.908504.

[30] Parul, M., Dr. Harish R. (2014). Optimized Image Steganography using Discrete Wavelet Transform (DWT). *International Journal of Recent Development in Engineering and Technology*, ISSN 2347–6435, 2(2):75–81.

[31] Prabakaran G., Bhavani R., Rajeswari P. S. (2013). Multi secure and robustness for medical image based steganography scheme. In Circuits, Power and Computing Technologies (ICCPCT), 2013 International Conference on, pp. 1188–1193. IEEE.

[32] Arunkumar S., Subramaniyaswamy V., Vijayakumar V., Chilamkurti N., Logesh R. (2019). SVD-based robust image steganographic scheme using RIWT and DCT for secure transmission of medical images. *Measurement* 139:426–437. doi:10.1016/j.measurement.2019.02.069

[33] Gunjal M., Jha J. (2014). Image steganography using discrete cosine transform (DCT) and blowfish algorithm. *International Journal of Computer Trends and Technology (IJCTT)* 11(4):144–150.

[34] Bagheri S., Ahmadi B., Zhang G., Wei S. (2020). Robust and hybrid SVD-based image watermarking schemes: A survey. *Multimedia Tools and Applications (2020)* 79:1075–1117. 10.1007/s11042-019-08197-6

[35] Durafe A., Patidar V. (2020). Development and analysis of IWT-SVD and DWT-SVD steganography using fractal cover. *Journal of King Saud University — Computer and Information Sciences* 34(7):4483–4498. doi: 10.1016/j.jksuci.2020.10.008

[36] Singh A. K., Dave M., Mohan A. (2014). Hybrid technique for robust and imperceptible dual watermarking using error correcting codes for application in telemedicine. *International Journal of Electronic Security and Digital Forensics* 6(4):285–305.

[37] Douglas M., Bailey K., Leeney M., Curran K. (2017). Using SVD and DWT based steganography to enhance the security of watermarked fingerprint images. *TELKOMNIKA* 15(3, September 2017):1368–1379. ISSN: 1693–6930, doi: 10.12928/TELKOMNIKA.v15i3.6437

[38] Singh S., Singh R., Siddiqui T. J. (2016). Singular value decomposition based image steganography using integer wavelet transform. *Advances in Signal Processing and Intelligent Recognition Systems*, vol 425. Springer, Cham. 10.1007/978-3-319-28658-7_50

[39] Murugan G., Uthandipalayam Subramaniyam R. (2020) Performance analysis of image steganography using wavelet transform for safe and secured transaction. *Multimedia Tools and Applications* 79:9101–9115. 10.1007/s11042-019-7507-6

[40] Subhedar M., Mankar V. (2020). Secure image steganography using framelet transform and bidiagonal SVD. *Multimedia Tools and Applications (2020)* 79: 1865–1886. 10.1007/s11042-019-08221-9

[41] Thanki R., Borra S., Dwivedi V., Borisagar K. (2017). A steganographic approach for secure communication of medical images based on the DCT-SVD and the compressed sensing (CS) theory. *The Imaging Science Journal* 65(8):457–467. doi: 10.1080/13682199.2017.1367129

[42] Thakkar F. N., Srivastava V. K. (2017). A blind medical image watermarking: DWT-SVD based robust and secure approach for telemedicine applications. *Multimedia Tools and Applications* 76:3669–3697. 10.1007/s11042-016-3928-7

[43] Jero S. E., Ramu P., Ramakrishnan S. (2014). Discrete wavelet transform and singular value decomposition based ECG steganography for secured patient information transmission. *Journal of Medical Systems* 38:132. DOI 10.1007/s10916-014-0132-z

[44] Xiao M., Heb Z., Quana T. (2015). A robust digital watermarking algorithm based on framelet and SVD. MIPPR 2015: Multispectral Image Acquisition, Processing and Analysis, Proc. of SPIE Vol. 9811 981119-1

[45] Prabakaran G., Bhavani R., Kanimozhi K. (2013). Dual transform based steganography using wavelet families and statistical methods, In: Proc. of the 2013 International Conference on Pattern Recognition, Informatics and Mobile Engineering, PRIME, pp. 287–293.

[46] Huang H.-Y., Chang S.-H. (2011). A 9/7 wavelet-based lossless data hiding. In: Proc. of IEEE Symposium on Computational Intelligence for Multimedia, Signal and Vision Processing, CIMSIVP, pp. 1–6.

[47] Xu J., Sung A. H., Shi P., Liu Q. (2004) JPEG compression immune steganography using wavelet transform. In: Proc. of the International Conference on Information Technology: Coding and Computing, ITCC'04, vol. 2, pp. 704–708.

[48] Zhang R., Dong S., Liu J. (2019) Invisible steganography via generative adversarial networks. *Multimedia Tools and Applications* 78:8559–8575. 10.1007/s11042-018-6951-z

[49] Baluja S. (2017). Hiding images in plain sight: Deep steganography. 31st Conference on Neural Information Processing Systems (NIPS 2017), Long Beach, CA, USA, pp. 1–11.

[50] Duan X., Guo D., Liu N., Li B., Gou M., Qin, C. (2020). A new high capacity image steganography method combined with image elliptic curve cryptography and deep neural network. *IEEE Access* 2021:14 pages. doi:10.1109/access.2020.2971528

[51] Wang R. Z., Lin C. F., Lin J. C. (2001). Image hiding by optimal LSB substitution and genetic algorithm. *Pattern Recognition* 34:671–683.

[52] Karakıs R., Guler I., Capraz I., Bilir E. (2015). A novel fuzzy logic-based image steganography method to ensure medical data security. *Computers in Biology and Medicine* 67:172–183. doi:10.1016/j.compbiomed.2015.10.011

[53] Karakis R., Guler I. (2014). An application of fuzzy logic-based image steganography, 22nd Signal Processing and Communications Applications Conference (SIU), Trabzon, pp. 156–159. doi: 10.1109/SIU.2014.6830189.

[54] Vanmathi C., Prabu S. (2018). Image steganography using fuzzy logic and chaotic for large payload and high imperceptibility. *International Journal of Fuzzy Systems* 20:460–473. 10.1007/s40815-017-0420-0

[55] Jain M., Kumar A., Choudhary R. C. (2017). Improved diagonal queue medical image steganography using Chaos theory, LFSR, and Rabin cryptosystem. *Brain Informatics* 4:95–106. 10.1007/s40708-016-0057-z

[56] Durafe A. (2020) Securing criminal records using R-Pi, QR code and steganography. *International Journal of Innovative Technology and Exploring Engineering (IJITEE) ISSN: 2278-3075* 9(6):684–689.

[57] Bremnavas I., Poorna B., Kanagachidambaresan G. R. (2011). Medical image security using LSB and chaotic logistic map. 3rd International Conference on Advances in Recent Technologies in Communication and Computing (ARTCom 2011). doi:10.1049/ic.2011.0086

[58] Singh A. K. (2015). Some new techniques of improved wavelet domain watermarking for medical images, PhD Theses, http://hdl.handle.net/10603/76453

[59] Eze P. U., Parampalli U., Evans R. J., Liu D. (2018). Spread spectrum steganographic capacity improvement for medical image security in teleradiology. 40th Annual International Conference of the IEEE Engineering in Medicine and Biology Society (EMBC). doi:10.1109/embc.2018.8512344

[60] Memon N. A., Chaudhry A., Ahmad M., Keerio Z. A. (2011). Hybrid watermarking of medical images for ROI authentication and recovery. *International Journal of Computer Mathematics* 88:2057–2071.

[61] Nipanikar S. I., Hima Deepthi V. (2018). A multiple criteria-based cost function using wavelet and edge transformation for medical image steganography. *Journal of Intelligent Systems* 27(3):331–347. DOI 10.1515/jisys-2016-0095

[62] Navas K., Thampy S. A., Sasikumar M. (2008). EPR hiding in medical images for telemedicine. *Proceeding World Academy of Science, Engineering and Technology* 2:292–295.

[63] Liaoa X., Yina J., Guoa S., Lib X., Sangaiahc A. K. (2018). Medical JPEG image steganography based on preserving inter-block dependencies. *Computer and Electrical Engineering* 67:320–329.

[64] Sampaio R. A., Jackowski M. P. (2013). Assessment of steganographic methods in medical imaging. *SIBGRAPI 2013 (XXV Conference on Graphics, Patterns and Images* 115732:1–5.

[65] Parrek N. K., Pachdi V. (2016). Medical image protection using genetic algorithm operations. *Soft Computing* 20:763–772. 10.1007/s00500-014-1539-7

[66] Prabakaran G. Dr, Bhavani R., Rajeswari P. S. (2013). Multi secure and robustness for medical image based steganography scheme, International Conference on Circuits, Power and Computing Technologies [ICCPCT-2013], pp. 1188–1193.

[67] Stoyanov B., & Stoyanov B. (2020). BOOST: Medical image steganography using nuclear spin generator. *Entropy* 22(5), 501. doi:10.3390/e22050501

Index

Note: Locators in *italics* represent figures and **bold** indicate tables in the text.

AAL. *See* Ambient-assisted living
ABP. *See* Arterial blood pressure
Acigna-G, 5
Adopting cloud computing in healthcare, 4
AI. *See* Artificial intelligence
Amazon, 207
Ambient-assisted living (AAL), 148–149, 204
American Recovery and Reinvestment Act of 2009, 201
Analytical network process (ANP), 58, 65
ANN. *See* Artificial neural network
Anonymization techniques, 64
ANP. *See* Analytical network process
Application of cloud-computing technology, 111–122
AR. *See* Augmented reality
Arnold transformation, 222, 224
Arterial blood pressure (ABP), 183
Artificial intelligence (AI), 228–229
    machine-learning and, 95–96
    steganography based on, 228–229, *228*
Artificial neural network (ANN), 70, 187
Augmented reality (AR), 96
Automated alarm signals, 177

Bayesian technique, 185
Benefits of cloud computing in healthcare domain, 199–200
BI. *See* Business intelligence
Big data, 54
Biomass conversion to fuels, thermochemical routes for, 58
BodyCloud SaaS approach, 149
Broadband network services, 105–106
BSSs. *See* Business support systems
Business intelligence (BI), 142

Business support systems (BSSs), 105

Chronic diseases, 2
CIoT. *See* Cognitive IoT
Client-server architecture, 64
Clinical device-centric approach, 186
Clinical environment-based approaches, 187
    dimension reduction, 187–188
    median filters, 187
Clinical knowledge-based approach, 186
    pattern match, 186
    team-based method, 186–187
Cloud computing, defined, 2
Cloud-driven healthcare services, *198*
Cloud infrastructure services, 3
"Cloud of things" concept, 148
CloudThings architecture, 148
CNN based method. *See* Convolutional neural network based method
Coalition game theory, 185
Cognitive IoT (CIoT), 205
Community cloud computing, 115
Conical matrix, **40**
Contextual relationship, 31, **32**
Convolutional neural network (CNN) based method, 228
COVID-19 pandemic, 5, 114, 126, 206
CPS. *See* Cyber-physical system
Cryptography, 218
CT scan, 101
Customised alarm signals, 183
Cyber-physical system (CPS), 24

DA. *See* Data analytics
Dan Schmidhuber, Hochreiter, 168
Data analytics (DA), 142

243

Data-source technologies, 115
DCT-based methods. *See* Discrete cosine
transform-based methods
Decision tree (DT), 58, 65, 70, 72, 74
Dell, 207
Delphi technique, 26
DEMATEL
analysis of enablers, 41
flow diagram of, *31*
methodology, 31
Denial of service (DoS), 61
DICOM. *See* Digital imaging and
communications in medicine
DICOMWeb, *133*, 140, *142*
capabilities service, 138–139
retrieve service, 135–136
search service, 134–135
storage service, 136–138
worklist service, 138
Digital imaging and communications in
medicine (DICOM), 5, 128, *129*,
132, 219. *See also* DICOMWeb
Digitalization, 203–204
Digraph and model, development of, 32, *37*
Discrete cosine transform (DCT)-based
methods, 224
Discrete wavelet transform (DWT), 222,
224, *226*
DSpace, 140
DT. *See* Decision tree
DWT. *See* Discrete wavelet transform

ECG. *See* Electrocardiogram
ECG signal, 164, *165*
Edge computing, 106–107, 158
EHMS. *See* enhanced healthcare monitoring
system
EHR. *See* Electronic health records
Electrocardiogram (ECG), alarm signals
from, 183
Electronic health records (EHR), 54, 200, 218
eMBB slicing. *See* Enhanced Mobile Broadband
slicing
Encryption, image steganography with, 229
Energy effectiveness, 87
Enhanced healthcare monitoring system
(EHMS), 58, 61, 66
Enhanced Mobile Broadband (eMBB)
slicing, 103
ESP. *See* Extended service provider
ETL techniques. *See* Extract, transform, load
techniques

Extended service provider (ESP), 151
Extract, transform, load (ETL) techniques, 142

False-positive alarms, 177–179, 181–182,
182, *188*
FBI. *See* Federal Bureau of Investigation
FCM algorithm. *See* Fuzzy C-means algorithm
Federal Bureau of Investigation (FBI), 54
Final reachability matrix, **35**
5G architecture, 103
logical structure of 5G, 103–105
slicing and integrating with broadband,
105–106
5G in healthcare
benefit of 5G to healthcare applications, 98
example application, 98–101
with high processing requirements, 97–98
5G technology, cloud computing and, 91, 101
edge computing, 106–107
impacts, 96–97
medical imaging, 93
augmented reality (AR), 96
machine-learning and AI, 95–96
processing, 95
storage, 94–95
visualization and virtual reality (VR), 96
opportunities provided by, 93
software defined network in 5G, 101–103
traditional healthcare applications, 92–93
FL-EM-GMM algorithm, 66
Fog computing, 79, 158
concepts in fog computing, 80–81
healthcare systems, 81–82
in IoT-based healthcare, 83
automatic fog computing, 86–87
computation center, 83–84
energy effectiveness, 87
latency and throughput, 84–85
reliability, 85
security, 85–86
properties of, 82
bandwidth, 82
dependability, 83
energy efficiency, 82
privacy, 82
scalability, 82–83
FreeWalker, 149
Fuzzy C-means (FCM) algorithm, 64
Fuzzy-logic–based methods, 229

GA based methods. *See* Genetic algorithms based
methods

GAN. *See* Generative adversarial network
Gated recurrent unit, 169, 172
Gaussian mixture model algorithm, 59
GDPR. *See* General data protection regulation
General data protection regulation (GDPR), 66
Generative adversarial network (GAN), 67
Genetic algorithms (GA) based methods, 229
Google Scholar, 56
Google search engine, 118–119
GRU, 165

Health 4.0 (H4.0) enablers, 23, **26–29**
    cause-and-effect diagram of, 39
    DEMATEL analysis of enablers, 39
    DEMETAL methodology, 30
    enablers of, 25–29
    implications of research, 45
    ISM methodology, 29
        flow diagram, *30*
        modeling the enablers of Indian
            healthcare industry by, 31–32
    limitations and future prospects of
        research, 46
    MICMAC analysis of enablers, 32–39
Healthcare services, cloud-computing technology
        and, 113–117
Healthcare technologies and services, 195
    analysis, 205–211
    benefits of cloud computing in healthcare
        domain, 199–200
    cloud computing, 196, 197–198
        deployment models, 197
        essential characteristics, 196–197
        service models, 197
    future scope, 211–212
    past of cloud computing in healthcare,
        200–202
    present trends in cloud-computing dynamics,
        202–205
Health data security
    using ML and DL strategy, 60–65
    using traditional approach, 65–69
HealthGuard, 60
Health Insurance Portability and Accountability
        Act of 1996 (HIPAA), 212
Health Level 7 (HL7), 128
Health monitoring (HM) architectural solutions,
        149–150
Heart-rate variability (HRV) index, 185
HIPAA. *See* Health Insurance Portability and
        Accountability Act of 1996
Histogram-based methods, 221

Histogram-preserving steganography based on
        block (HPSB), 221
HL7. *See* Health Level 7
HM architectural solutions. *See* Health
        monitoring architectural solutions
Horizon 2020 BigClouT project, 148
HPSB. *See* Histogram-preserving steganography
        based on block
HRV, 165, **167–168**
HRV index. *See* Heart-rate variability index
Hybrid cloud computing, 115
Hybrid domain, 224–226

IaaS. *See* Infrastructure as a Service
IBM, 207
ICT. *See* Information communication and
        technology
ICU. *See* Intensive care units
IDS. *See* Intrusion-detection system
IDWT. *See* Inverse discrete wavelet
        transformation
IEEE, 56, 60
IHE. *See* Integrating the Healthcare Enterprise
Image processing, 98
Image steganography, 217, *218*
    classification of, 219, *220*
        hybrid domain, 224–226
        spatial domain steganography,
            220–222, **223**
        steganography based on AI approaches,
            228–229, *228*
        transform domain steganography,
            222–224, *227*
    with encryption, 229, *230*
    medical, 219, *219*
    performance evaluation, 233–234
    performance pyramid, *233*
    spread-spectrum (SS) based, 230
    statistical and analytical measures used, 234,
        234–235
Industry 4.0 (I4.0). *See* Health 4.0 enablers
Information communication and technology
        (ICT), 210
Information object definition (IOD), 130
Information technology (IT), 2
Infrastructure as a Service (IaaS), 3, *3*, 115, 197
Infrastructure vs platform vs software, *199*
Initial reachability matrix, **34**
Integer wavelet transform (IWT), 222, 224, 226
Integrated offer beneficiary (IOB), 151
Integrated offer user (IOU), 151–152
Integrating the Healthcare Enterprise (IHE), 128

Intensive care units (ICU), alarms in, 177
Internet of m-Health Things (mIoT), 204–205
Internet of Things (IoT), 64–65, 66, 174
  architecture, 175, *175*
  characteristics of, 174
Internet of Things (IoT) and cloud computing,
    integration of, 147
  generic sensing service scenario, 150–151
  health monitoring (HM) architectural
    solutions, 149–150
  implementation scenarios, 157–159
  main roles and business interactions,
    151–152
  operation rules, 152–153
  service offer integrator (SOI)
    business model specifications, 153–156
    core entities of SOI-MIS data structure,
    156–157
Intrusion-detection system (IDS), 61
Intrusion detection tree ("IntruDTree"), 67
Inverse discrete wavelet transformation
    (IDWT), 224
IOB. *See* Integrated offer beneficiary
IOD. *See* Information object definition
IoT. *See* Internet of Things
IOU. *See* Integrated offer user
ISM methodology, 29, *38*
  flow diagram, *30*
  modeling the enablers of Indian healthcare
    industry by, 31–32
IT. *See* Information technology
IWT. *See* Integer wavelet transform

JpegJsteg, 224

KNN, 58

LCS. *See* Longest common subsequence
LDQN technique. *See* Learning-based
    deep-Q-network technique
Leadership, 39
Learning-based deep-Q-network (LDQN)
    technique, 59, 64–65
Longest common subsequence (LCS), 221
Long short-term memory (LSTM), 164,
    168–169, 170
LSB substitution methods, 220
LSTM. *See* Long short-term memory

Machine learning (ML) techniques, 54, 183–184
  and artificial intelligence, 95–96
  complexity analysis, 73–74

consolidated technique, 63
cyberattack identification with, *58, 59*
decision tree (DT), 72
future work, 74
health data security
  using ML and DL strategy, 60–65
  using traditional approach, 65–69
mathematical interpretation, 70
measure the computational complexity of, **73**
Naïve Bayes algorithm, 72–73
radial basis function (RBF) kernel, 71
research methodology, 55–56, *56*
research question, 56
  observation, 58–60
  search and selection strategy, 56–57
  selection criteria, 57–58
  thermochemical routes for biomass
    conversion to fuels, 58
support vector machine (SVM), 70–71
systematic search results, 60
Management and orchestration (MANO)
    plane(s), 104
MANO. *See* Management and orchestration
    plane(s)
Mapping-based methods, 221
MapReduce PaaS, 5
Massive machine-type communications
    (mMTC) slicing, 103
MCDM. *See* Multi-criteria decision-making
Medical image steganography, 219, *219*
MEDLINE, 201
m-health monitoring, 203, *203*
MICMAC analysis of enablers, 32–38
MIMAC analysis, **39**
mIoT. *See* Internet of m-Health Things
MITBPD dataset, 166
ML techniques. *See* Machine learning techniques
mMTC slicing. *See* Massive machine-type
    communications slicing
MR scan, 101
MSBN. *See* Multi-service broadband network
MSI-MDD platform architecture, 150
Multi-criteria decision-making (MCDM),
    58, 65
Multi-service broadband network (MSBN), 106

Naïve Bayes algorithm, 58, 65, 72–73
National Electrical Manufacturers Association
    (NEMA), 127
National Sleep Foundation, 164
NEMA. *See* National Electrical Manufacturers
    Association

Network functional virtualization (NFV), 101–102

Network slice, 105–106, *105*

NFV. *See* Network functional virtualization

On-demand self-service, 196

Operating system (OS), 3

OS. *See* Operating system

PaaS. *See* Platform as a Service

Past of cloud computing in healthcare, 200–202

Pattern discovery, 185–186

"Pay-as-you-go" model, 200

PCA. *See* Principal component analysis

Pentagon approach, 178, *178*
  clinical requirements, 179
  clinical trial and analysis, 180
  design and development, 180
  feedback loop, 180–181
  method selection, 179

Physiological data-based approach, 183
  coalition game theory, 185
  customised alarm signals, 183
  integration of techniques, 184
  machine-learning methods, 183–184
  pattern discovery, 185–186
  sensor fusion, 185
  time delay method, 184

Pixel/block indicator based methods, 221

Pixel value differencing (PVD) method, 220–221

Pixel-value prediction-based methods, 221–222

Platform as a Service (PaaS), 3, *3*, 115, 197

Precision medicine, 24

Present trends in cloud-computing dynamics, 202–205

Principal component analysis (PCA), 187

Private clouds, 207

Public cloud computing, 115

PubMed, 56, 60

PVD method. *See* Pixel value differencing method

QIDO-RS (Query Based on ID for DICOM Objects), 134, *134*, **134**, **135**

Radial basis function (RBF) kernel, 71

Random forest (RF), 58, 65, 67, 70

Random forest classifiers (RFC), 184

RBF kernel. *See* Radial basis function kernel

Reachability matrix (RM)
  development of, 32
  partitioning, 32

Remote patient monitoring (RPM), 173
  alarms in, 176–177
  application architecture, 176
  architecture for, 176
  clinical device-centric approach, 186, 189
  clinical environment-based approaches, 187, 189–190
    dimension reduction, 187–188
    median filters, 187
  clinical knowledge-based approach, 186, 189
    pattern match, 186
    team-based method, 186–187
  false-positive alarms, 177–178, *182*
  pentagon approach, 178, *178*
    clinical requirements, 179
    clinical trial and analysis, 180
    design and development, 180
    feedback loop, 180–181
    method selection, 179
  physiological data-based approach, 183, 189
    coalition game theory, 185
    customised alarm signals, 183
    integration of techniques, 184
    machine-learning methods, 183–184
    pattern discovery, 185–186
    sensor fusion, 185
    time delay method, 184

Resource pooling, 196

RF. *See* Random forest

RFC. *See* Random forest classifiers

RM. *See* Reachability matrix

Robotics, 97–98

Roentgen revolutionized medicine, 94

RPM. *See* Remote patient monitoring

RR interval, 166

SaaS. *See* Software as a Service

SDN. *See* Software defined network

SDO. *See* Sensor device owner

SDP. *See* Sensor data publisher

Search and selection strategy, 56–57

Selection criteria, 57–58

Sensing offer integrator (SOI) company, 151–152

Sensor data publisher (SDP), 151

Sensor device owner (SDO), 151

Sensor fusion, 185

Service management, 105, *106*

Service offer integrator (SOI)
  business model specifications, 153–156
  core entities of SOI-MIS data structure, 156–157

Singular value decomposition (SVD), 224–225, *225*, 226, *226*
Sleep-related disorders, 164
Sleep-stage identification, 163
  gated recurrent unit, 169, 172
  long short-term memory (LSTM), 168–169, *170*
    with peephole connection, 169, *170*
  MIT-BIH polysomnographic dataset, data collection of, 166
  model training and evaluation, 169
  pre-processing of data, 166–167, *170*
Software as a Service (SaaS), 3, *3*, 115, 197
Software defined network (SDN), 101–103
SOI. *See* Service offer integrator
SOI company. *See* Sensing offer integrator company
Spatial domain steganography, 220–222, **223**
Spread-spectrum (SS) based image steganography, 230
SS based image steganography. *See* Spread-spectrum based image steganography
SSIM matrix, development of, 32, **33**
Steganalysis, 228
Steganography based on AI approaches, 228–229, *228*
STOW-RS (Store OVer the Web), 136–138, *137*, **138**
Support vector machine (SVM), 58, 61, 64, 65, 67, 70–71
SVD. *See* Singular value decomposition
SVM. *See* Support vector machine

Thermochemical routes for biomass conversion to fuels, 58

3D ultrasound volumes, 100–101
Time delay method, 184
Traditional healthcare applications, 92–93
Transform domain steganography, 222–224, *227*
2D ultrasound images, 100

UbeHealth, 5
Ultra-high resolution video, 100
Ultra reliable low latency communications (URLLC) slicing, 103
UPS-RS (Unified Procedure Step), 138, *138*, **139**
URLLC slicing. *See* Ultra reliable low latency communications slicing
User-to-root (U2R) assault, 61

Vendor-neutral archive (VNA) service, 142
Virtualized network functions (VNFs), 102
Virtual machine (VM) implementations, 102
Visualization and virtual reality (VR), 96
VM implementations. *See* Virtual machine implementations
VNA service. *See* Vendor-neutral archive service
VNFs. *See* Virtualized network functions
VR. *See* Visualization and virtual reality

WADL. *See* web application description language
WADO-RS (web access to DICOM persistent objects), 135, *135*, **136**, **137**
WannaCry ransomware attack, 218
Wearable technology, 205
Web application description language (WADL), 138
WEKA platform, 65